Computer Supported Cooperative Work

Volume 36

TRUST IN TECHNOLOGY:
A SOCIO-TECHNICAL PERSPECTIVE

Trust in Technology:
A Socio-Technical
Perspective

Edited by

Karen Clarke
Lancaster University, United Kingdom

Gillian Hardstone
Edinburgh University, United Kingdom

Mark Rouncefield
Lancaster University, United Kingdom

and

Ian Sommerville
Lancaster University, United Kingdom

 Springer

A C.I.P. Catalogue record for this book is available from the Library of Congress.

005
T77
2006

ISBN-10 1-4020-4257-4 (HB)
ISBN-13 978-1-4020-4257-7 (HB)
ISBN-10 1-4020-4258-2 (e-book)
ISBN-13 978-1-4020-4258-4 (e-book)

Published by Springer,
P.O. Box 17, 3300 AA Dordrecht, The Netherlands.

www.springer.com

Printed on acid-free paper

CONTENTS

LIST OF CONTRIBUTORS

Graham Button - Xerox Research Centre Europe, Grenoble France

Karen Clarke - Department of Computing, Lancaster University, UK

Luciana d'Adderio - Research Centre for Social Sciences, University of Edinburgh, UK

Guy Dewsbury- Department of Computing, Lancaster University, UK

John Dobson - Department of Computing, Lancaster University, UK

Corin Gurr - Institute for Communicating and Collaborative Systems, Division of Informatics, University of Edinburgh, UK

Gillian Hardstone - Research Centre for Social Sciences, University of Edinburgh, UK

Mark Hartswood - Institute for Communicating and Collaborative Systems, Division of Informatics, University of Edinburgh, UK

Terry Hemmings - Department of Computing, Nottingham University, UK

John Hughes - Department of Sociology, Lancaster University, UK

David Martin - Department of Computing, Lancaster University, UK

Rob Procter - Institute for Communicating and Collaborative Systems, Division of Informatics, University of Edinburgh, UK

Mark Rouncefield - Department of Computing, Lancaster University, UK

Roger Slack - Institute for Communicating and Collaborative Systems, Division of Informatics, University of Edinburgh, UK

Ian Sommerville - Department of Computing, Lancaster University, UK

Alexander Voß - Institute for Communicating and Collaborative Systems, Division of Informatics, University of Edinburgh, UK

Robin Williams - Research Centre for Social Sciences, University of Edinburgh, UK

INTRODUCTION: A NEW PERSPECTIVE ON THE DEPENDABILITY OF SOFTWARE SYSTEMS

Graham Button
Xerox Research Centre Europe, Grenoble France

1. INTRODUCTION

The Chapters that make up this book all report on research that has been conducted within two strands of the Interdisciplinary Research Collaboration in Dependability (DIRC) project[1] sponsored by the Engineering and the Physical Sciences Research Council (EPSRC)[2]. The majority of the research on which this book is based has been conducted within the research strand entitled, 'Organizational Culture and Trust', with in-put from the 'Human Interaction in Real-Time Systems' strand of research. As the titles of these strands suggests, this book, and indeed the whole DIRC project, does not consider the matter of the dependability of software systems in the traditional terms and methodologies of software engineering and computer science.

Questions relating to the dependability of software systems have, in the main, been asked with respect to control and safety critical systems, iconic examples of these being systems deployed within the nuclear power industry, air traffic control, and carrier flight-deck operations. They have also traditionally been considered within software engineering and computer science in terms of formal metrics that model and measure the tolerances of systems. The DIRC programme, however, is providing a radical overhaul of

---

[1] DIRC includes researchers from five British Universities established in the area of dependable computer systems and related topics: City University, Lancaster University, The University of Edinburgh, The University of Newcastle and The University of York. DIRC aims to develop knowledge, methods and tools to ensure more dependable computer-based systems. The project started in September 2000, and is now half-way through its lifetime.

[2] The Engineering and Physical Sciences Research Council (EPSRC) is the UK Government's leading funding agency for research and training in engineering and the physical sciences.

the way in which the dependability of software systems is approached and assessed. It is radical in the sense that it is moving the issue beyond the confines of the disciplinary boarders of software engineering and computer science. It is doing so by bringing into consideration the cultural, organizational, interactional and psychological context in which systems are used, and also through the way in which dependability can be assessed through statistical methods. This radical overhaul brings together a multidisciplinary team of researchers drawn from the disciplines of statistics, sociology and psychology, in addition to computer science and software engineering.

DIRC is a seven year program, which began in September 2000. As evidenced by this collection, it has so far developed two foundationally innovative ways through which the dependability of software systems can be considered and which have set the tone for the research results that have so far been published.[3] The first is that the project has made dependability an issue that is relevant for software systems in the work place, *per se*, not just systems that are used in control and safety critical environments. This is an important step because even though the safety of an environment may not be at issue, nevertheless the dependence of an organization on, for example, its accountancy system may be crucial for its economic survival. Encouraging designers to view the dependability of any workplace system as at least a latent requirement emphasizes the need for design to understand the organizational context within which systems are placed. In this respect all of the chapters in this book investigate the issue of dependability outside of the confines of control and safety critical environments. For example, Clarke, Hughes and Rouncefield's study in Chapter 2 is situated within a large hospital trust in the North of England; Voß, Proctor, Slack and Hartswood's Chapter 9 investigation examines work in manufacturer of mass-customized diesel engines; Dewsbury, Sommerville, Clarke and Rouncefield in Chapter 8 move into the domestic setting, Rouncefield et al in Chapter 5 draws off work conducted in the diverse settings of a hospital, a steel-works, and an engine manufacturer, while Hardstone, D'Adderio and Williams in Chapter 4 is based on studies conducted in an automobile manufacturer, a high-end electronics company and another NHS hospital trust.

---

[3] DIRC has assembled an impressive list of publications to date which can be accessed at: www.dirc.org.uk/publications/index.php

The second innovation is to have extended the type of question that is relevant with respect to the issue of dependability. This has itself been done in two ways. First, not only has DIRC extended the range of systems to which questions of dependability can be addressed, as discussed above, it has also extended the whole idea of what a system is. Thus DIRC considers a system not just in terms of the computational technology involved, in DIRC terms the system includes the user and the organizational arrangements of use as well as the actual technology. This can be seen particularly in parts of Hardstone et al's Chapter 4 where they contrast two organizations using the same technology but with very different levels of reliability. It is clear from this chapter that assessing the dependability of the system inevitably has to involve reference to the organizational circumstances of the use of technology and that the dependability of the technology is a consequence of those circumstances. The upshot of expanding the idea of a system beyond the computational technology involved to also include users and the organizational environment and culture milieu within which the technology is deployed and used is that even if the computational technology itself is measured to be fit for its purpose according to formal models of dependability, problems with the usability, and acceptability of the technology, or the possibility of human error, bring into question the dependability of the system *as a whole*. Second, DIRC has not only extended the concept of 'system' it has also provided additional criteria to those of performance metrics for modeling the dependability of systems. Thus in Chapter 8 Dewsbury, Sommerville, Clarke and Rouncefield extend technically based models of dependability. They argue that Laprie's model needs to be expanded to include matters such as user acceptability and the ability of a system to be able to adapt to different environments of use and different users.

2. MAKING DEPENDABILITY AN EVERYDAY MATTER

This collection brings together research that represents the way in which DIRC researchers have accomplished an overhaul of the concept of the dependability of software systems through the examination of the social and organizational issues surrounding dependability. The idea of 'trust' that figures in the title is being used to gather together this new way of thinking about dependability as a culturally and organizational embedded matter. Dependability is a concept that has been appropriated by the engineering disciplines and given a technical meaning defined in terms of performance metrics and tolerances. Reapplied to the everyday world that technical definition of dependability would not be recognizable because in the everyday world dependability means much more than is meant by the technical definition. Yet, as DIRC research is showing, dependability is very much an everyday, not just a technical matter. The utilization of the concept of 'trust' is a way of freeing ourselves from the technical definition of dependability by making dependability a more everyday matter and thus freeing up the ideas involved from their technical specification. For example, systems that patently return false information, may, technically speaking in terms of their design parameters, be judged not to be dependable. However, as Clarke et al show in Chapter 2, in the everyday world of work, systems that may be formally defined in technical terms not to be dependable, may, nevertheless, be perfectly usable for the practical purposes of accomplishing the work they support. In these terms, although they may not be formally dependable they may be, nevertheless, 'trusted' by their users and within the organization. Within the everyday world, as Voß et al demonstrate in Chapter 9 they may be dependable enough for the practical purposes of getting the job done within the practical circumstances in which they are used.

Computer systems populate the everyday world. Systems pervade the everyday world of the work place: document systems, work flow systems, control systems, accountancy systems, and so on. The everyday world of the home is integrated into organizational systems: we use the phone, we receive bills generated by computer systems, and many people also explicitly use computer systems within the home. Systems exist within our everyday world of transport, holidays, leisure, medicine and the rest. Computer systems are just, quite simply, an everyday matter. And *trusting* a technology is also an everyday matter. That is, the determination of whether a system is trusted or not consists in the ways in which people make everyday judgments about trust which may accord, but which may also not accord with criteria that designers and engineers use to determine the dependability of a system. In this respect the question of how, in the everyday world, people determine that they trust something or someone is appropriate for understanding how people put, or do not put, their trust in a system.

So what does trust in the everyday world consist of? One of the points that Harold Garfinkel (1963) made in a paper on experiments with trust, is that trust is a background, taken for granted, expectancy in everyday interaction. So, for example, we take for granted that people will understand what we mean within a particular context: when we walk into the newspaper shop in the UK and ask for The Guardian we never think that instead of being handed a newspaper by that name we might be offered a person dressed up in a Superman like costume. We take for granted that when we tell someone to follow the signs to London they will follow the signs in the direction of the arrow head and not in the direction of the tail. It is just an ingredient of the way in which we conduct our everyday lives that there is a background expectancy that when we interact with people they have a commonsense knowledge of the social structure which they use to understand what they and others are saying and doing. To make this feature of social life explicitly visible Garfinkel would make trouble, and he describes how people become agitated when these background expectancies are breached (Garfinkel 1967) So, for example, he describes how he asked his students to continually question what members of their family were saying when they were watching television, and how quickly interactions deteriorated when they were constantly asked what they meant when they said something. In what they do and how they do it, people display that they just trust that they will be understood, unless understanding is marked as a particular, local problem. That trust comes to light when it is systematically breached.

In this respect, one of the ways in which we treat the issue of trust in the everyday world is that it is an *occasioned* matter. That is, we do not go around systematically asking if we trust or do not trust someone or something. Trust is a routine background expectancy in everyday interaction and in our everyday use of technology. To question this implicitly displayed trust is the result of something having occurred that brings it into question; it is a matter that has been brought about or occasioned by particular circumstances. For example, once discovered, the errant spouse may never be trusted again, or once someone misses an appointment we may wonder about their likelihood to do so again. We also do not go around our world making judgments that someone is trusting. We may make that observation but it is, again, occasioned by the circumstances. So we might say that the rock-climber standing on the crumbling ledge put his trust in his friend if we see him grasping for his fiends outstretch arm, but it is that occasion that makes relevant our observation about trust, for trust might not be part of the behaviour of just stretching out an arm. It is that action in the circumstances. We might also say that it takes time to build up trust in a new acquaintance or new things: we may have had doubts to begin with but we come to trust through experience that the new person in the office can be trusted to get the job done on time. Again, it is the circumstances, the fact of being new that occasions our question, once the new becomes familiar, the relevancy of the activity of trust disappears.

Computer systems are placed within the everyday world in which commonsense understandings of trust prevail, not into a world in which technical definitions of dependability rule. Like anything in that everyday world, they are therefore subject to commonsense everyday judgments with respect to their trustworthiness or their dependability. Thus, for instance, we may have had doubts about the new document repository system, but we come to trust, through experience, that it can be used to get the job done; as we near the end of the final quarter and the reporting deadline looms into view for tomorrow we might say of someone whom we observe setting off the long report to print overnight so that it is ready for the next day that they obviously trust the technology. We can also say that trust in technology is an occasioned matter. We regularly enter lifts without a moment's thought, but if the lift judders or stops short of a floor we may eye it suspiciously the next time we take it. In the everyday world we regularly use systems and our judgments as to their trustworthiness will be based upon our experiences; do those experiences with the technology occasion us to question their trustworthiness, or knowing their shortfalls do we trust them enough for them to be useful. We may have many occasions to wonder about the trustworthiness of systems per se, we read about large scale disasters involving air traffic control systems that result in the closure of airports, the UK stock exchange system that had to be scrapped, and the London ambulance fiasco. In is abroad in the world that the failure of computer systems can result in large amounts of wasted money and sometimes death. These reports may occasion us to be jaundiced about computer systems in general, yet our local experience of the system we use might mean that we log on at the beginning of the day without a moments thought.

All of the papers in this collection are about placing the issue of dependability on an everyday footing through the articulation of how, in the everyday world, people orient to the question of the trustworthiness of a system. They are also about making this everyday orientation a consideration in the design process. There are three themes that can be discerned that run through the chapters in this respect. First, trust as a practical matter in the situated affairs of users, the workplace and organizations. Second, the consequences of this for traditional software engineering and computer science understandings of dependability. Third, the utilization of ethnographic investigation as a design methodology.

3. DEPENDABILITY AS A PRACTICAL MATTER

There have been many ethnographically grounded studies of technology in use that describe the way in which technology in the workplace is made to work by those who use it, (cf. Luff et al 2000; Heath and Button 2002). Together, these studies have illustrated a number of themes with regard to the way in which people work to make technology usable in the workplace.

For example, it has been described how technology may be used in different ways or for different purposes to those intended by its designers (Bowers, et al 1995). Also, many studies have described how people have to work around a system in order to get the work done that the system is intended to support or automate. Quite simply, studies of technology in use have demonstrated that evaluating the role, efficiency, dependability and productivity gains of computer systems in the work place are complex matters which cannot be adequately appreciated through solely asking technical questions to do with performance, functionality, reliability, maitence and the like. The workplace is not just a space within which varieties of technologies are functioning according to their specifications and tolerances, it is a complex social milieu made up of matters of organizational and interactional contingencies which play into the very working, operation and assessment of technology. The technology found in the workplace does not stand outside of this social milieu, it is embedded within it, and it is no surprise, and in itself, no news, that technology is marbled through with social relevancies and social concerns.

Seen from a purely formal point of view the dependability and trustworthiness of a system may appear to be, in principal, the relatively straightforward matter of setting performance tolerances. This is not to say that it is straightforward to implement, indeed, it might involve the solution of difficult engineering problems but, in technical terms, a system either performs within the specified parameters or it does not. However, once a system is placed within the workplace it is placed within a social milieu within which organizational and interactional matters play upon how technology is considered. In the workaday world dependability may not then be *measured* but rather *judged*.

This idea is at the heart of Chapter 9 by Voß et al. They make the point that the dependability of a system is achieved through the actions and interactions of those involved in using the system. In this respect it takes interactional work by those involved to make a system dependable, for practical purposes. The starting point for this argument is to remember that 'dependability' is an everyday natural language expression used and understood in the daily round of everyday (including working) life. Voß et al thus want to understand what dependability means in everyday use within EngineCo a company that produces mass-customized diesel engines, and they make visible the ways in which, in their actions and interactions, the people involved at EngineCo come to view systems as dependable. They make visible the, borrowing a term from Livingstone (1986), 'lived work' that participants engage in, in order to make the systems they work with 'more or less dependable'. Thus for example, they describe the assembly control host which controls all processes within EngineCo and which interfaces with the company's EPR system (SAP R3) and with systems specific to the different functional units making up the plant. The idea of the 'buildability' of an engine might be thought of something that is verifiable by the system. That is, the buildability of an engine is dependent upon, for example, the necessary components being available. Thus the system can confirm or not that an engine can be built if the parts are available or not. However, there are a variety of contingencies that play into building engines, one of these is the short supply of some parts, and another is high customer demand. The buildability of engines is not then just dependent upon the availability of parts; work on building the engine may begin even if the parts are not available in order to work to meet demand. Work on the engine will be progressed until the absence of the part prevents them from continuing any further; but once the part arrives it can be finished off.

Working in this way means that more engines can be shipped to meet demand even though parts are missing at the time of starting to build the engine. Working in this way, though, requires co-ordination between different departments and Voß et al describe how the control room workers have to take account of the interests of the assembly workers in how they pace the flow of different types of engines to the assembly workers in order to have an even flow of complicated and less complicated assemblies that allow the performance targets to be achieved. The buildability of an engine is not then provided for in the verification by the system of the necessary components being available. The system may confirm or not confirm that it is possible. The buildability of an engine is an organizational judgment, which once made then requires organizational and interactional work to accomplish in such a way as to be done under the auspices of organizational constraints. The dependability of the system to verify or not the buildability of an engine is really irrelevant to those concerned; they work to make the system work for their situated purposes. Voß et al are thus making dependability a 'members' phenomenon' and argue that the professional understanding of dependability needs to be complemented with the practical view point of what dependability means for those who use systems.

One of the points raised in this chapter relates to an idea first introduced by David Sudnow (1993) in his account of the work of hospital staff: 'normal troubles'. Normal trouble are problems which arise in the course of work but which are just part and parcel of the work being done, and with which the people involved are familiar and which they have contended with and overcome on many occasions. The issue of normal troubles is relevant to how the dependability of a system is considered because systems can give rise to normal troubles in working routines. In this respect it might be supposed that a system is not performing properly, may not be dependable or trustworthy. However, the troubles that systems occasion may be very familiar and these troubles may be regularly and routinely handled with in the course of the work. Thus, although giving rise to problems a system may be deemed to be dependable and trustworthy for the practical purposed of doing the job. This is an idea that is articulated in Chapter 2 by Clarke et al.

They describe a 'bed crisis' inside a UK hospital trust. The management information system was alerting the Directorate Manager of Orthopaedics (DMO) that the hospital was 'minus nine beds'. That is to say, that the hospital trust, which was made up of three hospitals, would not have enough beds to cope with the number of patients they expected they would need to care for. There would be a shortfall of nine beds that was deemed to be a crisis level caused by a traffic accident. Clarke et al describe, however, that the DMO worked to normalize this crisis: "we go through our usual rituals for situations like these". These "usual rituals" turned out to be walking around the hospital wards, physically locating spare beds, inspected the 'bed boards' – physical representations of bed availability- asking ward sisters about their bed availability descriptions (data which is fed into the information system) and what they really meant. At the end of this 'hands on process' it was possible for the DMO to establish that rather than being nine beds short the hospital could in fact cope with the 'crisis'. The problem was handled in the routine of the practices through which the DMO made her calculations. Clarke et el describe how the apparent solidity and objectivity of managerial information (as proposed by the system involved) can be continually challenged in the activities of those involved in establishing how many free beds there are in practice. Clarke et al thus elaborate the theme on the work of using the systems 'the work of managing the bed management system, of making a system of calculability work'. However, they also elaborate how the fact that it requires work to make the system work, and that plainly the system did not reflect the real state of affairs on the wards does not mean that the system was viewed as not dependable, or trustworthy. It was just considered that this work of walking the wards and ascertaining the 'true' picture was part of using the system. Indeed, the system was very much viewed by those concerned as a support for their work, because it gave them, for their practical purposes, enough information to work with. The system, as Voß et al described with regard to their study, was more or less dependable for the practical affairs it was used, in part, to manage. Dependability viewed only in terms of a set of performance criteria would fail to capture the ways in which these performance criteria are both constituted and judged in the course of working with the system.

The issue of whether or not there are enough beds is, of course, a temporally located determination. Having, for example, five spare beds may be enough on this occasion, *this time*, but may not be enough on another occasion, at *that time*. In Chapter 5 Clarke et al consider the way in which *time* has been used to understand cultural aspects of technology and propose that 'timeliness' is a consideration in understanding how dependable systems are.

The social sciences have considered 'time' from the point of view of a number of social theories ranging from a Marxist interest in the regulation of time under modern capitalism to Giddens' concern with temporal change. In the vein of the studies presented in this collection, Clarke et al, however, eschew a theorizing approach to time and rather turn to the way in which time is actually oriented to in the actions and interactions of people working in organizations. By understanding the specifics of the way in which time is woven into organizational culture the authors intend to influence the design of systems whose dependability is, in part, measured temporally. Technologies which support 'just-in-time' manufacturing or IT systems which promise productivity improvements by enabling information to be organized and accessed in a more timely fashion cannot be assessed and judged just on an abstract and generalized measurement systems for time. Comparisons with a current state and a past state that show that it now takes, as measured in terms of speed, less time to perform an operation than it did before, miss the point of the way in which time may be calculated in organizational life. In this respect the dependability of a system that it will deliver in time or that it can be relied upon to be faster than its predecessor may not so much turn on a precise mathematical calculation but rather on the way in which time is accounted for and measured within the organizational context in which a system is to operate. To this end Clarke et al range across a variety of studies of the workplace to bring out how time is oriented to and impacts the organizational structure and work done within in it that a system will support. With those understandings in hand designers have a more sensitive appreciation of the situational relevance of time, and how to accommodate it in their design, than they would otherwise have through a purely generalized measurement system for time that stands outside of the situation in which 'the clock ticks'.

4. IMPLICATIONS FOR FORMAL MODELS OF DEPENDABILITY

The second theme that permeates the book concerns the implications that this work has for the formal conceptions of dependability found in software engineering and computer science. Most of the chapters invite systems' designers and builders to consider elaborating on the formal characterization of dependability through a consideration of the practical character of dependability and trustworthiness displayed in situated judgments. The Chapters 8,7 and 3, by Dewsbury, Sommerville, Clarke and Rouncefield; Martin and Sommerville, and by Dobson, however, explicitly address this issue. In Chapter 4, Hardstone, D'Adderio and Williams bridge between both the theme of dependability as a practical matter and that of the implications this has for formal methods of dependability, and in that capacity I will introduce this chapter first.

Hardstone et al consider the way in which formalists have approached dependability through the *standardization* of information structures and organizational practice. This is particularly relevant with respect to systems and practices that are operated across geographically dispersed sites where the need for coordination is important. Standardization is seen to be a way in which sites can come to trust each other's operations and reciprocal inputs. Hardstone et al, through a study of three organizations that were moving towards standardization, suggest, however, that standardization is really a practical matter, and more negotiable than is suggest by formalist approaches. As Hardstone et al explain, formalist accounts of standardization and classification in system design emphasize that ensuring consistency, completeness and mutually exclusive categories of classification will result in systems that are both usable and dependable. In reality, however, looseness in the system and trade-offs are required to make the standardization process workable. Hardstone et al thus draw conclusions about how formalists and information systems designers should approach the issue of standardization.

The three case studies that are presented represent different levels of organizational heterogeneity and diversity. ComputerCo, a manufacturer of high-end electronics, was attempting to standardize a product and its production processes across two geographically separated sites; MotorCo, an automotive manufacturer was trying to bring about standardization within a single organization, while NHS Urban, a UK National Health Service Trust hospital was introducing standardization of recording clinical practice across different professional bodies of healthcare practioners. In the case of ComputerCo the heterogeneity they were attempting to handle through standardization was differences in culture and labour structures, while within MotorCo it was the different ways in which two engineering groups who were cooperating in the production of a product worked and how they used different database languages, and within NHS Urban it was the fact that the different bodies of professionals had their own and different bodies of knowledge and practice. In ComputerCo the move towards standardization involved creating and implementing rules and methodologies to ensure that the product and processes to produce the product were exactly duplicated at each site; within MotorCo it involved the introduction of new software supported product structure and a single database, and within NHS Urban it consisted of introducing a computer based records system.

Hardstone et al acknowledge that all three organizations partially succeeded in their standardization attempts; however, what is of interest here is that they also partially failed because in the process of standardization new forms of undependability developed. In the case of ComputerCo not all lower level knowledge could be codified and transformed, within MotorCo, contrary to the arguments of codification economists, standardization did not resolve the existing incompatibilities between the sites and led to new bottlenecks, and for NHS Urban the difficulties of fitting the system to some of the activities of the different groups and the difficulties of negotiating a common ground between them emphasized how mediation between the groups had been necessary to make the data dependable. This was now difficult to accomplish and the consequence was that the data was undependable. The lesson that Hardstone et al draw for formalist approaches to dependability and for designers of information systems is that local meaning and practice are important and that coordinating systems need to be flexible enough to handle necessary local variations. A conclusion that echoes, and is thus reinforced, by arguments previously made about workflow systems (Suchman 1994).

In Chapter 8 Dewsbury, Sommerville, Clarke and Rouncefield focus on Laprie's dependability model. They argue that work on dependability has been mainly concerned with control and production systems. However, in the spirit of DIRC research they argue that with the proliferation of computer systems in the work place it is not just production and control systems that are critical; business and governments are in some cases totally reliant upon a system for crucial aspects of their operation, and the dependability of such systems is as critical as it is for the systems traditionally driven by dependability requirements. However, it is not only within the work place that dependability is of concern; some domestic-based computer systems, in the instance with which Dewsbury et al are concerned, assistive technology systems for older people, must also be dependable for they can involve life critical matters. A consequential feature of such domestic based systems is the extent to which the system is *acceptable* to a user and how well the system can adapt to different users and user environments. Thus the installation of domestic-based systems should not just be concerned with the need to make the system failure free, instead the overall dependability of a system also involves the issue of whether or not it fulfils its intended purpose from the user's point of view. Dewsbury et al make the point that technically based dependability models such as Laprie's do take account of users. However, users should be considered as elements in the system that are comparable with other elements such as hardware and software elements. In this respect 'interaction faults' can be seen as resulting from 'human errors' just as they can be considered as resulting from hardware and software. Dewsbury et al, based upon their experiences of designing assistive technologies for older people, propose extending the technical models of dependability to encompass the human element so that dependability can be rearticulated in terms of human aspects as well as the nature of error and faults. To this end they bring into modeling process matters such as fitness for purpose, adaptability, acceptability, and trustworthiness.

One way in which 'the human element' can be taken into account with regard to issues of dependability, or for that matter, other questions related to systems' design, that is stressed throughout this book is through the actual study of the work of people who will use the system and the study of how they use current systems. However, engaging in detailed ethnographic studies of work is time consuming and is also dependent upon the availability of good ethnographers, whether they are the designers themselves or dedicated professionals. In Chapter 7 Martin, Rouncefield and Sommerville address this issue by proposing a resource through which designers can systematically draw of the existing body of ethnomethdologically informed ethnographic studies of work (Randall et al 1995). One of the problems that designers face is the ability to find or draw generalities from out of particular studies, and the resource that Martin and Sommerville build is, in part, an attempt to provide a resolution to this problem.

To this end they detect patterns of what they call cooperative interaction. These are regularities, revealed by the corpus of studies, in the way in which work activities and interaction are organized. Martin and Sommerville identify a number of regular themes or topics that these studies have encountered: sequentially and temporality; a working division of labour; plans and procedures; routines, rhythms, patterns; coordination; awareness of work and ecology and affordances. The idea of 'patterns of cooperation' is that it is possible to generate generalized descriptions of interaction based upon specific studies of the various topics. Martin and Sommerville have so far documented ten such patterns. They have created a series of web pages that describe these patterns in a structured way, in each case moving from a high level description of the phenomena, 'The Essence of the Pattern', to three sections entitled 'Why?', 'Where Used', and 'Dependability Implications'. The reader can then drop into a vignette giving greater detail of the pattern and described in terms of the five topical headings. The idea is that designers can gain a quick insight into the social and interactional matters that might surround dependability issues for a system being designed for a situation that may correspond to one of the patterns of interaction. Simply, the patterns are thus a resource for considering dependability issues for new situations but which have similarities to the situation described in the patterns.

Martin and Sommerville are tackling a very complex, and for some, vexing issue in this chapter which is how to make studies of the workplace tell for situations not covered by a particular study and of making these studies a general resource for design as opposed to being a resource for a particular design for the situation studied. This is the first serious attempt to grapple with this issue and from the point of view of systems designers it is a welcome and important development.

While Martin and Sommerville are developing a radically new resource for the design of systems with respect to dependability, Dobson in chapter? considers the implications of a DIRC perspective on dependability for a more traditional design tool: modeling. Modeling is done to reduce the complexity of socio-technical systems, and Dobson describes how complexity can be handled by constructing different models of different parts of the system thus producing a suite of models. The distinctiveness of the approach is described by Dobson as residing in the fact that the models making up the suite related to one another within a conceptual framework, that of responsibility. Dobson's chapter is built up as a tutorial in such a modeling procedure. This chapter stands out from the rest of the collection because it is articulating a more usual tool in the methodological repertoire of design; nevertheless Dobson is using this tool to provide a DIRC type insight into dependability, for the conceptual framework for his models is the social matter of responsibility within an organization.

5. ETHNOGRAPHY AS A DESIGN METHODOLOGY

The strand of the DIRC project that most of the chapters in this book are drawn from is one within which the social considerations of systems' use predominate, and thus is the one within which the human science, especially sociological considerations are articulated. However, the Human Sciences in general, and sociology in particular, seethe with perspectival rivalry and methodological debate, something that can be clearly seen in Clarke et al's Chapter 1, in their review of different perspectives on the idea of trust. The fact that the Human Sciences is a battleground of competing perspectives means that the very idea within the DIRC program that a consideration of dependability issues in systems design should be grounded in the social world in which the systems will be used, is not a simple matter of turning to the appropriated discipline and using its findings. Computer scientists who have turned to sociology for insights into their problems are often surprised by the range of theoretical and methodological positions within sociology, and the intense disputes and rivalries between them. Given this situation then it might well be the case that turning to sociology to broaden an understanding of dependability might actually confuse matters, for there is no one social perspective that they could appeal to, there are a variety of them. For instance, from the point of view of labour process theory, making systems more and more dependable may be viewed as part of the general deskilling of labour under modern capitalism. From the point of view of postmodernism, however, dependability may be part of the objectification of society rendered by technological and scientific disciplines. While from yet another perspective, social constructionism, dependability may the product of rhetorical processes.

Sociology has often turned its attention to particular matters, for example, education, health, race relations, and the list of 'the sociology ofs...' is impressive. These subject areas, however, then become battle grounds on which the historical perspectival disputes of sociology are fought, and edited collections of sociological articles proliferate and articulate the various ways in which different sociological perspectives apprehend the phenomena. However, if we consider the point of view of systems designers rather than the point of view of the human scientist, this sort of internecine perspectival warfare may not be productive. Designers are not interested in a sociology of technology, and with understanding how different sociological factions reinterpret what they, the designers, do, from inside any particular sociological theory. The designers of systems who are interested in what sociology may offer have a very practical orientation. Thus, with respect to the issue of dependability they are interested in the way in which sociology can support them in tackling the issue of dependability as an engineering or design issue.

In this respect this current book, which is predominantly a sociological book, differs from the general run of sociological considerations of a phenomena. It is not attempting to provide different, sociological perspectives on, or push one sociological perspective about dependability in the manner of sociological collections on other topics might do. This is because it not *about* a sociology of design and engineering with regard to the issue of dependability, rather it is a sociology *for* design and engineering. The question this book raises is not about making dependability and trust topics for sociology, but how the way in which dependability and trust is articulated in the commonsense world of social relationships can inform design and engineering. This book is thus not about theories that provide different and competing interpretations of what, really, engineers are doing in building dependable systems. It is, rather, intended to have an actual impact upon the way in which designers consider building in the issue of dependability in the design of their systems. In this respect this book continues a research direction that has been established between some sociologists and the relevant design and engineering disciplines and which is to trade the analysis of work, and analysis of the use of technology, into the actual design of technology.

Those who have pursued this interdisciplinary research in general and those in this present collection in particular, have developed the relevancy of *ethnographically* gathered materials for design. This idea has been particularly promulgated in the field of Computer Supported Cooperative Work (CSCW) where ethnographers and computer scientists have been working together for more than a decade to articulate studies of work and organizations into computer systems' design. Ethnography, as practised within CSCW emphasizes the observation of work and technology use as it unfolds as a real time phenomena, and the apprehension of the participants' point of view. As a way of gathering data it stands in contrast to surveys and questionnaires. Given designers practical interests, it is not surprising that the field work methodology of ethnography has interested them more than the theoretical or statistical strands of the human sciences. Ethnography emphasizes investigating matters of work and use empirically, as opposed to theoretically; in real worldly circumstances, as opposed to contrived experimental situations; in real time, as opposed to generalized time; and as work and use unfolds, as opposed to after the fact stories about work. This gives designers a further methodology through which to develop requirements for systems and to assess systems in use. Many of the authors of this book have been at the forefront of developing ethnography as a methodology for design in the field of CSCW, and through this book all they are showing its relevancy for yet another area of systems design, that of dependability.

However, ethnography is not all of a piece. There are a number of sociological positions that gather materials through the fieldwork of ethnography: symbolic interactionism, social studies of science and technology, and ethnomethodology being some. What these different sociological positions then do with those materials can, however, be very different. For example, within social studies of science and technology there is an emphasis on understanding how the science or the technology is a construction of social processes, while in ethnomethodology there is an emphasis upon the uniquely adequate features of work. It is a curious fact, however, that the ethnographers within CSCW tend to emphasize ethnomethodology, and this is also reflected in this book, for the position adopted by most, though importantly not all, within this collection is also that of ethnomethodology. This is not something that, in the main, is overtly announced, but it is discernable in the character of most of the studies, and in the invocation of other relevant studies. In one respect it may not matter to the designer that this is ethnomethodology; it is just the utility of the sociology for design purposes that is important. In another respect it is, for the utility may actually rest upon the character of the study as ethnomethodological. An introduction to a collection is not the place, however, to explore this matter, and readers can now turn to the actual chapters themselves to start to form their own opinions.

REFERENCES

1. Bowers, J., Button, G. and Sharrock, W.W. (1995). Workflow From Within and Without: Technology and Cooperative Work on the Print Industry Shopfloor, in H. Marmolin, Y. Sundblad, and K. Schmidt. *Proceedings of the Fourth European Conference on Computer-Supported Cooperative Work* Dordrecht: Kluwer Academic Publishers.
2. Garfinkel, H. (1963). "A conception of, and Experiments with, 'Trust' as a Condition of Stable Concerted Actions. " In *Motivation and Social Interaction.* Edited by O.J. Harvey, 187-238. New York: The Ronald Press.
3. Garfinkel, H. (1967) *Studies in Ethnomethodology* . Englewood Cliffs, NJ: Prentice- Hall.
4. Heath, C. and Button, G. (eds) (2002). Special Issue on Workplace Studies, *The British Journal of Sociology*, Volume 53, Number 2.
5. Randall, D., Rouncefield, M. and Hughes, John (1995) Chalk and Cheese: BPR and Ethnomethodologically Informed Ethnography in CSCW. In H. Marmolin, Y. Sundblad and K. Schmidt (eds.) *Proceedings of the Fourth European Conference On Computer Supported Cooperative Work.* Dordrecht: Kluwer Academic Publishers.
6. Livingston, Eric (1986). *The Ethnomethodological Foundations of Mathematics.* London: Routledge & Kegan Paul.
7. Luff, P., Hindmarsh, J. and Heath, C (eds) (2000). Workplace *Studies: Recovering Work Practice and Informing Design.* Cambridge: Cambridge University Press.
8. Suchman, Lucy (1994). Do categories have politics?: The Language/Action Perspective Reconsidered, *Computer Supported Cooperative Work* 2.
9. Sudnow, D. (1993). *Normal Crimes: Sociological Features of the Penal Code in a Public Defender Office.* Ivington Publishers.

Chapter 1

TRUST AND ORGANISATIONAL WORK

Karen Clarke[1], Gillian Hardstone[2], Mark Hartswood[2], Rob Procter[2] and
Mark Rouncefield[1]

1 Department of Computing, Lancaster University, UK.
2 Institute for Communicating and Collaborative Systems, Division of Informatics, University of Edinburgh, UK.

"For most of us, most of the time, our natural attitude in the taken-for-granted world is one which enables us to maintain our sanity in our passage through life and the daily round. Routines, habits ...and the consistencies with which our interactions with each other conform to expectations, together provide the infrastructure for a moral universe in which we, its citizens, can go about our daily business. Through learning to trust others we learn, one way or another, to trust things. And likewise, through learning to trust material things we learn to trust abstract things. Trust is therefore achieved and sustained through the ordinariness of everyday life and the consistencies of both language and experience." (Silverstone)

".. there is no relationship of trust with a computer "(Shneiderman 2000)

1. INTRODUCTION: NOTIONS OF TRUST

"Without trust only very simple forms of human cooperation which can be transacted on the spot are possible ... Trust is indispensable in order to increase a social system's potential for action beyond these elementary forms"(Luhmann 1990)

K. Clarke, G. Hardstone, M. Rouncefield and I. Sommerville (eds.), Trust in Technology:
A Socio-Technical Perspective, 1–20.
© 2006 *Springer. Printed in the Netherlands.*

This book looks at trust as a 'lived condition', that is, not as some defined state of affairs but as woven into the very fabric of everyday social and organizational life. Trust has previously been explored and analyzed in any number of ways. Issues of trust form an important part in much of the work of the early sociologists, Durkheim, Weber, and Simmel for example, concerned as they were with the rise of an industrial and modern society and the dependence or trust in abstract social systems – such as the exchange of goods and services or the use of money or credit. Trust in modernity resides in these abstract systems that produce some form of certain in the face of risks and hazards. Simmel (1978), for instance, writes: "Without the general trust that people have in each other, society itself would disintegrate, for very few relationships are based entirely upon what is known with certainty about another person, and very few relationships would endure if trust were not as strong as, or stronger than, rational proof or personal observation" (Simmel 1978: 178-9). For Weber too, one of the preconditions for the rise of modern capitalism was the transition from personal to impersonal trust. More modern writers (Beck 1992), that emphasize the increasing complexity and the extent to which a 'risk society' has emerged similarly point to trust as a way to facilitate decision making in the face of complexity and risk. As Dunn (1984) argues: "Trustworthiness, the capacity to commit one's self to fulfilling the legitimate expectation of others, is both the constitutive virtue of, and the key causal precondition for the existence of, any society" (Dunn 1984: 287).

The electronic edition of Gambetta's (1988) *Trust: Making and Breaking Cooperative Relations* seems a good place to start when trying to summarize the various conceptualizations of trust, not only because of ease of access to the material but also because the collection is based on a series of seminars in which some 'key thinkers' in the field were involved e.g. Luhmann, Lorenz, Gellner. At least on first inspection the collection examines a number of issues that are of interest to the DIRC project. Gambetta's interest stems from a concern with the lack of regional economic development in Southern Italy. His point is that for development to occur, collective interest is not both necessary and sufficient. In outlining the approach of the collection he says that it: -

> "tries to address the underlying problems, shared by many other
> political and economic areas where cooperation fails to emerge
> irrespective of the collective interest. It explores the causality of
> cooperation from the perspective of the belief on which cooperation is
> predicated, namely *trust*." (Foreword: vii)

Although we are not particularly interested in 'causal' analysis in this sense, the collection also approaches issues of trust in a way that would hold some sway with the DIRC approach. This follows from Gambetta's view that trust 'demands' a wide-ranging perspective. The papers in the collection range from looking at trust in the sense of differentiating it from other related concepts (e.g. Luhmann) to looking at 'trust in action' in particular settings (e.g. Lorenz). This chapter starts by looking at Luhmann's attempt at differentiating trust from other related concepts i.e. Luhmann's approach to the 'elusive notion'

There are a number of different theoretical approaches that have been taken to the study of trust, from Axelrod's (1997) calculative model, through to Luhmann's (1979; 1990) processual model. Luhmann's approach to the 'elusive notion' of trust starts by looking at the problem of conceptualizing trust. He argues that because trust has been theoretically 'ignored' then conceptual clarification has not been particularly attended to. He also argues that empirical work has muddied the conceptual waters by confusing trust with other issues, e.g., positive/negative attitudes, confidence, alienation, solidarity, participation - the issues it gets interchanged with being dependent on the setting being studied. Luhmann argues that such studies are merely re-rehearsing Gemeinschaft and Gesellschaft, and that further conceptual clarification is needed if we are to make any useful insights on what he calls 'trusting relations'. He argues that all approaches fail to pay attention to the social process of trust production, that they leave unspecified "the social mechanisms which generate trust." The notion of trust as a social process is the key question for Luhmann, within the idea of the function of trust as a general concern. A functional perspective on trust would seem to be a way in to its analysis, and relates to the DIRC project in terms of the notion of trust and its relationship to uncertainty, risk and dependability. Rather than emphasizing what trust does, however, investigations of how trust is achieved, how it can be seen in action, are needed. This would hopefully avoid some of the pitfalls of trying to talk about trust in an abstract sense, without reference to lived experience Luhmann's first aim is to differentiate trust from other related concepts. The first concept that Luhmann wants to distinguish from trust is familiarity. Luhmann sees familiarity as "an unavoidable fact of life, whereas trust is a "solution for specific problems of risk""(1990: 95). He sees familiarity as the broader context within which trust takes place, and the 'familiar' lebenswelt/lifeworld as our shifting but constant location. However, the main conceptual distinction, which Luhmann wants to make, is between trust and confidence. He says that both concepts refer to "expectations which may lapse into disappointments" but that,

> " If you do not consider alternatives ... you are in a situation of
> confidence. If you choose one action in preference of others in spite of
> the possibility of being disappointed by the action of others, you
> define the situation as one of trust. In the case of confidence you will
> react to disappointment by external attribution. In the case of trust you

will have to consider an internal attribution and eventually regret your trusting choice." (1990: 97-98)

Luhmann ascribes confidence to situations where we have no real choice; Luhmann argues that trust is required when a negative outcome would make you regret your action. However, confidence may revert to trust, and vice versa, when your potential for choice or influence changes in a given situation. Thus, "the relation between confidence and trust becomes a highly complex research issue" (1990:98).

Luhmann's central point is that all approaches fail to pay attention to the *social process of trust production*, i.e., they leave unspecified "the social mechanisms which generate trust" (1990: 95). Rather than emphasizing what trust does, investigations of how trust is achieved, how it can be seen in action, are needed. Our studies in DIRC take on board Luhmann's recommendation to look at trust accomplishment as a social process, for the idea of trust is manifested in organizational life in a number of different ways. So, for example, the emerging notion of the 'audit culture' (Strathern, Power) embraces a particular form of 'trust' – in making actions accountable, warrantable and punishable. Within such 'audit cultures' one has to be seen to be auditable, even if the actual efficacy of the audit itself is often difficult to demonstrate. As Power (1994) suggests, this kind of 'performed' audit is more concerned with 'rituals of verification' than with interrogating the content of actual work practice. Although a comparatively recent perspective the notion of audit culture can be seen as an extension of some of the ideas of Yates and 'control through communication' (Yates 1989). In this view, new communication genres – documents, records, memos and their storage technologies – developed as a product of organizational needs and available technologies. Older customs of form and style gave way in the face of a desire to make documents more efficient to create and use. Systematic management represented an attempt to impose standardized procedures on routing managerial work through 'method' or 'system'. This involved a careful definition of duties and responsibilities coupled with standardized procedures, a specific way of gathering, handling, analyzing and transmitting information whereby 'system' became the means by which information became trustable. However, the view explored here is, as Garfinkel (1963) suggests, that trust is more than the notion of audit, but is woven into the very fabric of everyday organizational life – the workaday world – as part of the 'taken for granted' moral order.

Our interest is in how trust is accomplished as a mundane feature of everyday work – looking in particular at two, inter-related and sometimes interchangeable, features of organizational life – paperwork and computer work. Our focus on trust in paper records and documents includes how trust is accomplished in everyday work, in particular work with and around records; and how trust can therefore be viewed as a product of work on the record, and incorporated in various ways into the record. The features we are interested in include a consideration of how, and in what ways, the organization of the record creates and sustains certain 'trustable' features as a recognizable sedimentation of activity, as a record of activity and actions. Another feature relevant to an analysis of records concerns trust and habit – the 'taken for granted' nature of social life. This includes the notion of physical location: the trust that records will be in their usual place and the need to account for any departures from the norm. These 'trustable' features of records come from, and reinforce, the way they are embedded in a moral order. As Zimmerman (1971) writes: "The taken for granted use of documents ... is largely dependent on an ordered world – the ordered world of organizations, and the ordered world of society at large."

Paper records are one of the ways in which the interdependencies within a division of labour are achieved. What emerges from our fieldwork in different organizational settings in the DIRC project is that records are not simple detached commentaries on activities but integral features of them. Records have a procedural implicativeness for the actions of organizationally relevant others because they represent organizational events and, consequently are tied to the production and the performance of organizational activities. Documents are typically part of transformation processes by which one set of actions initiates another set and are often 'glosses' of the work that goes into their production. It is in knowing what the record represents which provides for its use within the setting concerned. 'Knowing what the document represents' means knowing about the work that produced it, what it means within *this* activity, within *this* organization and how it might be used.

Our interest in trust and technology, trust and computer work stems from a concern with whether, as technology and work organization changes, different forms and problems of trust emerge? Kipnis (1996) for example, clearly links the nature of trust to the organization of work and the character of technology. Our interest is in what mutual trust exists within the organizational system (the socio-technical system), how this trust (and culture) is achieved and supported (or undermined) by IT systems, and the extent that the overall dependable delivery of organizational work is reliant on this trust. Within healthcare, for example, the electronic patient record (Hartswood et al 2000; Fitzpatrick 2000; Ellingsen and Monteiro 2001) has been presented as a means to provide timely and location-independent access to comprehensive, integrated patient data. Supporters have pointed to apparent shortcomings of the traditional paper-based medical record, suggesting not only is paper inferior as a record-keeping medium, but it also encourages various 'undesirable' record-keeping practices - for being hard to access, poorly organized, incomplete, inaccurate, hard to read, lacking consistency in format and so on. The electronic record, in healthcare and elsewhere, is consequently seen as providing the conditions for the imposition of greater discipline and structure on record-keeping practices and it has also become a major factor in the drive for standardization.

2. TRUST AND PAPER RECORDS

Paper records, their creation, keeping and use have been the subject of research for some time, documents and document work are often a principal locus for cooperative work, but this interest has been given a new momentum by the move towards computerization and electronic records (Heath and Luff 1996; Hertzum 1999; Hughes et al 1996; Komito 1998). This research has examined both the organizational factors and reasons behind the varied activities of document work, the socially organized practices and reasoning associated with routine, 'workaday' use; as well as the 'affordances' of paper with an interest in how such affordances of paper, might be reproduced electronically. As Berg comments: *"When it is acknowledged that the medical record is interwoven with the structure of medical work in fundamental ways, that different medical record systems embody different notions of how work is organized, different modes of configuring patient bodies, and so forth, we are in a position to better understand and intervene upon the issues that are at stake."* This section continues and extends this interest in records, their organizational justification and the various forms in which records can appear, through an ethnographic examination of record keeping, organizational change and issues of trust. 'Trust' here relates to the generalized ability to "take for granted, to take under trust, a vast array of features of the social order". As records and record keeping proliferate, and as the technology and organizational culture changes, with organizations becoming increasingly distributed, so issues of trust and related notions such as risk become notable. Put simply, our interest is particularly in 'how' (rather than 'why') people in organizational life often appear to place great trust in the often less than pristine, and heavily and (allegedly) illegibly annotated pieces of paper.

Our interest lies in trying to understand *in detail* how and in what ways and in what precise circumstances artefacts such as records and the various representations they contain come to be trusted or trustable. What features of the record and the work that surrounds it and goes into its production, do we need to understand, capture and represent in order to maintain or develop trust? How do documents get worked up and enter into everyday work as trustable, reliable artifacts? One perspicuous setting for the study of documents in DIRC was the toxicology ward within a large Edinburgh hospital. The Deliberate Self Harm (DSH) unit is a specialised inpatient service that allows for joint medical and psychiatric assessment of patients who typically have been referred following a suspected self-harm incident. The patient record epitomizes the traditional, much criticized, departmentally oriented, paper-based record. It consists of a set of paper records that accumulate over the course of the treatment and subsequent disposal of a patient. The patient record contains a heterogeneous series of paper documents associated with the patient's current admission. Each of these documents has a particular sort of modularity and stands in relation to the other components of the record and the disciplines that attend to them in particular sorts of ways.

Looking at everyday use of the records gives some insight into how records become trustable features of mundane working practice. Record folders for each patient are kept in a trolley that follows the cycle of activity within the ward. During the morning ward round (usually held between 8.30 and 9.00am) it is wheeled from bed to bed and each of the record folders are accessed. Then at 9.00am a handovers takes place where the consultant toxicologist runs through the medical status of each of the patients, and a nurse gives a 'psychosocial' handover. The records trolley is wheeled into the ward at the beginning of this meeting, allowing sequential access to the records as each patient is discussed. A nurse produces each of the records in turn, referring to the progress notes to give a brief synopsis of salient factors of each presentation. At the end of the morning meeting the patients are allocated to team members for assessment, who then avail themselves of the relevant notes. Team members will typically read through these notes prior to seeing the patient. The records are consulted and updated during the ongoing process of assessment.

What emerges from these observations is the tie between the location of the records as a collection, and the particular activities carried out on the ward, and variations in the organization of the records as a collection depending on the activity. The record as a central focus of activity entails brings members involved in different activities associated with the patient into alignment. Furthermore, the obligations and rituals associated with the keeping and sharing of records allow members to demonstrate a regard for each other's work and to maintain the impression of the work as a collaborative, team effort, carried out by members with notionally different statuses. Records and recording practices then are used as resources for maintaining relations or 'trust' between members, what Goffman (1982) terms 'ritual supplies'. The progress notes, for example, provide a temporal account of the work performed with the patient. They tell the story of the patient's visit, from the perspectives of those involved in the patient's care. The toxicology inpatient assessment form codifies parts of the assessment (by employing devices such as labeled fields, tick boxes, lists of actions and the like) and again is organized chronologically, detailing the admission by the nursing staff, the medical clerking of the patient, some components of the patient's ongoing medical care, the psychiatric assessment, and the discharge procedure. In addition, there are a number of documents that are incorporated into the record by placing them in the file, including blood test results, cardiogram traces etc, as well as suicide notes, letters faxed from other hospitals etc. Without making too much of such simple interaction what is also going on here - and it is clearly one of the 'affordances' of a paper record as well as fundamental to notions of 'trust' - is what Goodwin (1994) refers to as 'professional vision'. It is through such routine, everyday document work and its associated annotation, coding, highlighting and so on that 'participants build and contest *professional vision*, which consists of socially organized ways of seeing and understanding events'; an accredited way of seeing within a professional discipline. Examining such shared use of records also facilitates an understanding of what it means for groups, defined by their different expertise and responsibilities, to work together 'as a team'.

Any account of routine work in the toxicology ward raise important questions about the role of documents in work activities. In particular, documents/records as 'trustable' artefacts; how this trust is an accomplishment of various forms of organizational work; how such features of the record as its 'trustability' enter into and are a part of everyday work with documents and patients. Through their public character, paper records provide the knowledgeable member, that is, anyone who has been with the organization long enough to 'learn the ropes', with status information that can be 'read off' from the environment without undue effort through 'peripherally attending' to the surroundings. As we have already outlines, as they pass or progress through the organization, documents gather additions that provide a 'story' making plain who has handled the document, and what action has been taken as a result. In such cases the document can be seen as a 'stratified trace' of the activities of the organization and can be interrogated to this effect. A paper document can facilitate co-ordinating tasks across a complex division of labour, by making socially available the allocation of tasks – who has done what. The use of documents and the accompanying informal interaction can then be seen as integral elements in the generation of the orderliness of activities and part of the routine accomplishment of trust. Furthermore, the emphasis on paper, as it is in so many other organizations, is closely linked to the need for an audit trail and to questions of accountability should these arise. The supposed 'completeness' of the paper record is part of its 'trustability' and permits it to act as an audit trail;

providing an outline of, and justification for various decisions, for records, despite their mundane, 'seen but unnoticed' status, are normatively regulated, and enter into the moral order where their status as trustable artefacts is clearly important.

3. TRUST & COMPUTER SYSTEMS

It is unlikely that anyone who has ever spent any time observing, or working in, an environment in which computer systems are an integral part of the work will have failed to notice the cries of anguish, frustration and occasional anger as computers supposedly fail to 'do what they are supposed to'. Trust can be observed to be an important feature, if not 'the' important feature of everyday work with computer systems. One increasingly important aspect of this, as new software and systems are introduced, is the interaction with and issues surrounding the replacement of, 'legacy' systems.

The DIRC fieldwork provides a number of other examples of the problems that arise with legacy systems in everyday use, with, for example, systems unable to 'talk' to any of the other databases or management information systems. Such 'legacy' issues can arise relatively rapidly due to the fast changing nature of organizational priorities and organizational life. These concerns are not merely technological in focus but also organizational in the sense of being intimately wrapped up in 'trustability', and the everyday accomplishment of work. Because such trust is important in everyday work, an appreciation of legacy needs to move away from a purely technological stance - with its emphasis on ageing systems and outdated code - to admit the importance and impact of organizational issues. Any attempt to resolve legacy issues will depend for its success on understanding that organizational change will necessarily have to confront legacies as the practical issues of daily work; understanding how technologies become embedded and are oriented to within everyday working practice. Issues of trust are relevant here since trust arises not simply from the technology but from the ways it is embedded in social and organizational processes and relationships. The paradox of legacy systems is that despite their outdated or outmoded character they are often trustable and adhered to long after their usefulness has become limited, if not a positive block on the progress of management, precisely because of the way in which they are embedded in longstanding social and organizational processes

Our first example of the trust issues involved in the use of technology as an everyday feature of organizational life is drawn from a study, a field trial, of an expert system for the detection of breast cancer. Here the trust issues centred around whether, and to what extent, the expert system was 'reliable and trustable' – the degree to which readers might come to believe and trust the output of the system when it tells them a feature on a mammogram is, or is not, suspicious. The study, an extended investigation of reading practices, formed part of a 12 month HTA/EPSRC funded field trial of a computer aided detection (CAD) tool, considering issues of usability for the deployment of the proposed system within the NHS breast screening programme. Our interest was in the effects of the tool on reader performance and how (and if) readers made sense of the tool's behaviour. The tool itself targeted micro-calcifications, as well as ill-defined and spiculated lesions. Suspicious areas on the mammogram were identified by prompts - calcification clusters were marked by a shaded triangle; ill-defined lesions were marked with an asterix; and circle was drawn around either prompt type if the system's confidence was high. The expert system on trial consisted of two components, a scanning and processing unit and a film viewer to display the prompts. As with conventional reading, films on the viewing box were scrolled up and down. However, when the button used to scroll the next set of films into view was pressed then the prompts screens were 'switched off' and a further button needed to be pressed to see the prompts. In this way readers were encouraged to examine the films in the conventional fashion prior to examining the prompts.

Our previous studies have shown how readers reflexively adapt their working practices in order to build and sustain their 'professional vision' (Goodwin, 1994), and that this, in turn, contributes to the management of individual and collective performance. Readers have evolved an 'ecology of practice' for performance management that is deployed as part of the routine of screening work. (Hartswood, Procter and Slack, 2000; Hartswood, Procter, Slack and Rouncefield, 2000). For example, readers use a repertoire of manipulations to make certain features on the mammogram 'more visible'. A magnifying glass may be used to assess the shape, texture and arrangement of calcifications or, where the breast is dense, the film may be removed and taken to a separate light box. In cases where a suspicious feature was seen on one view readers might use their fingers or an object such as a pen for measurement and calculation. These repertoires of manipulations were an integral part of the embodied practice of reading.

We have noted elsewhere (Hartswood et al 2001) that readers make use of 'worldly interpretations' (Driessen, 1999) of the significance of the object - through ideas about 'territories of normal appearance' and 'incongruity procedures' (Sacks 1972). There are objects that do not belong in a 'normal' (i.e. non-recallable) film, and the positioning of an object in a particular area of the breast renders it more suspicious than if it had been elsewhere. At the same time certain areas within the mammogram are regarded as more difficult to interpret and readers particularly oriented to them in their examinations. As one reader noted:

"..I have areas where I know I'm weak at seeing .. you know ones that you've missed .. one is over the .muscle there .. if you don't make a conscious effort to look there you tend not to see that bit of breast .. and the other area is right down in the chest wall - breast and chest wall area .. because in older women the cancers tend to be in the upper outer quadrant so I look in that area very carefully .. it depends on the type of breast really .. I try to look at the whole film, because I know if I just glance at it and don't make that conscious effort I don't look.."

Bearing these existing skills or 'professional vision' in mind, the main strengths of the CAD system lay in picking up subtle signs - that some readers felt they might have missed - and stimulating interaction between film reader and the technology by prompting them to re-examine the mammogram. As one reader said:

"Those micros that the computer picked up .. I might have missed it if I was reading in a hurry .. I'd certainly missed them on the oblique.." "I thought they were very useful, they make me look more closely at the films .. I make my own judgment .. but if the prompt is pointing things out I will go and look at it again"

There was also a perception that the CAD system was more consistent than readers:

".. its just the fact that its more consistent than you are .. because it's a machine.."

Readers also frequently expressed the opinion that they had skills or deficiencies in noticing particular types of object within films. Here CAD prompts were seen as useful, both compensating in some (consistent) way for any individual weaknesses of the reader and as a reminder of 'good practice':

"My approach tends to be to look for things that I know I'm not so good at ... there are certain things that you do have to prompt yourself to look at, one of them being the danger areas."

"I'd made up my mind about where the cancer was .. but I was looking at all these other areas .. because one has to look at the other breast from experience because one has to look for the second cancer that maybe difficult to see .. and also you're looking for multi-focal cancer .. "

Amongst the weaknesses of the tool identified by readers – weaknesses that impacted on its 'trustability' - was the distracting appearance of too many prompts:

"this is quite distracting .. there's an obvious cancer there (pointing) but the computer's picked up a lot of other things.." "there's so many prompts .. especially benign calcifications .. you've already looked and seen there are lots of benign calcs.."

In addition the system was also seen to prompt the 'wrong' things, in particular benign features of artefacts of the film process:

" .. what the computer has picked up is benign .. it may even be talcum powder.."
'I'm having trouble seeing the calc its picked up there ..(pointing) . I can only think
its an artefact on the film (a thin line at the edge of the film)"

At the same time the system was seen to be missing obvious prompts that
raised wider issues to do with trusting and 'understanding' the machine:

" That's quite a suspicious mass on the CC .. I'm surprised it didn't pick it up on
the oblique.." (Points to area) "I'm surprised the computer didn't spot it .. its so spiky
.. I'd definitely call that back.." "I'm surprised the computer didn't pick that up .. my
eye went to it straight away.."

That the CAD system did not detect 'obvious' cancers (because the
system deliberately ignored obvious or massive cancers over 20mm –
something many readers simply forgot) leads us to ask how readers used the
prompts to make sense of the system's prompting behaviour. Readers
occasionally held incorrect notions about the system and were often baffled
by the high level of false prompt (again this was related to the sensitivity and
prompting rate built into the tool). In these instances any lack of trust
engendered was a product of not clearly understanding how the machine
worked. The (in)ability to make sense of how the tool behaved evidently
impacts on issues of dependability and trust. How readers use prompts to
inform their decision-making, and how they make sense of a prompting
tool's behaviour, may be important for maximizing effectiveness
(Hartswood et al., 1997b; Hartswood and Procter, 1998; 2000a). We found
that readers rationalized 'false' prompts by devising explanations or accounts
of its behaviour that were grounded in the properties of the mammogram
image itself - that it was talcum powder, or an artefact of the developing
process. This points to general issues concerning trust – users' perception of
the dependability of the evidence generated by such tools - and how trust is
influenced by users' capacity for making sense of how the tool behaves. The
question, of course, is how *do* readers construct, achieve or *make* sense of
the machine? Following Schütz (1967) we might argue that readers render
mammograms intelligible using a mosaic of 'recipe knowledge'. While the
common experiences and rules and, importantly, trust embodied in the
'mosaic' are always open to potential revision they are, nevertheless,
generally relied upon for all practical purposes as furnishing criterion by
which adequate sense may be assembled and practical activities realised – in
this case reading the mammogram -.

Of course in everyday interaction any breakdown in sense is rapidly
repaired and 'trustability' restored. However, when the other participant in
the interaction is a computer, difficulties can arise as readers rush to
premature and often mistaken conclusions about what has happened, what is
happening, and what the machine 'meant' by a prompt. The problem is, of
course, that the machine generally provides no account of its actions – and is
unable to 'repair' people's mistaken beliefs. As Dourish (2001) writes:

" In just the same way as they approach all other activities, they (users) need to be able to decide what to do in order to get things done. In everyday interaction ... accountability is the key feature that enables them to do this. The way that activities are organized makes their nature available to others; they can be seen and inspected, observed and reported. But this feature - the way that actions are organized - is exactly what is hidden by software abstractions. Not by accident either but by design. .. (what) is hidden is information about how the system is doing what it does, how the perceived action is organized .. It requires a technical approach that provides three primary features. First we need to find a way to ensure that the account that is offered of the system's behaviour (that) is strongly connected to the behaviour that it describes. .. Second, we need to find a way to allow this representation to be tied to the action in such a way that the account emerges along with the action rather than separately from it ... Third, we need to ensure that the account that is offered is an account of the current specific behaviour of the system.." (Dourish 2001: 83-85)

Our next example comes from some studies of the introduction and use of expert systems and databases within a large commercial bank. As Smith and Wield (1988) suggested some time ago - massive organizational changes and the changes in consumer behaviour has increasingly moved bank work away from the supposedly 'classical model':

"The classical model of bank work involved customers and staff in face to face trust relations. Banking was thus far from an exclusively impersonal set of accounting calculations and ledger entries. It was, and to a declining extent still is, based on intensive and often long standing personal relations."(Smith & Wield 1988)

The range of technology available to the financial services industry has increased markedly in terms of the increasingly sophisticated usage of standard accounting and relational database packages, and in the development and provision of a range of communications technologies and 'expert' programs. The accounting and database packages provide an obvious representation of the customer in terms of the history of the working of an account and the varied dealings with the bank and its products. Expert programs similarly incorporate and depend on a whole series of models, predictions and scenarios of customer behaviour such that the 'customer in the machine' can be depicted as a complex but knowable entity. Our interest was in how the technology within the bank, by giving access to a customer's account or relationship history, or through 'expert' programs with their typifications of customer behaviour, was regularly brought into play as a 'trustable' technology and as an aspect of everyday, mundane customer work. Within this particular bank – responding to a wide range of commercial pressures – the technology developed a typology of the bank's customers in terms of utilizations of bank products, spending and income patterns. Analyses of the working of the customer's account and the database of 'Customer Notes' (which contained a record of every contact between the bank and the customer) were used to construct a 'picture' of the customer which then played a part in the complex interaction between the customer and the bank. This record was valuable through its procedural implicativeness in informing and guiding the actions of others, comprising an important component in the individual worker's 'sense of organization'.

This attempt to ensure standardization and consistency in decision-making and procedure through increasing reliance on the technology produced a conflict between traditional ideas of 'relationship management' (in the sense of managing accounts according to what was 'known' about the customer as the product of a longstanding relationship) and management according to expert risk grading and assessment packages. As one manager said of the increasing reliance on technology: *"...the machine will give you a recommendation. if the machine says 'No' and that decision is overridden its 90% likely to go down the pan...loans 'down the pan ' have reduced considerably since the introduction of machines"*. Furthermore, the suggestion was that any relevant local knowledge will in the future be available 'in the machine' through a standardized approach to maintaining their customer relational database. In these circumstances what became important in such customer work was orientation to the technologies containing the customer record. Attentiveness to the 'virtual customer' represented in organizational records and attentiveness to unraveling the history of the customer's account and complaint using the available technology became especially important for organizational actions. The importance of the electronic record was manifested in the everyday fact that practically every instance of customer contact began with the provision of an account number so that details of account working or customer notes were available before the customer came 'on line'.

This short extract from the fieldwork observations illustrates some of the subtleties involved in the use of, and trust in, the technology. This case unfolded over several hours and involved a businessman whose account cards have been retained by the bank's ATM but who claims that somebody at the Lending Centre - 'Mark' - had already verbally agreed an increase in his overdraft limit. Here the Manager uses the technology to provide information as he mediates between the 'real' customer, angry because he cannot get access to any money; and the 'virtual customer' presented in terms of an account with a borrowing and relationship history on the Manager's computer screen. In this first section the customer has gone into the branch where his cards have 'been eaten', has related his story, and is now 'playing merry hell', so the branch have contacted the Lending Centre;

> Phones Team Member (PTM): "I've got .. branch on the phone .. card retained.." explains case - "a high risk grade account.. we've got all the markers on .. he said (Mark) agreed ..." "he said are you calling me a liar .. I said No, I'm just trying to

determine the facts .. " "he's now gone into QQQ branch and is playing merry hell"

Manager goes with (PTM) to her workstation to look at the account (836) on screen - using screen to examine working of the account - "I think he's trying to pull a fast one"..

Some hours later, having perused the customer's account history and notes, and the bank's staff attendance database that informs him that 'Mark' was on holiday on the day in question, the Manager is preparing to phone the customer about his complaint. Again he uses the accounting package and the relational database to look at the working of the account prior to and during the call.

Manager: "Hello Mr X.. my name's .... I understand we've sent a couple of letters (can see that this is the case from 'Customer Notes' on screen) .. now you've been into .. branch and it's (the card) been retained and you went into QQQ branch (to complain).

You spoke to someone called Mark I understand .. Normally what happens . if you ring up and we agree .. we mark an interview note to that effect..

You're saying it was definitely last week?.. .. There's no interview note to say it

I know you spoke to Mark on 8th February (looking at Customer Notes) .. but you say you spoke to Mark since then .. and there's no notes on this at all"

In this potentially fraught customer interaction the manager uses the computer and specifically the accounting and database packages containing customer notes, account working, and transactions through the account, to carefully manage the situation, demonstrating a mastery of the details of the account's working. He then carefully explains the way forward, again using the technology, weaving it into his telephone conversation.

".. When you have a conversation with someone at the Lending Centre .. for us to bear with you (to let borrowers exceed their agreed borrowing terms) ... they have to mark a limit on the account..

Now we have to sort it out today.... The way the system works now is you have to stay within an agreed limit .. We have to mark the limit ahead of time .. (otherwise account will automatically appear as 'out of order')

"I'm just getting some info on the screen.. (looking at account) .. What sort of work are you doing at the moment? .. What sort of turnover?.. OK.. That's not what's been going through the account recently has it?.. (using machine - customer notes) .... I'm just looking at some of your customer notes ..

What's your business card limit at the moment .. cos that was increased back in December wasn't it .. yeah .. Have you sent a business plan?

The things to do for today .. We can look at increasing your limit.. the re-issue of your business card .. and the getting of a (new) business card for you ..

If we were looking to increase your limit what would you want it increased to? ....
Let's just (using machine to check balance) .. You stand at .. your balance on
uncleareds is 791 OD against a limit of 400 .. until cheques cleared .."

Here the Manager is dealing, through the technology, with a customer he
has never seen, negotiating a 'fit' between the customer as represented in the
computer records and the customer as presented through the telephone. This
process is facilitated by frequent reference to the electronic customer record.
Within the bank such expert systems and databases are not only trustable and
useful but are an essential part of the everyday, taken for granted, mundane
world.

But this is skilful *use* of the technology, not a simpleminded trust in the
technology alone. For the numbers representing certain kinds of activity on a
customer's account have no *absolute* significance in themselves. Rather it is
the situated arrival at some kind of *meaning* for those numbers. The numbers
that drive the machine-based representations of the customer have no
inherent meaning outside of their situated use. It is rather that the way
numbers provide for a working representation of necessarily contingent
phenomena in such a way that those phenomena can be classified and
communicated in a form that is commonsensically recognisable to anyone
else engaged in similar activities. It is mathematization of the necessarily
unique, contingent, and unpredictable in such a way that it becomes
generalizable and predictable *in the context of particular working practices*.
Workers in the bank draw upon a common stock of knowledge regarding
what any set of numbers might or might not mean in a certain set of
circumstances. This is not used as a rule for what those numbers will always
mean, but rather as a visibly oriented to resource for arriving at just what this
set of numbers means in this particular set of circumstances. However,
despite the increasing importance of the 'customer in the machine', issues of
skill, local knowledge, or cooperation and coordination do not 'go away'
when mundane activities are machine mediated. 'Local knowledge' remains a
stubbornly persistent feature of decision-making. Whatever the classificatory
regimes imposed by expert systems, the problem of determining exactly
what each 'case' is a case of, especially in relatively unusual circumstances,
remains one of 'occasioned determination' in the course of the work itself.
And the single most noticeable thing about the introduction of new
technology, is the extent to which it becomes a tool through which to
achieve 'business as usual'. The introduction of new technology in the bank
has then not so much completely re-written the relationship between the
bank and its customers as necessitated the development of new 'routines',
and new competencies. These competencies relate to the continued
maintenance of trust and to the continued production of accountable,
trustable, decisions in particular circumstances.

4. CONCLUSION: OCCASIONING TRUST

Computer systems, databases, expert systems etc pervade the everyday world of work. Using this technology is an everyday matter and part of this 'everydayness', part of its mundane, taken for granted character lies in trusting the technology – at least until given a good reason not to. As Garfinkel (1963) argues trust forms the background expectancy of everyday interaction. The issue of trusting or not trusting technology in the everyday organizational world is then an *occasioned* matter. Since trust is such a routine background expectancy in both everyday interaction and in our everyday use of technology, the interesting design issue becomes determining, investigating, exactly how, in the everyday world, people orient to the question of the trustworthiness of a system.

Some general conclusions about trust and organizational work have emerged from DIRC's empirical work on trust; especially work with paper and electronic records. So, for example, our studies have explicated: how records handle information incorporating notions of trust that the record is accurate or checkable; how records add meaning, incorporating the trust that the information is meaningful or can be made meaningful, that it can provide some form of stratified trace of the orderliness of activities. Similarly while records provide organizational members with some notion of a history of an activity, an account, a patient, a customer etc, and provide a means for coordinating actions, important elements of trust reside in such an historical record, that it presents an accurate account of the order of events. This implies that using a record is not simply a question of 'reading the record' but translating the circumstances of a patient or a customer into an appropriate organizational formulation and the apparent solidity and objectivity of information – its 'trustability' - can continually be challenged as new data appear and as circumstances change. Our empirical data points to a number of trust issues - related to the way that record use is a fundamental aspect of the moral order of the working division of labour - that may be relevant to the introduction of the electronic records. There are implications both for the collection and recording of information, as well as for the access and use of information by others. Our studies document ways in which while members' work practices clearly show all the signs of attending to predictable, formalized and repeatable procedures, at the same time they also display elements of unpredictable, improvised and situated activity and in that fashion maintain the trustable status of the record (the patient record, the customer record etc), and it is precisely such ad hoc interventions of local routines that trade upon, reinforce and modify the trust status of the record. While information gathering and sharing is central to organizational work, its accomplishment often has little to do with the formal structure or content of the record. Instead, mundane interactional competences - knowing how to preface, repair, produce formulations, tell stories, develop scenarios - are routinely observed to play an important part in the work, incorporating instances of the working up of a sense of shared experience that draws upon assumed sets of common-sense, taken for granted, trustable understandings about 'how we do this kind of work'. While our research points to the continuing relevance of various forms of 'local knowledge' the suggestion is that any relevant local knowledge will in the future be available 'in the machine' through a standardized approach to maintaining databases. However, whereas face-to-face interactions can be maintained by the simple expedient of asking questions, relevant knowledge 'in the machine' relies on other operatives having regularly, rigorously and routinely input information. It also makes important demands on the technology in an evolutionary sense. Thus and for instance, the reconfiguration of these technologies to incorporate these 'informal' knowledges implicates the operative in 'making the knowledge fit'. Database fields have standard sizes, and may well have standard notations. For the operative, the job of work is to 'fit' their knowledge to these standard formats in such a way that relevant knowledge of the customer is trustably incorporated. The point is that within the database this information has to be such that *other people* can work with the data and thereby maintain levels of trust. The 'trust' issue poses interesting and challenging issues for systems design and the 'dependability problem' becomes not so much concerned with the relatively simple creation of new technical artefacts or the 'computerization' and replacement of work practices but with the effective integration of computer systems with existing and developing work practices.

REFERENCES

1. Axelrod, R. (1997) Complexity of Co-operation: agent based models of competition and collaboration. Princeton. Princeton UP.
2. Beck, U. (1992) Risk Society: Towards a New Modernity. London. Sage.
3. Berg, M. (1997). Rationalising Medical Work: Decision Support techniques and Medical Practices. Cambridge: MIT Press.
4. Dunn, J. (1984) The concept of 'trust' in the politics of John Locke. In Rorty, R. Schneewind, J.B. and Skinner, Q. (eds) Philosophy in History. Cambridge. Cambridge University Press. Pp 279-301.
5. Ellingsen, G. and Monterio, E. (2001): A patchwork planet: The heterogeneity of electronic patient record systems in hospitals. In Proceedings of the Information Systems Research Seminar in Scandinavia (IRIS'2000, Uddevalla, Sweden, August).

6. Fitzpatrick, G. (2000) Understanding the Paper Record in Practice: Implications for EHRs. In *Proceedings of HIC'2000*.

7. Fogg, B. and Tseng, H. 'The elements of computer credibility'. In *Proceedings of CHI'99*, pp 80-87, ACM Press, New York.

8. Fukuyama, F. (1996) Trust: The Social Virtues and the Creation of Prosperity. London. Penguin.

9. Gambetta, D. (1990) (ed). Trust: Making and Breaking Cooperative Relations, Oxford.Basil Blackwell.Available online at www.sociology.ox.ac.uk/trustbook.html

10. Gambetta, D. (ed). Trust: Making and Breaking Cooperative Relations, electronic edition, Department of sociology, University of Oxford, www.sociology.ox.ac.uk/papers.

11. Garfinkel, H. (1963) A conception of, and experiment with 'trust' as a condition of stable, concerted actions. In Harvey O.J. (ed) Motivation and Social Interaction. New York. The Ronald Press. pp 187-238.

12. Garfinkel, H. (1967). Studies in Ethnomethodology. Englewood Cliffs, NY.

13. Goffman, E. (1982) Interaction Ritual: Essays on Face to Face Behaviour. Pantheon Books

14. Goodwin, C. (1994) Professional Vision. American Anthropologist 96(3): 606-633

15. Hartswood, M., Procter, R., Rouncefield, M. and Sharpe, M. (2000) Making a Case in Medical Work: Implications for the Electronic Medical Record. In press - The Journal of CSCW.

16. Heath, C. and Luff, P. (1996). Documents and Professional Practice: 'bad' organizational reasons for 'good' clinical records, in *Proceedings of CSCW '96* (Boston MA, November), ACM Press, 354-362.

17. Hertzum, M. (1999) Six Roles of Documents in Professional's Work. In *Proceedings of ECSCW'99*. Kluwer. 41-60.

18. Hughes, J., King, V., Mariani, J, Rodden, T and Twidale, M. (1996) Paperwork and its Lessons for Database Systems: an Initial Assessment. In Shapiro, D., Tauber, M and Traunmuller, R. (1996) (eds) The Design of Computer Supported Cooperative Work and Groupware Systems. Amsterdam. Elsevier. 43-66.

19. Kipnis, D. (1996) Trust and Technology. In Kramer, R and Tyler, T. (1996) (eds) Trust in Organizations: Frontiers of Theory and Research. London. Sage. 39-50.

20. Komito, L. (1998) Paper 'Work' And Electronic Files: defending professional practice. Journal of Information Technology 13 (4): December 1998.

21. Luhmann, N. (1979) Trust and Power, Chichester, Wiley.

22. Luhmann, N. (1990) 'Familiarity, Confidence, trust: problems and Alternatives' in Gambetta, D. (ed) Trust: Making and Breaking Co-operative Relations, electronic edition, Department of Sociology, University of Oxford, chapter 6, pp 94-107. http://www.sociology.ox.ac.uk/papers/luhmann94-107.pdf.

23. Mistzal, B. A. (1996) Trust in Modern Societies: The Search for the Bases of Social Order. Cambridge. Polity Press.

24. Power, M. (1994) The Audit Explosion. Demos, London,

25. Power, M., The Audit Society: rituals of verification, Oxford University Press, Oxford, (1997)

26. Simmel, G. (1978) The Philosophy of Money. London. Routledge.

27. Star, S. L. and Griesemer, J. R. (1989). Institutional Ecology, 'translations', and boundary objects: amateurs and professionals in Berkeley's Museum of Vertebrate Zoology, 1907-39. Social Studies of Science vol. 19: 387-420.

28. Strathern, M. (2000) (ed) Audit Cultures: Anthropological studies in accountability, ethics and the academy. London. Routledge.

29. Yates, J. (1989) Control through Communication: The Rise of System in American Management. Baltimore. John Hopkins University Press.
30. Zimmerman, D. (1971) Record Keeping and the Intake Process in a Public Welfare Organization. In Wheeler, S. (ed). On Record: Files and Dossiers in American Life. Russell Sage Foundation, New York.

Chapter 2

WHEN A BED IS NOT A BED: CALCULATION AND CALCULABILITY IN COMPLEX ORGANISATIONAL SETTINGS

Karen Clarke, John Hughes, Mark Rouncefield, Terry Hemmings
Departments of Computing and Sociology, Lancaster University

1. INTRODUCTION

This chapter presents preliminary findings from the Dependability Interdisciplinary Research Collaboration (DIRC) project, a collaborative six-year research project examining issues of dependability in a number of organisational settings. We are in the process of ethnographic fieldwork at three hospitals in the North-West of England, examining managerial work at each of these three sites. The fieldwork has involved shadowing the clinical and directorate managers of various departments, clinics and wards in order to explore the managerial work that they do. The focus of the DIRC project is on trust in technology and the data from our empirical studies are being used to look at trust as a process embedded in the daily work practice of the clinicians, managers and other staff involved in a given area. With this project focus in mind, this chapter examines the use of computerised and paper-based information systems on a particular day, and how a dependable or 'trusted' state of affairs is established in a 'crisis' situation. Here we pay attention to one aspect of this managerial work, namely 'bed management': how the availability of beds is managed on a day-to-day basis.

This research has been carried out within the context of a large organisation undergoing a shift in its approach to record keeping. The hospitals where we have carried out our fieldwork, as part of a national policy process, are using information technology more and more for record-keeping purposes, replacing and supporting previous paper-based systems.

K. Clarke, G. Hardstone, M. Rouncefield and I. Sommerville (eds.), Trust in Technology:
A Socio-Technical Perspective, 21–38.

policy process is one whose aim is standardisation of work practice along with assumed improvements in the delivery of healthcare. The UK National Health Service (NHS) is experiencing enormous growth in the deployment of information and communications technologies (ICTs). Extensive use of technology serves to 'reconfigure the organisation' through its application in data analysis, communication and decision support. Recent policy shifts in healthcare in the UK have been towards an evidence-based healthcare approach and clinical governance, approaches that have emphasised the need for standardisation of professional practice in healthcare settings. An increased role for new technology is at the heart of these policy shifts, with increased use of, for example, computerised information systems as the purported route to a more effective healthcare service (Berg, 1997; Bloor & Maynard, 1997; Department of Health, 1997). Standardisation and computerisation are seen as the solutions to the 'health problem', and in this way it is argued that information systems in healthcare will become more trustworthy. Fitzpatrick argues that that all technology design for healthcare settings "should start with the question 'how do we support clinical practice', which requires that we understand more about the realities of that practice" (Fitzpatrick, 2000). This policy approach is central to the issues in this chapter.

Shared information displays in Healthcare settings are intended to provide major benefits in support of the co-ordination of patient care; in organising and locating clinical information; in coordinating and managing patient healthcare; and in organisational integration. Providing IT support for contingent managerial work however requires that systems necessarily pay attention to the occasioned character of activities. We propose to discuss issues surrounding the affordances of an existing non-digital display and the ways in which features such as calculation and calculability, and annotation are taken for granted by users and often ignored by designers.

Findings from the ethnographic studies bring to the fore issues regarding the production and utilisation of information in everyday managerial work. The factors relevant to information use in managerial working practices point to issues which must be addressed in the design of digital displays This chapter will examine the use of an existing non-digital display – the 'beds board' – and its use in the management of patient care. The beds board is used within a management process that also uses a computerised Management Information System (MIS) in the provision of bed information. As the use of the 'beds board' indicates, the task of supporting complex, collaborative work is not a matter of simply automating existing records or procedures.

For practical purposes we propose to introduce examples that allow us to focus on everyday managerial work in a hospital trust, namely 'bed management', how the availability of beds is managed on a day-to-day basis. We will deal with some of the complexities involved in the use of technology in the provision of information, the production and utilisation of that information in everyday managerial work, and the factors relevant to information use in managerial working practices. On the DIRC project (www.dirc.org) we deployed ethnographic research techniques that have increasingly been utilised in studies of technologies in use (Bowers, Button & Sharrock, 1995; Button & Sharrock, 1997; Hughes, King, Randall & Sharrock, 1993; Hughes, King, Rodden & Andersen, 1994; Hughes, Rouncefield & Tolmie, 2002). The advantage of this approach lies in the 'sensitising' it promotes to the real world character and practical context of activities. Concrete examples will be incorporated that provide 'live' insight into activities surrounding a 'beds crisis' on a particular day with a specific Directorate Manager (DM), and the use of a non-digital beds board within the management of the crisis.

2. GOOD REASONS FOR BAD RECORDS: REPRESENTING THE WORK

Historically, notions of the information age assume a major role for technology in the shaping of work and its day-to-day organisation (Robins & Webster, 1999). Complex organisations most obviously display forms of organisational knowledge in the Weberian sense (Weber, 1978): simply put, information formally collected, collated and archived about the organisation and its activities. The focus here is on what may loosely be termed 'management information'. What is meant by the term 'management information' differs in different contexts. Other ethnographic studies have looked at the production of representations of managerial work (see for example: Hughes, Rouncefield & Tolmie, 2002) that are used by managers to account for their working activity. Here, we shift in emphasis away from management information used to account for the work of managers themselves, to the use of management information used alongside other sources of local knowledge in the everyday routines of managerial work. The main 'other source' examined in this chapter is the 'beds board' – a notice board consisting of a representation of the occupancy of beds on a ward area. Here we see the 'representation' of the bed occupancy on the ward as a practical, situated activity within the 'real world, real time' work within the hospital. The representation involves the use of the local skills and knowledge of those involved in its production and use. In this way, our interest is in the interactional work involved in the use and monitoring of management information. Through our examination of a 'beds crisis' we will highlight issues regarding the mooted benefits and affordances of public displays. As Bowers, Button and Sharrock recommend (Bowers, Button & Sharrock, 1995; Button & Sharrock, 1997,) the key to 'optimal use' of the new communications infrastructures is the appropriate development of systems to support work co-ordination. We also want to keep in mind the cautionary note about displays that:

" What anyone can find them to say or to mean will depend on interpretation of the displays. Running your eye down the print-out, whizzing through the file returns, tells you very little unless you know what to look for and where" (Anderson, Hughes & Sharrock, 1989)

Garfinkel (in Turner, 1975) reported on the 'normal, natural troubles' that may be encountered by the researcher in attempting to utilize clinic records for research purposes. The title of Garfinkel's paper – 'Good' Organizational Reasons for 'Bad' Clinic Records' – refers to the context of seemingly 'bad' records as seen by the researcher:

" Any investigator who has attempted a study with the use of clinic records, almost wherever such records are found, has a litany of troubles to recite. Moreover, hospital and clinic administrators frequently are as knowledgeable and concerned abut these 'shortcomings' as are the investigators themselves … the term 'normal, natural' is used in a conventional sociological sense to mean in accord with prevailing rules of practice". (1975: 114)

Developed from Garfinkel's notion of 'normal, natural troubles', we examine the ways in which a 'beds crisis' is managed on a particular morning in one of these hospitals. Before we look at the specific events relevant to this paper, perhaps a brief outline of the idea of 'normal, natural troubles' would be useful here.

For Garfinkel, 'normal, natural troubles' refers to the troubles that were encountered by the researcher in trying to collect information from clinic records. The paper goes on to explore the moral and practical organisational rationale for its mode of record-keeping, such that there can be seen to be 'good' reasons for what may appear as 'bad' records on first examination. For example, for Garfinkel a 'reason' for bad records is the idea of the "marginal utility of added information" (ibid: 115) – personnel may not understand the purpose of certain forms of information collection or may be suspicious of them, seeing them as ranging from "benign, to irrelevant to ominous". Such records, in terms of both the idea of the records from an organisational perspective and in the member's use of the records from the clinic context fit with the "prevailing rules of practice" of the clinic, and clinic personnel "as self-reporters, actively seek to act in compliance with rules of the clinic's operating procedures that *for them and from their point of view are more or less taken for granted as right ways of doing things* ...

[they] are integral features of the usual ways of getting each day's work done." (1975: 114).

We wish to extend this idea of 'normal natural troubles' from the use for research purposes of clinic records to examine how apparently 'bad' records are utilised and also how a manager in a particular situation uses 'workarounds' where the 'official record' is flawed. Without a detailed understanding of the practices in the setting of the hospital, we cannot get a nuanced view of what may first appear to be simply bad records. In this way we will look at the 'prevailing rules of practice' that should be taken into account prior to the design and implementation of computer-based display systems. Here we are not looking at the use of patients' clinic records or medical files, but at other forms of record keeping. Although we started off thinking abut good reasons for bad records as in Garfinkel's work, this led us to look at other forms of record keeping and the ways in which such records are incorporated into daily work practice. Specifically here we examine bed management practice in the form of: -

1. The use of the information available on the computer-based Management Information System (MIS) at the hospital, a system beset by its own problems of apparently 'bad' records

2. The use of a 'state of play' notice board on a surgical ward, and

3. The managerial work involved in coming to an 'acceptable' account of the situation for the purposes of the manager involved.

We will argue, as does Garfinkel, that the "least interesting thing that one can say about them [the records] is that they are 'carelessly kept'" (1975: 114).

Related to the notion of apparently 'bad' records, is the idea of records and displays as 'representing work'. How best to represent the work of an organisation, or group of workers within an organisation, is central to the design of display artefacts to support everyday work. In this chapter we also explore the practical ways in which 'representations' and 'information' are produced and utilised as part of routine and ongoing managerial work. Whilst hospital work cannot be wholly categorised as information work, the increased use of new information and communication technologies (ICT's) to allow more flexible and mobile patterns of working is relevant to the health sector. The directorate managers in the NHS Trust study, for example, have responsibilities and work 'domains' across three geographically separate hospitals and may have discrete ward and clinic areas under their jurisdiction within each hospital. They will also have regular working patterns with human resources departments, other directorate managers, waiting list sections and so on. Thus much of their work is about the exchange and flow of information, in the form of accounts, policy initiatives, waiting list figures, and bed availability to name but a few.

3. THE ABIDING CONCERNS OF THE ORGANISATION: BED MANAGEMENT.

It is important to note here that although we are examining here the events on one day in a particular hospital, these events have a wider relevance. Bed management is an abiding concern, common throughout the National Health Service (NHS). Thus there are generic issues that can be explicated through the use of ethnographic study. For example, bed management can be seen as the broad 'problem', but contained within it are more specific issues e.g. 'winter planning', when the hospitals try to plan for 'known' seasonal problems. Hospital waiting lists and the availability of hospital beds is a highly charged political issue. At the time of the observations detailed here (November 2000) a great deal of concern was given to 'winter planning' which was related to national press reports, from the previous year, of hospitals being full and effectively closed to new patients. As one manager commented; " .. it came down from on high that this year there would not be a Winter crisis .. and I mean from On High..".

This concern over 'winter planning' was reflected not just in a daily managerial focus on bed numbers but also related statistics connected to waiting time on trolleys and the 'escalation policy'. Again this was linked to national press reports of patients spending enormous amounts of time on hospitals trolleys as they waited for beds to become available. The 'escalation policy' was linked to a government requirement that no patient should be kept on a trolley for more than 12 hours. Trolley waiting times were closely monitored and the Trust had contingency plans to open up a day-case theatre to accommodate more beds and patients. Bed management was associated with a system of alerts that instigated various managerial responses: "to go to red (alert) the Directorate Manager has to go and count.. if the position is that we (the Hospital) are ..closed to admissions the Directorate Manager has to come in and physically count the beds … Ward Sisters can be naughty .. if they know they have five admissions coming in tomorrow …   you can understand where they're coming from .. " . The managerial focus on bed management was supported by the collation of a weekly site report circulated by email. For example;

" Weekly site rep attached for your information. Large volume of medical sleepouts at both main sites. Current position:

XXX: no available beds now although position will change. Some elective admissions for today being cancelled and admissions for next 2 days under review with relevant clinical directorates..

ZZZ contacted by GGG last night to take medicine emergencies from south of GGG area... some patients at ZZZ still waiting for beds at DDD to become available "

(letters indicate areas covered by the hospitals)

The Bed Manager (BM) coordinates the availability of hospital beds across the two sites. The BM is based at H1, with no dedicated office accommodation at H2 or H3. The 'bed availability' data as available on the Management Information System (MIS) may be seen as a 'bad' record for a number of reasons to do with the lack of a standardized approach to information collection, time lag between information collection and its appearance in the MIS database. The role of the BM is to constantly monitor and maintain the process of bed management in such a way as to avoid a situation where no beds are available. At a more local level, the directorate managers and ward managers monitor bed management. Here we explore the actions of the directorate manager of orthopaedics (henceforth the DMO) as she deals with a scenario of being "minus nine beds". We will examine what she calls "the usual rituals" used to manage the crisis, and the ways in which the 'bad' record from the Management Information System is used in conjunction with the 'rituals' of ward rounds.

'Activity' monitoring

Patient treatment, (and in particular the number of patients treated) is referred to by hospital management as 'activity', and frequent discussions were had assessing whether or not enough 'activity' was going on in the directorate. At the time of the fieldwork there were several policy strategies going on which aimed to increase 'activity' through better record-keeping e.g. the production of process maps was being used to potentially identify what are known as "bottlenecks" which delay "knife to skin" time, i.e. those parts in the 'processing' of patients which cause delays to or cancellation of treatment for a variety of reasons e.g. pre-op assessments not being done e.g. trying to standardise practice of record-keeping especially with regard to the Accident and Emergency department, who "don't care" about anything other than the patient, and therefore don't always fill out the required documentation. This shows the highly contingent nature of the hospital work, or, as one manager put it, "It's always crisis management in the NHS". This then feeds into concerns over attempts to standardise practice, for example, the soon to be implemented Electronic Patient Records (EPR's), for which standardisation seems to be a pre-requisite. The electronic record will not afford the kind of flexibility offered by a paper-based system. We write about these issues elsewhere, but point them out to demonstrate that there are many areas of record-keeping which may contribute to a representation of 'good' or 'bad' records.

Bed management and the bed management figures impact on other aspects of managerial activity and reporting - most notably in managerial calculations of activity, bed occupancy and patient turnover, all of which are relevant in national calculations and audit of performance. A great deal of managerial work is consequently devoted to untangling, interpreting and re-calculating the statistics on activity and patient turnover to take into account the process of bed management. It is not that the case that the statistics are not trusted They are not regarded as 'just any old numbers', but their limitations are recognised and related to how there are collected and collated. For example, although activity figures are provided on a Ward basis, this is affected by factors such as 'sleepouts'. An example of this would be when a 'stroke' patient is given a bed on a 'geriatric' ward. The Manager needs to extract 'her patients' and 'her doctors' from the figures in order to gain an accurate account of occupancy and length of stay to generate any performance indicators.

4. 'MINUS NINE BEDS'

Observations of the ways staff orient to existing shared displays illuminate the complexity of managerial work with the figures produced by the MIS needing to mesh with more local, changeable and situated information. The following example illustrates this with reference to the previously mentioned 'beds board' (see Fig.1) On arrival one morning at one hospital (in a three hospital trust) the Directorate Manager of Orthopaedics' (DMO) first words were "We're minus nine beds". Some kind of 'bed crisis' was happening - assumed to be caused by a road traffic accident by the staff present - and the DMO would be taking some action to determine the position of her directorate. The DMO had received an 'end of day report', produced daily by the MIS, and this had alerted her to the potential shortfall in bed availability. The reference to 'minus nine beds' was to the state of play across all three sites, not only within the orthopaedic directorate. Although the 'minus nine' was referred to as being the "state of play", it actually referred to the future situation if all patients were admitted as expected for that day. The MIS 'end of day report' shows the figure for 8 November, surgical as minus six (see fig. 2). The DMO said that she needed to go to the orthopaedic wards to assess the situation, adding, "we go through our usual rituals for situations like these". She explained that it was essential to physically survey the wards rather than trying to get information another way for example, by telephone. She said that this was a process of "chivvying people up". Exactly what this meant became apparent once we arrived on the wards.

Fig. 1 The Beds board

First, the DMO walked around the floor of orthopaedic wards and did a count of seemingly empty beds. She then went to the nurses' station where there is a beds board (see Fig. 1) that represents the bed situation. The beds board represented the total ward area, with each ward 'bay' (usually comprising six beds) marked separately. Each bed is indicated by a metal slot where a card, with the patient's details, can be placed. Cards that have been placed straight into the slots represent existing in-patients. Cards placed diagonally in the slots represent patients due to be discharged, pending a visit by social services, a consultant, the physiotherapist etc.

The presence of diagonally placed cards forced an immediate re-count for the DMO, as her count was based on a 'head-count' of patients present. The DMO then discussed available beds with the ward sister, who explained the expected time/date of discharge for the 'diagonals'. The ward sister also pointed to two slanted cards for existing in-patients and explained that they were acutely, terminally ill but said that she *"couldn't guarantee a day or time for them"*. The DMO then left the nurses' station and went to speak to the physiotherapist to ascertain whether there were any other patients who were fit for discharge or who were likely to become so that day. Through these processes, the DMO established that there were enough beds to see them through the 'crisis'. On leaving the ward area, the DMO said that establishing the availability of beds is *"a very physical thing"*.

END OF DAY REPORT

	NOV 6 6.30PM	NOV 7 6pm	NOV 8 7pm	NOV 9 4.30pm	NOV 10
PRESTON-BEDS AVAILABLE					
MEDICAL	5	7	2	9	
SURGICAL	0	0	-6	0	
ORTHOPAEDIC	0	2	0	1	
BURNS/PLASTIC	2	2	0	2	
NEUROSURGERY	1	1	0	4	
NEUROLOGY	1	3	2	4	
ONCOLOGY	0	3	1	0	
HDU	1	1	1	2	
RENAL	0	2	2	0	
OPHTHALMOLOGY	0	1	0	0	
ENT	2	0	2	2	
TOTALS	12	22	4	24	0
ITU	1	1	2	1	
GYNAE SGH	6	5	6	12	
SLEEPOUTS-RPH					
MEDICAL	16	12	15	14	
ORTHOPAEDIC	0	0	0	1	
SURGICAL	5	3	10	6	
NEURO	0	0	0	0	
RENAL	2	3	0	0	
ONCOLOGY	1	0	0	0	
BURNS & PLASTIC	0	0	0	1	
TOTALS	24	18	26	22	0
EMERGENCY ADMS-RPH					
CANCELLED OPS-RPH (NO BEDS)	0	0	0	0	
COMMENTS	med surg very busy	both sites remain very	CDH unable to sustain	came Surg take remains	
CHORLEY-BEDS AVAILABLE					
MEDICAL	3	5	7	8	
SURGICAL	5	4	4	7	
HDU	0	0	1	0	
ORTHOPAEDIC	3	4	4	7	
GYNAE	6	5	4	3	
TOTALS	17	18	20	25	0
ITU	1	3	2	4	
SLEEPOUTS-CDH					
MEDICAL	15	19	20	18	
ORTHOPAEDIC	0	0	0	1	
SURGICAL	2	1	2	1	
TOTALS	17	20	22	20	0
EMERGENCY ADMS- CDH					

Fig. 2 MIS'end of day' report

5. CALCULATION AND CALCULABILITY

The observations reveal how apparent solidity and objectivity of managerial information can thus continually be challenged as new data come to the fore, for example, where supposedly 'occupied' beds become available. Understanding of the data is facilitated through reconstructing the available information; that Ward Sisters were 'being naughty' or that some of the beds are occupied by 'walking wounded'. Thus readings of the bed management data are 'defeasible', capable of being re-interpreted to fit with new items of information and presented to different audiences.

What we observe in the work of bed management is that the process is difficult and eventually what emerges is a few 'quick and dirty' figures on which to make a judgement. The bed management figures and the bed management board are then the end product of a series of procedures. These procedures make up a system of calculation and are designed to give a picture, a representation, of the 'bed position' of each ward. But this picture is neither clear nor unambiguous since the figures are embedded in a nest of interactional, organisational and operational contingencies and gets their meaning from them.

Any explication of the work of managing the bed management system has to address what, for specific occasions, constitutes correctness, allowable error and so on. The practical monitoring of the bed availability situation is thus a system of calculability. Whenever there is a 'crisis' - an accident, political pressure, demands on targets or whatever - the figures are subject to reinterpretation and the calculations are subject to change. Such a finding has some repercussions in terms of the extent to which existing systems can be automated or computerised. The knowledge, which anyone working within the system possesses and uses, is a locally organised corpus and is unavailable to analytic reconstruction as a collection of abstracted cases and idealised procedures. There is no authoritative list of what personnel know about the bed management system in any particular medical ward and their peculiarities, or when this knowledge is to be relevantly applied as a set of general guidelines. At best all that can be achieved is to attempt to apply the system of calculation as consistently as possible. However, any application of the public display system must allow others to follow it to see how the result - in the form of discharging walking wounded, setting up extra beds and so on - was arrived at.

What clearly emerges from our observations of managerial work is its complexity. Much of the 'organisational knowledge' regularly utilised in the managerial work of co-ordination and decision-making is not of a kind that is immediately visible in procedures or simply facilitated by reference to the record. Providing IT support for such contingent work requires that display systems necessarily pay attention to the occasioned character of activities. If the aim is to embed knowledge properties in management information systems then it needs to be captured, managed and displayed in a way that will make it accurate, available, accessible, effective and usable. Such a task is hardly a matter of simply digitalising existing records. These accounts of everyday managerial work would merely be a series of interesting stories were it not for the implications such accounts have for the design of new technologies and the support of working around shared displays. Our research highlights a need to attend to some of the everyday realities of organisational life. As designers attempt to accommodate some of the complexities of organisational working, so the challenges facing systems display designers necessarily increase. These new challenges involve attending to the lived reality of organisational groups - much as we have described it here - in order to design effective systems.

The use of such notice boards for calculation and planning purposes is written about elsewhere. For example, Button and Sharrock (Button & Sharrock, 1997) have written extensively about a fieldwork study carried out in a sector of the print industry. Here too the organisation concerned was about to undergo a change in the nature of calculation and planning through the utilisation of new technology. In this study Button and Sharrock focus on the use of, what is referred to as, a 'forward-loading-board' which "is an organisational artefact that is used to work up the daily array of jobs into a rational production order and by means of which the AM [Administration Manager] is able to perform his necessary calculations" (1997:5). In terms of our study, similar calculation work is being done. Whilst we are careful not to 'see things that aren't there' (Coulter & Sharrock, 1998), it is evident from the fieldwork that calculation relevant to the 'activity' of the hospital is done through the use of artefacts such as the beds-board and through information available via the MIS.

The practical value of numbers

The specific nature of print jobs and hospital treatment may differ, but calculation is nevertheless done with regard to similar salient features – in the previous scenario – how many beds do we have available? However, the calculation work of the manager may be directed at many other aspects of her managerial work – how much time have we got? What equipment is available? Which staff are available? Will this earn enough money? The direction of the calculation work towards such a range of questions can be seen in the following fieldwork extract and the way in which different categories of orthopaedic surgery are brought into play to meet certain ends. On the morning before the apparent 'beds crisis', the DMO had a meeting with the financial advisor for the Trust where a financial shortfall for that month was discussed. The financial advisor asked, "Have we started that big back yet?" This was referring to a potential earning source of £15K against the monthly shortfall. At a meeting later on in the same day, the DMO had a meeting to discuss the management of waiting lists, the hospital policy of 13 weeks maximum waiting time being under threat, where strategy was discussed to do "more fingers, then joints, then spines", fingers being the quickest to treat and spines the slowest, thus addressing the excessive waiting list figures. The point to be made here is that the categories of patient or of surgical need/status are brought into play when calculations for different ends are required i.e. for bed management, financial or policy purposes.

In the everyday work of the Hospital Trust patients and their representations become the focus for calculation and accounting work. The bed management figures are only one such locus for calculation work and they are interlinked with other sets of figures and calculations. Such accounting work is socially organized in a number of ways.

1. Calculation and calculability is a members problem i.e. it is achieved through the practical action of those involved. It takes the form of the achievement and display of 'proper' calculation. We are interested in the examination of the routine work that goes into making such a system of calculability operate.

2. Our interest in 'calculability' arises in relation to the variety of ways in which calculative rationalities interweave with other rationalities in the context of negotiations over 'beds' - and thus patients, operations, resources, targets.

3. As in other forms of distributed working, calculation work within the hospital - in this case in terms of 'beds' - is calculation within a division of labour. In this fashion calculation work and organization work are harmonized in and through competent practical action. Related to what Anderson et al (1989) refer to as the 'lore of numbers' - "capacity to play off the requirements for representing a set of activities through a system of calculation against the practicalities and obligations involved in performing those activities effectively and efficiently" (1989: 104)

Of course the calculation process is difficult and subject to rules of thumb and so on, and eventually what emerges is a few 'quick and dirty' figures on which to make a judgment. This is what can be clearly seen in the 'beds crisis' example. Our interest is not in the premise of calculability but the work which medical personnel do to make their activities fit with what might be characterized as 'accountants' terms. " This work involves grappling with the sheer practical difficulties of determining which figures are wanted, pulling them out, and then knowing how to manipulate them and assess their product." (105-6) The idea of 'accountability' that emerges from this is not merely in terms of members' accounts but as a specific form of members account - that conforms with particular 'rules' etc.

Explicating this work is not simply a question of medical staff seeing what is 'in the bed management figures' and then automatically working out what should be done. 'What is in the figures' is itself something that has to be worked out, and working it out involves balancing operational and organizational objectives and priorities. The bed management figures and the beds board are the end product of a series of procedures. These procedures make up a system of calculation and are designed to give a picture, a representation, of the 'bed position' of each ward. But this picture is neither clear nor unambiguous since the figures are embedded in a nest of interactional, organizational and operational contingencies and get their meaning from them.

Any explication of the work of managing the bed management system, of making a system of calculability work has to address what, for some specific occasion, constitutes correctness, allowable error, the margins of probability and calculability. Whenever there is a 'crisis' - an accident, political pressure, demands on targets or whatever - the figures are subject to reinterpretation and the calculations are subject to change. Essentially, the work involved in 'bed management' consists in a system of rules and their application in contexts - that is it is a system of calculability. The bed management figures and the bed management board are themselves the products of socially organized accounting work. They are 'displays' (Lynch in Hughes, Rouncefield & Tolmie, 2002) of the methods used to produce them - what anyone can find them to say or to mean will depend on interpretation of the displays.

If we examine the bed management system as an empirically observable set of activities, as the operation of a system of calculability, we note that the knowledge that anyone working within the system possesses and uses is a locally organized corpus (Pollner, 1987). It is a body of knowledge that makes itself available to those who know how to do *these calculations* with *these materials* in *this ward*. As a corpus it is unavailable to analytic reconstruction as a collection of abstracted cases and idealized procedures. There is no authoritative list of what personnel know about the bed management system in any particular medical ward and their peculiarities, nor when this knowledge is to be relevantly applied as a set of general guidelines. At best all that can be achieved is to attempt to apply the system of calculation as consistently as possible. However, any application of the system must allow others to follow it to see how the result - in the form of discharging walking wounded, setting up extra beds etc - was arrived at - the systematicity of the procedures is both an achievement and a resource.

The at-a glance visibility of order

This calculation work also has some resonance in the idea of the 'at-a-glance' visibility of order. In their case study of the print industry Button & Sharrock look at the use of a 'forward-loading-board' in the day to day management of print jobs and discuss the board as a public display of the order of production available to those who need to see it (Button & Sharrock, 1997). The forward-loading-board is:

"an organisational artefact that is used to work up the daily array of jobs into a rational production order and by means of which the AM [Administration Manager] is able to perform his necessary calculations" (ibid)

The forward-loading-board has a vertical axis and a horizontal axis – the former showing print machines and weeks and the latter showing the number of hours in a week to a maximum of a hundred. In brief, it is used by the Administration manager to project, review, consider different production orders, fine tune the production order and organise timings from origination to finishing. The board may be on the desk of the Administration Manager, but it is still publicly available to others such as the Production Manager (PM). In the same way, the beds board, although sited next to the ward sister's desk, is publicly available to other nursing staff, physiotherapists, occupational therapists, consultants, and in our example, the DMO. This public display allows for the re-calculation outlined above in our beds crisis scenario.

Although the nature of the work being undertaken in the hospital differs from the print centre, the beds board is used in similar ways by 'organisational toolsmiths' (Bittner: in Turner, 1975) in the day to day running of the hospital ward such as the ward sister or the DMO. However, their use of the board is oriented to different priorities. For the DMO, there is the at-a glance visibility of order afforded by the beds board and the public nature of it as an artefact. She can use and recognise the order shown by the beds board and all its features – empty slots, slanted cards and so on. The beds board helps the DMO to make bed management and, in this case, crisis management, a calculable phenomenon. The DMO has a range of organisational responsibilities – some oriented to the priorities of the Trust as a whole in the form of Trust policies, and some oriented to her domain – the orthopaedics directorate – and its staff and patients. In the case shown here, although there is an apparent beds crisis across the three hospital sites, the DMO is concerned to establish an acceptable state of affairs in her local domain rather than attending to the broader concerns of the Trust.

From the starting point of the MIS figures that indicated a crisis, the DMO establishes what is 'behind the numbers' in a local sense. The beds board makes the status in the ward "available to others in a format that they can work with" (Hughes, Rouncefield & Tolmie, 2002). Where other studies have looked at the use of 'management information' in the sense of information used only for managerial purposes on one level, we have explored the way in which management information is used alongside other local knowledge in the everyday routines of bed management. The MIS figures are not used here as accounting devices for managers to demonstrate some kind of performance indicators for the Trust management board (although they are required to do this at specific times), but are an alert to a potential problem which the DMO then deals with via her 'usual rituals'.

The DMO has established an acceptable situation in her own directorate, and the broader bed availability crisis is something that she "can let pass for now" (ibid).

6. CAUTIONARY TALES FOR THE DESIGN OF SITUATED AND PUBLIC DISPLAYS

The strength of the ethnographic approach is in that it uncovers the mundane and taken for granted routines in the everyday management of the hospital. Although the daily working practices of those in the orthopaedics directorate may be reasonably described as mundane and taken for granted, this should not be read in a way that belies the skills and experience of the staff involved. The hospital staff routinely avoid serious, sometimes life-threatening, crises, and, as a design community, we must make ourselves aware of factors to be considered before the implementation of new forms of public display. We would suggest that designers revisit their unexplicated assumptions regarding the uses of new ICT's. The nature of the organisation involved is key here. For example, many studies of the use of new forms of situated and public displays, including some in this volume, explore the use of large whiteboards for distributed workers and they have been installed and evaluated in a quite 'experimental' fashion. This is inappropriate a for a safety critical setting such as a hospital, where 'failure' of the technology can have serious results.

The calculation work in the 'minus nine beds' situation detailed above is directed at a number of ends all related to 'activity' in the hospital. Garfinkel's notion of 'normal, natural troubles' led us to think about record-keeping practices as displays that are the result of socially organised accounting work and which are or may be re-interpreted according to the contingent matters of the moment. It is not the case that representations and displays here are 'trusted' or 'not trusted'. They are used within known limitations and in conjunction with other artefacts and local knowledge. Information is, as Pettersson et al (2002) put it, "*made* reliable by this complex amalgam of artefacts and practices" (2002: 287).

Although we have said that the DMO established an 'acceptable' situation within her domain, this was still dependant to a certain extent on the ward sister's interpretation of the 'story' told by the beds board. It may be suggested, for example, that there could be a digital version of the beds board that the DMO could access from her office. However, when bed availability is not a problem she would not need to look at it, and when bed availability is a potential problem, she is still dependant on the local knowledge of the ward sister (and others) to give her a more precise information e.g. that certain beds currently indicated as slanted cards will be vacated that day or the next. Some benefits may be seen in the introduction of a digital beds board accessible on the hospital network e.g. such that the DMO could monitor the situation from any of the three hospital sites. However, in the same way that Bowers, Button and Sharrock (1995 & 1997) warned that the design community should develop 'measures of value' for proposed systems for organisations, we suggest that it should not be assumed that a digital display would bring enough benefits to warrant its design and implementation. The affordances of the current displays, practices and 'usual rituals' carried out by the DMO indicate that such a measure of value is not immediately apparent.

In considering some new form of beds board display, other issues that need careful consideration. The existing beds board is situated in the ward sister's office and as such its 'public' character is limited to those deemed appropriate members to view it i.e. hospital staff. It would not be suitable, for example, to place the beds board in an area of the wards where patients and their friends and family could view it – they might start to ask why a certain 'card' was slanted. In this way, any computerised display should also not be on 'public' view. The location of the board has also evolved as the 'appropriate' location for other pieces of information relevant to the ward (see Fig. 1). Thus, policy change announcements, memos and other documents are routinely pinned to the edges of the board because it is known that staff will see them there. For the hospital staff, much work has already gone into placing the appropriate artefacts in the place of optimal use. This is not to say that there could not be some kind of digital display that may benefit the hospital staff, but that this should not be assumed.

REFERENCES

1. Anderson, R., Hughes, J., and Sharrock, W. (1989) Working For Profit; the social organisation of Calculation in an Entrepreneurial Firm (1989) Avebury, Aldershot
2. Bannon, L. & Bodker, S. 'Constructing Common Information Spaces' in ECSCW'97: Proceedings of the 5th European Conference on CSCW. Hughes, J.A., Prinz, W., Rodden, T. & Schmidt, K. (eds) pp 81-96
3. Berg, M. (1997). Rationalising Medical Work: Decision Support techniques and Medical Practices. Cambridge: MIT Press
4. Bloor, K. and Maynard, A. (1997), Clinical Governance: Clinician Heal Thyself. Institute of Health Services Management
5. Bowers, J., Button, G. & Sharrock, W. 'Workflow from Within and Without: Technology and Cooperative Work on the Print Industry Shopfloor' in ECSCW'95: Proceedings of the 4th European Conference on CSCW. Marmolin, H., Sundblad, Y. & Schmidt, K. (eds) pp 51-66
6. Button, G. & Sharrock, W. 'The Production of Order and the Order of Production: Possibilities for Distributed Organisations, Work and Technology in the Print

Industry' in ECSCW'97: Proceedings of the 5th European Conference on CSCW. Hughes, J.A., Prinz, W., Rodden, T. & Schmidt, K. (eds) pp 1-16

7. Coulter, J. & Sharrock, W. "On What We Can See" in Theory And Psychology, Vol. 8, No. 2, 1998.
8. Department of Health (1997), The New NHS: Modern, Dependable, The Stationery Office, London, December 1997, ISBN 0 10 138072 0.
9. DIRC see http://www.dirc.org.uk/
10. Fitzpatrick, G. (2000) Understanding the Paper Record in Practice: Implications for EHRs. In Proceedings of HIC'2000
11. Hughes, J.A, King, V., Randall, D., Sharrock, W. (1993). Ethnography for system design: a guide. COMIC Working Paper, Computing Department, Lancaster University, UK
12. Hughes, J., King, V., Rodden, T., Andersen, H. (1994). 'Moving out of the control room: ethnography in system design', in Proceedings of CSCW'94 (Chapel Hill NC), ACM Press, pp. 429-438
13. Hughes, J., Rouncefield, M. & Tolmie, P. 'Representing Knowledge' in The British Journal of Sociology Vol. 53 Issue No.2 June 2002 pp 221-238
14. Petterson, M., Randall, D. & Helgeson, B. 'Ambiguities, Awareness and Economy: A Study of Emergency Service Work' in CSCW2002: Proceedings of ACM 2002 Conference on Computer Supported Cooperative Work, ACM Press, pp.286-295
15. Pollner, M. (1987) Mundane Reason: Reality in Everyday and Sociological Discourse Cambridge: Cambridge University Press
16. Robins, K. & Webster, F. (1999) Times of the Technoculture: From the Information Society to the Virtual Life London: Routledge
17. Turner, R. (ed) (1975) Ethnomethodology Penguin
18. Weber, M. (1978) Economy and Society, Vols 1 and 2, Berkeley, CA: University of California Press

Chapter 3

ENTERPRISE MODELING BASED ON RESPONSIBILITY

John Dobson with David Martin
University of Lancaster

1. INTRODUCTION

Trust and responsibility are closely related concepts. If I trust someone to do something, then I have implicitly given them a responsibility to do it. failure to carry out such a responsibility is a breach of trust — and trust, once broken, is not easy to repair.

In the design of information systems for use in organizations, it is important to establish the patterns of trust and responsibility that exist in the organization, since these patterns tend to get inscribed in the system. It is a common enough observation that information systems that do not match the patterns of trust and responsibility in an organization are not well received by their users. Making models of these patterns is an important way for the system architect to reflect them in the structure of the system, for where there are no models, there is no understanding.

So in describing one particular method of modeling responsibilities in an organization – a method that is one example of what is generically called 'enterprise modeling'– we are providing the system architect with a way of understanding, and therefore enabling to make explicit, the implicit patterns of trust and responsibility that structure all human organizations.

K.Clarke, G. Hardstone, M. Rouncefield and I. Sommerville (eds.), Trust in Technology:
A Socio-Technical Perspective, 39–67.

Modeling a Socio Technical System

In this chapter we shall describe an enterprise modeling technique based on the idea that to make sense of a socio-technical system in order to design an information and communication technology (ICT) system which is intended to be deployed in the socio-technical context requires an analysis of the responsibilities that exist in that context and the way these responsibilities are mapped on to the various actors. This mapping of responsibilities to actors constitutes the roles of the actors.

We will not attempt to give a philosophical definition of *responsibility*, (readers who are interested may wish to consult the book by Lucas [Lucas 1995]), though we hope our use of the term will become clear (and there is indeed an underlying philosophical stance). What is important about it for our purposes is that it is something laid on, or assumed by, a moral agent who may be an individual, a group or an organization (or anything else to which we are prepared to ascribe moral agency). The normal expectation is that responsibilities will be discharged, but they can of course also be laid down, ignored, abrogated, or delegated to another moral agent. A *role* is a collection of responsibilities held by an agent that in some sense go together. An agent will normally hold several roles simultaneously, e.g. an individual might be a parent, a citizen, an employee, a doctor. What set of responsibilities go together to form a role is a social construct. Each role is defined in terms of the responsibilities it entails.

Starting from responsibilities is important for four reasons. *Firstly*, many forms of organizational restructuring can be described as re-articulations of responsibilities: existing responsibilities are mapped on to actors in a different way, and some new responsibilities are created and old ones laid down. *Secondly*, many information and communication requirements derive from responsibilities: to whom does an actor in a particular role need to talk to, and what information needs to be exchanged in order to discharge the responsibilities of that role, and what needs to be recorded to show that they have in fact been discharged? *Thirdly*, trust is closely related to responsibility. Although we are not going to advocate any particular one of the many social theories of trust that have been proposed [Parsons 1951; Luhmann 1979; Axelrod 1984], trust can, we assert, always be operationalised as meaning *not having to check*: trusting an actor means not checking whether the actions associated with that role have been performed, and a trusted piece of software is one whose correct functioning does not have to be checked every time it is used. Of course, trust can always be misplaced. *Fourthly*, any analysis of an ICT system as part of a larger socio-technical system must (at least partially) answer the question: What can go wrong? For the failures in the technical domain of the system, the answers to

the question are technical ones and ways of finding them are laid down in many methodologies, though alleviations and countermeasures may involve, as well as technical fixes, the creation of new responsibilities in the social domain. But to answer the question what can go wrong in the social domain? cannot stop –though it may start– with the classic dichotomy of sins of omission and sins of commission; issues of conflict of interest, misplaced trust, (mis)delegation of inalienable responsibility and so on, have also to be examined. In fact, our style of enterprise modeling was designed to permit this latter kind of examination.

It is important to realise at the outset that our responsibility modeling concepts and process embody a particular philosophy and that this should permeate the modelers' approach to the problem. In other words modeling is first and foremost a mental process, and the construction of diagrams representing the models should be regarded solely as a tool or aid to this process. We have endeavoured to be explicit about our philosophy throughout this chapter.

The need for modeling arises because socio-technical systems are very complex. We therefore use models that each describe only a certain aspect of the system. We can then handle the complexity by using one model at a time to give us a simplified view of the system. The strength of our approach to modeling lies however not just in the suite of models that has been developed, but in the fact that the models relate to one another within a conceptual framework.

By itself, the approach of developing different models each with a single perspective does not handle problems of interaction. We deal with interaction through our abstraction of a conversation, which in turn is built on a model of messages and communication.

There are certainly dozens and possibly hundreds of methods of so-called 'enterprise modeling'; and to provide yet another certainly needs some justification. Our claim is that because our method starts from the concept of responsibility as a primitive social construct and proceeds by abstracting away from the way responsibilities are mapped on to actual work roles and structures, it is better adapted to discuss issues of organizational change than any purely descriptive method. It is so often the case that change involves re-articulation and reallocation of responsibilities, while keeping the core set of responsibilities intact.

For those who are familiar with the literature, we can say that our method is based on the soft systems methodology [Checkland 1981; Checkland and Scholes 1990], with responsibility taking the place of activity in the elaboration of the root definition. For those not so familiar, it is not necessary to read Checkland's books to understand the present chapter, though they provide a useful introduction to one particular influential and successful method of looking at socio-technical systems.

In the following sections the way in which the modeling framework is built up, starting with the concept of responsibility, is explained in a tutorial style. This is followed by an example of responsibility modeling applied to healthcare and to a particular case of public service (an environmental planning office, in fact). These two examples have been chosen because we wish to show how our approach can be applied to systems of both broad and narrow levels of granularity.

The Core Concepts: Role and Responsibility

The first step in an analysis is to decide precisely to what ends the analysis is aimed, i.e. the modeler must pinpoint what aspects or areas of the organization are of interest by identifying goals, forces for change, issues and concerns. Choosing such a perspective is another part of the simplification strategy. It helps to focus the modeling on the chosen organizational goals and provides a basis for evaluation. Typical perspectives are efficiency, worker satisfaction, safety, security, reliability, cost and suchlike. Perspectives should not be confused with viewpoints of individuals, although these may contribute to a perspective.

The core concept in our way of looking at organizations is **role**. We describe roles as the primary manipulators of the state or structure of the system. Most often they are people or groups of people in the sociotechnical system, although it is possible for a machine to behave as a role, as for an example an expert system in sole charge of a piece of automated equipment, such as a fly-by-wire aircraft[4] . What a role represents (here meaning 'is an abstraction of') is an 'office' in the sense of a role holder, and this can be any size of group from an individual to a whole organization.

Following from the concept of the role is the concept of the relationship between roles. We call these **structural relationships** because we regard them as the skeleton of a socio-technical system. Every relationship between one role and another implies a conversation (see section 3) and the need for some sort of communication link between them permitting the exchange of information. Structural relationships are thus central in two respects, in that they embody the organizational structure in terms of authorization and power structures, and in that they impose requirements

---

[4] When, in such circumstances, we say the expert system has the responsibility for flying the aircraft, we mean that it is not the pilot — though it may be the designer of the expert system or the aircraft designer who chose to use that expert system.

in terms of information and communication structures on any IT system installed.

Figure 1. A structural relationship between roles

The key to modeling structural relationships is the realization that they are basically relationships of responsibility between roles. (As explained in section 2.5 the 'flavour' of structural relationships is determined by the relative positions of the roles within the organizational structure, but it is only very exceptionally that they are not based on a responsibility relationship at all.) This brings us to the other core concept in our modeling scheme, that of **responsibility**. The function of the organization is manifest in the responsibilities held by the roles that constitute it, and that the structure of the organization is manifest in the responsibility relationships between them. The rationale behind this view will therefore be explained in depth as it forms the central tenet of our conceptual modeling framework.

2. RESPONSIBILITY AND THE RESPONSIBILITY RELATIONSHIP

The Nature of the Responsibility Relationship

Being responsible can mean either being accountable for a state of affairs without necessarily any implication of a direct causal connection with the state of affairs, or being the primary cause of (or preventer of) a result. We have named these two distinct types of responsibility **'consequential'** and **'causal'** responsibility respectively. Consequential responsibilities are indicative of the objectives[5] of the organization and the enduring organizational structure whereas causal responsibilities are dynamic in nature being the relationship between a role and an event. An example taken from the 'Herald of Free Enterprise' disaster illustrates the distinction. The ship's captain is always consequentially responsible for the state of the ship,

---

[5] By 'objectives' here we mean not just what the organisation does for a business, but also how it achieves it such as being a good employer, financially prudent and so on.

and in this case was blamed (with others) for the disaster although he did not cause it directly. However consequential and causal responsibilities are often closely associated as in the case of the deckhand who did not close the hold doors. He was causally responsible when the ship capsized, but he also held consequential responsibility for the state of the hold doors all the time he held the role of deckhand. Here we are attempting to model the enduring organizational structure so the responsibilities referred to throughout this document are only of the consequential type implying accountability, blameworthiness or liability of the responsibility holder.

We define responsibility as a relationship between two roles regarding a specific state of affairs with respect to a particular mode such as bringing about, preventing, maintaining and so on, such that the holder of the responsibility is responsible to the giver of the responsibility, the responsibility principal (Figure 2).

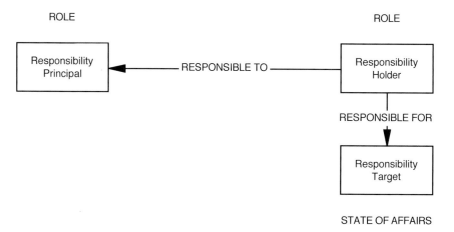

Figure 2. A responsibility relationship between two roles

Our characterization of a responsibility consists of:

a) who is responsible to whom;

b) the state of affairs for which the responsibility is held;

c) a list of obligations held by the responsibility holder (what the holder must do to fulfill the responsibility);

d) the mode of responsibility (these include accountability, blameworthiness, legal liability).

The important point here is that responsibilities cannot be looked at on their own but must always be considered as a relationship between two roles. The states of affairs for which responsibilities are held may be at any level of granularity of the organization. For example the responsibilities may be at a very high level such as for the adequacy of the service provided, for the continuity of a process, for safety, for security, for the accuracy of information and suchlike, or they may be at an individual level for a very specific state such as whether a door is closed, or whether a form is correctly filled in.

The Responsibility – Obligation – Activity Relationship

The distinction between **responsibilities**, **obligations** and **activities**, and the relationship of activities to responsibilities through obligations is central to our conceptual modeling framework. This is based on the concept that people execute activities, thereby using resources, in order to discharge the obligations imposed on them by virtue of the responsibilities they hold. These obligations effectively describe their 'jobs' or roles, and are the link between their responsibilities and the activities they execute. We can choose whether it is more appropriate to model responsibilities, obligations or activities depending on what view of the organization we want to take and what stage we are at in the development process.

The distinction between responsibilities and obligations is apparent from the words we use: a responsibility is **for** a state (of affairs), whereas an obligation is **to do** (or not do) something that will change or maintain that state of affairs. Thus a set of obligations must be discharged in order to fulfill a responsibility. As such, obligations define in what way the responsibility holder is responsible, and what must be done to fulfill the responsibility. Take for example a hospital doctor with responsibility for alleviating the medical condition of patients. To fulfill this responsibility, obligations must be discharged that change or maintain the patients' condition. These may include obligations to diagnose, to treat, to monitor and to prescribe. Responsibilities therefore tell us **why** roles do something, whereas obligations tell us **what** they should do. Although we make a clear distinction between responsibilities and obligations, (since this distinction is particularly valuable in that we can choose to model either responsibilities or obligations), it should be understood that responsibilities and obligations are closely linked: every responsibility must have obligations attached to it and every obligation must be related to a responsibility.

The distinction between obligations and activities is that obligations define **what** has to be done rather than **how** it is done. As such we regard obligations as an abstraction away from activities. Activities are defined as operations that change the state of the system. Role holders may (or may not) have a wide choice of activities that discharge the obligations they hold. Consider again the hospital doctor who has an obligation to make a diagnosis. The actual activities undertaken may be one or more of several: examining the patient, ordering x-rays or doing tests.

It should be emphasized here that, although we have suggested that the activity – obligation – responsibility sequence is progressively more abstract in nature, responsibilities are not abstracted activities, and the reason that we prefer to approach the problem of enterprise modeling from the responsibility angle is that a responsibility model tells us much more about the organization than an activity model can. Responsibilities represent aspects of structure and policy as well as function, and are, for example, indicative of commitment by the responsibility holder. We also focus on obligations in preference to activities since an obligation model provides us with an abstract template of the process within the organization and avoids the partial and inadequate analysis arising from working only from a model of activities as they are instantiated at present, which gives little understanding of *why* things are done and how changes in working will affect people's interpretation of their responsibilities.

Delegation of Responsibility

The concept of the responsibility relationship allows us to give an account of the delegation process in terms of responsibilities and obligations. We shall see below that the delegation process is essentially a transfer of obligations from one role to another thereby establishing a new responsibility relationship between them.

Although it is common to speak of responsibilities being transferred or delegated, and thus as having a dynamic aspect, the fact that a responsibility is a relationship between two roles means that a responsibility holder cannot independently transfer those responsibilities to another role. However, what may be happening in the case of apparent transfer is that the responsibility is reallocated to a new holder by the responsibility principal by destroying the relationship with the previous holder and establishing a new one with a new holder. The case of apparent delegation of responsibilities is accounted for by the fact that, although responsibilities cannot be transferred, a responsibility holder can transfer *obligations* to another role. The result of this process is the establishment of a new responsibility relationship between the two roles. The first role becomes the principal of the new responsibility relationship and the other role is the new responsibility holder. We will now examine this process in detail.

Obligations or duties placed on one role by virtue of the responsibilities held may be passed to another role provided that it is permitted by their relationship within the organizational structure. This process is illustrated in Figure 3. The top diagram shows the initial situation where role A holds several obligations associated with a particular responsibility. Even when an obligation is transferred to role B (lower diagram) role A still retains the original responsibility since this is not transferable, and we will see in the next section that this responsibility is still fulfilled. Meanwhile role B has acquired an obligation relating to the state of affairs for which role A holds responsibility. Role B must now also hold responsibility for that same state of affairs, as well as role A, because it will be affected when the obligation is discharged. However role B's responsibility is to role A who delegated the obligation; in other words a new responsibility relationship has been created between them. The lower diagram in Figure 3 illustrates how the process of delegation creates a new responsibility relationship between the two roles.

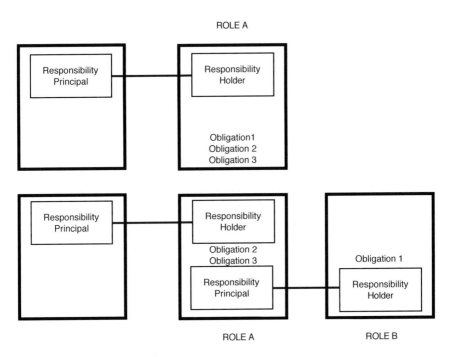

Figure 3. A responsibility relationship created by the transfer of an obligation

An example of this process is where the captain of a ship is responsible to the directors of the company for the safety of the ship. This responsibility to the company is retained even if the obligations to take safety precautions are delegated to the crew. The crew then acquire responsibility for the state of safety in their respective areas of operation, but their responsibility is to the captain and not directly to the company.

A chain of responsibility relationships can thus be created as obligations are passed from one role to another, with each link in the chain being a responsibility relationship between two roles. Within each individual responsibility relationship both roles have a responsibility for the same state of affairs, although their obligations differ. It should be noted that this delegation process will frequently be implicit rather than explicit, and may be used to explain how the hierarchical organizational structure and distribution of responsibilities has come about over time.

Functional and Structural Obligation

So far we have only encountered obligations that are functional in nature. They are what roles must do *with respect to a state of affairs* (e.g. execute an activity), in order to fulfill any responsibilities they hold regarding that state of affairs. These we term **functional obligations**. They are indicative of the relationships between the roles and the state of affairs.

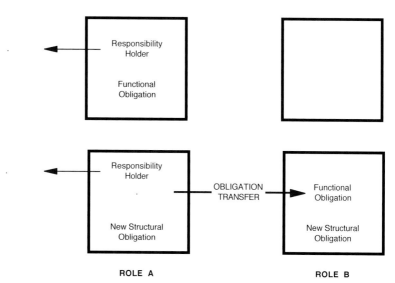

Figure 4. New structural obligations created by the transfer of an obligation

We have seen however that when a role delegates an obligation to another role, responsibility for the resulting state of affairs is still retained by the principal. In order to fulfill this responsibility the principal must ensure that the transferred functional obligation is discharged satisfactorily by the other role. A new obligation of a structural nature is created whenever an obligation is delegated. This is an example of a **structural obligation**. It is to do whatever is appropriate *with respect to another role* in order to fulfill a responsibility, such as directing, supervising, monitoring and suchlike of the other role. This other role also acquires a new structural obligation of a complementary nature: to *be* directed, to *be* supervised etc. (Figure 4). For example if a director passes an obligation to a manager, the director acquires a structural obligation to direct the manager in the discharging of the transferred obligation, and the manager acquires an obligation to accept direction. In this case the director holds a structural obligation and the manager holds both functional and structural obligations (Figure 5). This can also be expressed as: *Role A directs (Role B executes activity)*, where the modal operator 'directs' is the structural obligation, and 'executes' is the functional obligation.

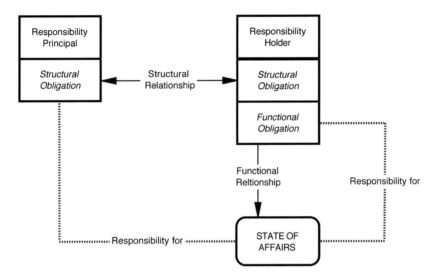

Figure 5. The responsibility relationship in terms of obligations

Structural obligations come therefore in pairs and are indicative of the relationships between roles. It is these paired structural obligations that largely determine the flavour of the structural relationships between roles at the level of roles. Again these structural obligations are very often implicit in the hierarchical structure of the organization rather than arising dynamically from explicit delegation.

The nature of structural obligations arising from the delegation process has been described here, but it must be pointed out that structural obligations are attached to any responsibility relationship, not just those arising from the delegation process (see Section 2.5).

The distinction between functional and structural obligations is particularly valuable from the point of view of modeling organizational structure, but it should be noted that in reality both types of obligations imply function in that both are realised as activities. Note also that no assignment of obligations is made to either an entity type or a relationship type; for example obligations may be regarded as entities linked by a relationship as in the role diagrams in section B, or alternatively as relationships between roles (structural obligations) or between a role and an action (functional obligations).

Types of Structural Relationship

Two categories of structural relationship have been identified on the basis of different patterns of responsibility. Within these categories many types or 'flavours' may exist depending on the relative positions of the roles within the organizational structure and their involvement in the particular context.

These two categories are the **contractual** type of relationship between organizations or between distinct organizational units within an organization, and the **co-worker** type of relationship between roles within an organization. The distinction is that in a contractual relationship there is no concept of shared responsibility whereas in the co-worker relationship the roles do share responsibility, although their individual responsibilities for the same state of affairs may be different.

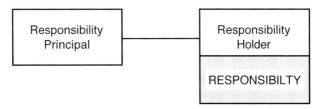

Figure 6. The contractual responsibility relationship

In a **contractual relationship** the responsibility holder contracts to fulfill the responsibility that is imposed by the responsibility principal (Figure 6). The most typical example of this category is the **service** type of relationship where the server contracts to provide a service to the client. Note that only the server holds responsibility for the provision of the service, i.e. there is no concept of shared responsibility. Of course the responsibility principal may hold other responsibilities, such as for payment for the service provided.

In this type of structural relationship the responsibility holder, the server, apparently holds only functional obligations that must be discharged to fulfill the responsibility, i.e. to provide the service. There are however structural obligations on both sides, implicit in the nature of the contract. The client is expected to behave in a 'client-like' way to the server, e.g. in the form of the request, acknowledgement of and payment for the service, while the server should behave in a 'server-like' way by providing the appropriate service, under certain mutually agreed conditions.

Most structural relationships between roles at an inter-organizational level will be of this type. Within a large organization, relationships between departments will often be of this type, for example the physiotherapy department in a hospital may be run as a service to the other departments. By looking at the contractual relationships between a role (organizational unit) and other roles, we can ascertain what responsibilities are held within the role of interest and to which roles it is responsible. At this stage a role can be regarded as a black box (a container which we do not wish to see inside); we are interested in what responsibilities it holds, and not how they are distributed within the role (this follows at a later stage). These high level responsibilities define the purpose of the role.

Responsibilities held by such a role are distributed within that role by the delegation process, whether explicitly or implicitly. This process results in a network of responsibility relationships giving rise to structural relationships of the co-worker type. **Co-worker relationships** are distinguished from contractual relationships in that both roles hold responsibility, although in different ways, for the same state of affairs. The main type of co-worker relationship is that which results from the responsibility relationships set up by the delegation process, whether implicit or explicit (Figure 7). The roles are linked by the holding of structural obligations to each other that are created during the delegation process. Examples of these paired structural obligations are direct—accept direction; advise—request and accept advice; supervise—be supervised.

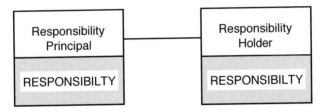

Figure 7. The co-worker responsibility relationship resulting from delegation

The nature of these co-worker structural relationships is strongly flavoured by the relative positions of the roles within the organizational power structure insofar as it affects the context in which they are working together. For example a structural relationship will have a strong element of **power** in it if one role is senior to another with regard to the specific task and can make and enforce demands on the other. Alternatively it may be what we term a **peer** relationship if the roles are equals and work together as colleagues without any element of enforcement. This power element largely determines the character of the paired structural obligations, i.e. whether the superior role is directing, managing, supervising or merely collaborating.

A variation on the peer relationship is that of collaboration where there is shared responsibility for a given state of affairs, but no responsibility relationship exists between the two roles, since no element of delegation has taken place. In this case each role would hold responsibility to a third party but a structural relationship would exist between them by virtue of working together (Figure 8).

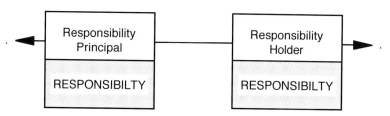

Figure 8. The co-worker relationship resulting from collaboration

A model of co-worker relationships can be of particular value for the identification of role mismatches and in general for checking whether the organizational structure is well formed. It can help in job design and generation of future scenarios, and in particular can be used to check that every structural obligation held by one role holder is related to an appropriate structural obligation held by another role holder.

3. CONVERSATIONS

In order to describe relationships between roles, we introduce the idea of **conversations**. Conversations take place wherever there are structural relationships between roles. A conversation is defined as a sequence of speech acts (not necessarily spoken face-to-face) between two or more roles. The nature and sequence of these speech acts can tell us much about the type of structural relationship between the two roles. For example the speech acts will be different between roles in a power relationship from those in a peer relationship. The conversations may refer to activities, obligations or responsibilities held by the roles, or the conversations may be activities in their own right as for example conversations between a bank clerk and a client.

In addition our method of conversation analysis is a valuable link between the enterprise and information aspects of the system and thus a useful tool in the requirements capture process, since most conversations (excluding face-to-face) are mediated by some sort of resource whether paper or electronic, and are therefore indicative of requirements on the IT system. We refer to this resource as the **instrument** of the conversation.

Attributes of Conversations

We use the term "conversation" to identify the relationship between two roles. At this stage in our argument, we are considering roles in the abstract, prior to their allocation to individuals or groups. This means that we are treating roles in the normative sense and are trying to characterise what is meant, for example, by a doctor—patient relationship rather than to evaluate the motivation or performance of any particular doctor or patient.

For a conversation to take place, intention (what the parties mean) and extension (what they do) have to be combined and operationalised in some observable behaviour which is interpreted by the conversing agents. This is the process of instrumentalisation; the *instrument* is the resource which mediates the association between the intentional and extensional events, the act and the action. The term "instrument" is a rich one combining the legal connotation of the documentary embodiment of a contract, the scientific or medical connotation of a tool for acquiring, recording or presenting information and the musical connotation of the means of performance. In the theory of conversations, we use the term to denote any resource which serves to signal or witness an intended act and which carries information associated with that act, concerning the state of the conversation in which it is performed. Thus a document may be an instrument, and so also may a handshake. In the latter case, the resource involves the co-located attendance and activity of the participants.

It is fundamental to the concept of a conversation that it provides some benefit for either or both of the participants, that they have some stake in its outcome. The benefits generated by or exchanged in a conversation may be of different types or even belong to different value systems for each of the participants. Each makes an individual evaluation of the conversation and so a conversation has different *significance* for each of the parties. Conversations with high significance imply that the benefits at stake or the consequences of failure for one or both of the parties are high. Two classes of conversations can now be distinguished on the basis of the intended balance of benefits:

Symmetrically significant conversations are intended to produce benefits that are judged as fair and more or less equal for each of the parties.

Asymmetrically significant conversations occur where the main derivation of benefit is by one party. Benefits derived by the other party may be the consequence of factors outside the immediate conversation such as a sense of vocation or kinship or the acquisition of esteem from third parties; it may, indeed, be regarded as ineffable.

A conversation can also be characterized in terms of *mutuality*. This refers to the level of responsibility each party is expected to accept for the benefit to be derived by the other party and for protecting the other party form any harm associated with breakdown or misapplication of the conversation.

Mutuality also has a magnitude and a distribution within a conversation. A relationship with high, symmetrical mutuality implies partnership and co-operation whereas asymmetric mutuality, higher on one side than on the other, implies a relationship of care such as parent—child or teacher—pupil. Clearly, if the significance of a conversation is asymmetrical then there is a requirement for it to exhibit an appropriately distributed mutuality: the parent accepts responsibility for the child receiving the main direct benefit from the relationship. Zero mutuality is associated with the *"caveat emptor"* principle of the consumer—supplier relationship. Mutuality can also be considered to be negative, as in a competitive relationship where the win of one participant implies the loss of the other.

Significance and mutuality are **intentional** attributes of a conversation. They are static in the sense that they are attributes of the conversation as a whole and are constitutive of the participating roles. They are intentional in the sense that they cannot be deduced by a third party simply by examining the interaction between agents; some prior knowledge of the purposes and interests of the participants is required. It is in this sense that they characterise a normative framework within which the conversation is defined and the respective roles institutionalised.

There are two **extensional** attributes of a conversation which complete its normative framework. The first of these is *capability,* which defines the set of resources required by each agent to properly fulfill the responsibilities of its particular role. These include the appropriate rights and capabilities in relation to the communications and information resources required to instrumentalise the conversation and also to the resources that must be deployed and possibly consumed in the discharge of the responsibilities associated with the role.

The second extensional requirement of the normative framework of a conversation is the distribution of *control* between the participants. For example, the pupil may only speak when the teacher grants permission. The party which has the right to initiate a conversation, or cause a transition from one phase to the next, exercises power in doing so and it is a normative principle that imbalance in the distribution of control and the power it confers, should be compatible with asymmetries in significance, mutuality and capability.

It is clearly a requirement on the normative definition of a conversation that the configuration of significance, mutuality, capability and control are coherent and compatible. It is a requirement for the effective conduct of a conversation that each of the parties has a compatible conception of the attributes of their role. One of the uses of the theory of conversations presented here is as a tool for analyzing the causes of breakdown in real conversations that may result from mismatches of perception and of intention.

The idea of a pure role and a pure conversation is an abstraction that can be used as a synthetic and analytic tool. In architectural discourse we may be either combining roles together in the formulation of organizational structures and policies or we are analyzing observed behaviour in order to discover the structure of institutionalized combinations of responsibilities. In both of these processes, the issue of conflict and synergies of interest arise.

The Composition of Roles

The process of defining an enterprise projection in terms of the division of responsibility proceeds to a level of granularity required for problem owners and policy makers to express and explore all the possible configurations and mappings of responsibility that are of interest to them.

The synthetic process by which composite roles are constructed by composing a set of basic roles and the conversations they imply, may operate at one of three distinct levels:

Composite, theoretical roles which combine basic roles but which are still considered as abstract and normative.

Individual roles, where the set of responsibilities defined in the role are intended to be allocated to a person who will bring all their pre-existing roles, relationships and interests to the organizational context, e.g. wife, mother, citizen, member of a trade union, etc.

Collective roles that will be allocated to an organizational structure such as a team, a department, a division or a company.

In the case of theoretical role definition, the evaluation of the coherence and compatibility of role combinations depends on an examination of the distribution of significance, mutuality, capability and control of the component role relationships. We will consider the principles of this process in the next section. In the case of individual and collective roles, the assessment is based on the composition of the proposed, already composite theoretical role, with some model of the target organizational unit: employee, group or company.

The particular models of the target unit will depend on the political stance of the stakeholders and the purpose of the analysis. For example, modeling the employee as a hostile who is pursuing a role with large negative mutuality is a form of threat analysis, identifying the vulnerabilities and failure modes of a proposed organizational structure to internal attack.

Similarly, an organizational unit could be modeled as a participative, democratic team or, alternatively, as a hierarchically controlled unit. For example, if the theoretical role under consideration is the commander of a military operation, then we are comparing a guerrilla versus the regular army approach to the commander—subordinate relationship.

Combining Theoretical Roles

There are two basic cases of composition of dyadic roles which can be used to illustrate the principles of our method of conversation theory. These are illustrated in Figure 9, below.

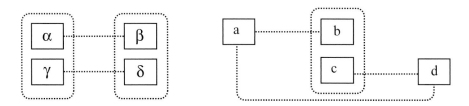

Pairwise composition of roles.   Transitive composition of roles

Figure 9: Composition of roles

In pairwise composition, the relationship α-β and the relationship γ-δ are combined. For this to be plausible and acceptable, each of the conversations needs to be of comparable and compatible significance for each party. For example, the combination of a doctor—patient relationship with that of experimenter—subject, which occurs when medical research is conducted within a health care enterprise, can lead to potential conflicts of interest, since the doctor takes more responsibility for the benefit obtained by the patient than the experimenter does for the subject. Hence the special protocols which apply in such cases. In cases of very asymmetric mutuality, e.g. borrowing money to create a creditor—debtor relationship, the concept of collateral is introduced to equalise the asymmetric significance. Thus, the lender's dependence on the borrower's continued commitment to repay is balanced by the borrower's dependence on the lender for continued access to pledged collateral.

In the case of transitive compositions, the key issues concern the nature of the relationship between (a) and (d). If they are independent, then the composition of (b) and (c) onto a job or mission for an individual or organizational unit is also an independent consideration. If, however, the (a - d) conversation is significant then a conflict may arise. For example, if the doctor (b) becomes the commissioned sales representative (c) for the drug company (d) and the patient (a) becomes the customer of that company because the doctor prescribes its drugs rather than drugs from some other producers, the doctor—patient mutuality has been compromised by a conflict of interest. In contrast, if the doctor as a member (c) of a golf club (d) introduces the patient as a guest, then neither of the relationships can be said thereby to have been compromised.

In the case where the roles (a) and (d) are not independent of each other then transitive composition produces a role (bc) which is a common third party. In the case where the composite role, (bc) removes the need for direct interaction between (a) and (d), we have a intermediary or broking role. In cases where (a) and (d) continue to have a direct relationship, the third party role may either be supervisory in relation to this conversation or it may be supportive and infrastructural to it.

A different set of considerations arise when we consider capability and control in composite roles. Capabilities imply access to and use of resources, facilities, information and skills. These may interact when combined to create overloads or interferences rendering the composition of the roles inadvisable. Alternatively, combinations of roles can create efficiencies and economies through the reuse of capabilities.

Finally, the distribution of control implied by roles which are to be combined must be broadly compatible: expecting the subordinate to be the teacher of the superior can be threatening and lead to tensions arising from role conflict.

Applying the Normative Framework to Market Conversations

Consider the conversation between the market roles of vendor and purchaser. The basic significance of such a conversation is dictated by the monetary value of the purchase; however, this does not exhaust the significance issue. The vendor's reputation within the market place may be at stake and in the case of certain goods, the purchaser's health and safety may also be a consideration. The mutuality of the relationship is institutionalized in law, which, in the case of the sale of goods to the public, may place a responsibility on the vendor for the basic protection of the purchaser.

The capability required of a purchaser concerns an appreciation of the need to be satisfied, the rights and ability to select an offer and to transact; and the capability required of a vendor is the right, the ability and the intention to transfer the ownership or other rights over whatever is offered through the market transaction.

The allocation of control between the vendor and the purchaser in the selection and the transaction phases of market conversation is a matter of convention or regulation, producing a range of market protocols including auctions, open outcry, tendering, etc. Each protocol is differentiated by the distribution of control over the instruments of communication and of the progress of the conversation between phases. Each of these protocols is an instantiation of a logically prior definition in terms of a sequence of acts. For example, the generic purchaser—vendor "act flow" is:

1 The vendor's offer to trade, which may be either unconditional or conditional on the negotiation of an acceptable price with an acceptable purchaser.

2 A purchaser's bid to purchase at a specified price.

3 A vendor's and purchaser's re-offer, commitment or withdrawal.

4 A vendor's discharge, which transfers the traded right over the offered resource to the purchaser.

5 The purchaser's discharge, which transfers the payment or other consideration to the vendor.

6 A claim for recourse in the event of a complaint by either transacting party.

This generic outline may be subject to constraints in particular cases. For example, as a consequence of the distribution of significance and control in normal retailing, only the vendor is able to initiate a conversation with an offer at a fixed price and haggling is not admissible. By contrast, in a procurement exercise, the purchaser initiates a conversation by publishing a call for tenders and trade takes place at the price selected or negotiated by the purchaser.

The means by which vendor—purchaser acts are instrumentalised depends on the nature of the specific market relationship. In the purchase of goods in a department store, customer commitment is implicit in selection, whereas if the significance of the market conversation is high and the context is highly institutionalized, as is the case in house purchase, commitment may be signaled by signing a legal document. It is interesting to note that in commitments of very high significance in non-institutionalized contexts, only direct negotiation and a personal handshake may be acceptable. The parties need to be able to look each other in the eye and evaluate whether they trust each other or not. Such commitments cannot be mediated by any other instrument.

In some procurement contexts, which are intended to provide a fair opportunity for potential suppliers to compete in the interests of the purchaser, bids may be recorded and communicated in sealed envelopes. In an auction, bids will be broadcast openly because the interests of the vendor are served by competition between potential purchasers.

For dyadic conversations to be transitively composable, then, either
- The uncomposed roles are independent, or
- The composed role is mediating between the uncomposed ones, or
- It must be supervisory in relation to the two roles, or
- It must be infrastructural to them.

4. HEALTH ENTERPRISE: AN EXAMPLE OF RESPONSIBILITY MODELLING

Introduction

In this section, we present an example of the use of responsibilities to model some aspects of health care. These models identify agents, i.e. those to whom responsibilities, as we have defined them, are ascribed, and locate the conversations that take place between them. We have chosen this example because its subject is accessible and because it provides a good illustration of a number of the properties of such models.

The Basic Model

At the most abstract level, health enterprise is modeled as three internal responsibilities:

The *funding agent* accepts responsibility in relation to external agents, the *civil persons*, to provide health care on the demand of *patients*. The context of the conversation between funding agents and civil persons may be social, as in a public health environment, commercial, as in a private health environment or charitable, where the patient and the civil person are quite separate. It may be intermediated by a third party agent such as an insurance enterprise or the state. The instruments of the funding conversation may include:
- The medical prospectus defining the range of health care which is offered.
- The contribution or payment.
- Some token of membership by which qualifying patients may be identified if required.

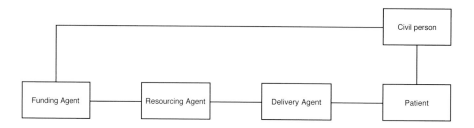

Figure 10. The basic model of health enterprise

The conversation between the funding agent and the resourcing agent is concerned with the responsibility to convert general resources into specific ones which are adequate to meet the care delivery obligations of the health care enterprise. Funding responsibility includes the prediction of demand, whereas the resourcing agency is responsible for planning and resourcing Figure 10 presents this most abstract enterprise model of health enterprise. It will be used in two ways: firstly we look in greater detail into delivery agency to see how this responsibility is structured and how its component responsibilities are mapped in different ways in the context of primary and secondary health enterprises. We will then show how the basic model can be used as a component of a wider enterprise model of a health sector, which shows the distinctions and relationships between health care enterprises, public health, medical research, and education and medical supply.

Health Care Delivery

In the western tradition of medicine, health care delivery responsibilities are structured into the following conversations:

Diagnosing: the responsibility to assess the patient's medial condition, which implies the right to enquire into symptoms and history. The patient has the responsibility to answer fully and honestly but the responsibility for assessing the completeness, relevance and reliability of the information presented lies with the agent who has a responsibility to generate a diagnosis.

Prescribing: is the responsibility to select a treatment from those that have been resourced within the enterprise, which is appropriate for the diagnosis. This may include referral. If diagnosing and prescribing responsibilities are composed together into the role of an individual, then the diagnosis may not be effectively externalized as an item of information in an instrument such as the medical records — which thus becomes a history of treatment rather than a full record of medical encounter.

Dispensing responsibility is concerned with ensuring that medical resources are consumed only on the basis of prescription and administered only to the patients for whom they are intended.

Administering responsibility is concerned with the correct and timely delivery of treatment.

Counselling agency reflects the principle of informed consent in the Western medical tradition.

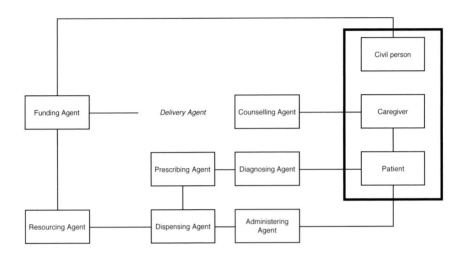

Figure 11. Medical care delivery agency

The responsibilities of health care delivery are allocated and shared in different ways in primary and secondary health care and also vary in different national settings. We will consider the United Kingdom model where, in the case of primary healthcare, we find the roles of general practitioner and pharmacist and a mapping of responsibilities as shown in Figure 12. Note that, in the case of simple medications and common, non-acute illness, the consumer—supplier relationship between the pharmacist and client may be activated with self or shared diagnosis and prescription. This is not an example of health enterprise as we have constituted it but is an example of commercial enterprise albeit with some special medical characteristics.

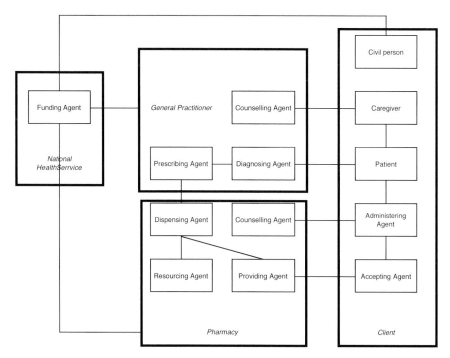

Figure 12. Primary health care delivery – the U.K. model

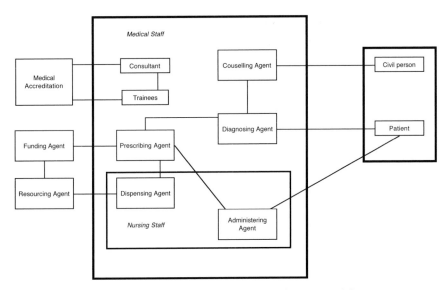

Figure 13. Secondary health care delivery – the U.K. model

In the case of secondary health care, which is situated in a hospital, the responsibilities are mapped between medical, nursing and surgical staff. In each of these cases, care delivery and medical education and accreditation are combined. It is the composition of responsibilities, and the consequent potential for misconstruing conversations, which gives rise to one of the failure modes of the enterprise. Thus, the need to counsel the patient and the need to train doctors leads to a conflict of roles: does the consultant address the patient as carer or the students as teacher when a round of the ward is conducted? And if the latter is the case, what has the role of patient become?

Despite the differences between these two models of primary and secondary delivery, we can see that they both represent delivery of care by health enterprises because we see the same set of responsibilities and the occurrence of the same set of conversations albeit distributed in different ways on to roles for people.

Constructing a Health Sector

Having considered a basic model of the health enterprise, we can observe three distinct applications of the model which are distinguished by the nature of the benefit that is delivered and, consequently the nature of the conversation between the enterprise and the health care client. These are:

Health Care Enterprise where the benefit is treatment and the client is a patient.

Public Health Enterprise where the benefit is information and protection and the client is a constituency and an audience.

Medical Research Enterprise where the benefit is improved medical capabilities and treatments and the client combines the roles of subject and of beneficiary, although these may occur at different times and be represented by different sets of individuals within the client community.

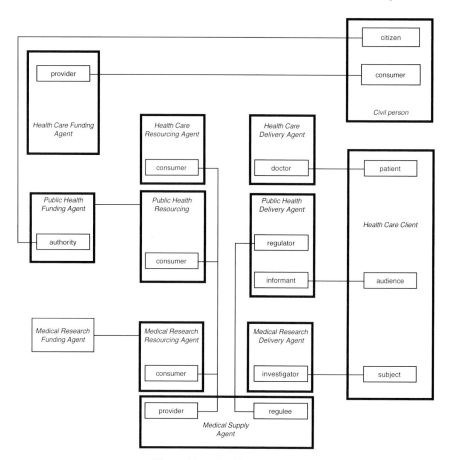

Figure 14. A health sector

It can be seen in Figure 14 that medical supply does not fall within the scope of medical enterprise as we constitute it. There is, however, a strong link between medical research and medical supply, which results in potential conflicts of interest when they are composed together. It is for this reason that the regulatory relationship controls a public health enterprise to ensure that it is independent of the supply sector and acting in the collective interests of the clients.

Instruments, conversations and activities

The names of the agents represented in our models all denote activities such as diagnosing and prescribing, but, it must be stressed, the definitions we have given them have been strictly in terms of responsibilities. The discharge of these responsibilities involves the generation and interpretation of information as well as the allocation and consumption of resources. These exchanges between agents we call conversations.

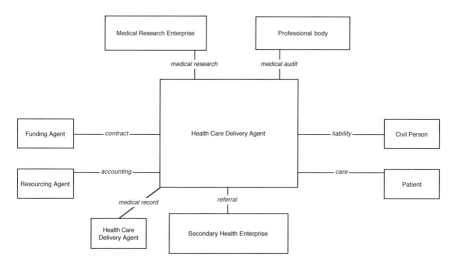

Figure 15. Conversations which include the information item <diagnosis>

We have not represented the instruments of the conversations in the models presented here. The instruments are embodied in documents such as medical records, prescriptions and audit records.

Figure 15 represents the set of conversations which a health care delivery agent engages in and in which an information item <diagnosis> appears. The following brief observations can be made on these contexts:

Medical records: this represents a conversation between doctors in the interests of the patient.

Care: in this conversation, the good of the patient may justify dissembling; the doctor does not always reveal the true nature of the diagnosis and the patient may not want to hear it.

Liability: certain diagnoses can have implications beyond the purely medical — for example, on the employment prospects or other rights of the civil person who is the patient.

Medical audit: here the issue is the competence and quality of the diagnosing agent's performance. In practice, diagnoses in medical audit tend to be very generic thus maximizing the probability that they are correct.

Accounting: certain diagnoses imply standard treatments which have a cost. If the required resources have not been allocated, there is a conflict with resourcing: we may not be able to afford that particular diagnosis, perhaps it would be better if the patient had something cheaper.

Contract: the doctor is a professional and has a career to pursue. In these contexts, certain diagnoses can become admissible or not admissible, fashionable or otherwise.

Medical research: diagnoses can have significant impacts on the profitability of drugs and the share prices of the companies that invent and manufacture them.

The context in which these models were constructed was the definition of data models for medical information systems. The conclusion drawn from the identification of this range of contexts of generation and interpretation is that to follow the "write once, read many times" design rule, which is a principle of many data modeling and database applications, represents the imposition of a complex set of unintended and often unacceptable policies.

5. RESPONSIBILITY MODELLING IN THE DESIGN PROCESS

In this final section, we shall say something about the role of enterprise models in the design process.

Recall that the enterprise model shows separate responsibilities and the instruments that mediate conversations between the responsibility holders. It is a matter of organizational configuration how those responsibilities map on to organizational roles and entities, and how allocations of channels and media are constituted to form the instruments. A lot of organizational redesign in preparation for, or consequent upon, the introduction of an information and communication system is concerned with changing these mappings and allocations and the introduction of new responsibilities. The system may also require or result in distributing a single responsibility among two or more work roles. By representing what is invariant under organizational change, the models allow for discussion of different configurations.

Similarly, the models can be used to promote discussion of the boundaries of the system. It is a matter of common experience of system analysts that in the early stages of system design, determining where the system boundaries are to be drawn is possibly the most time-consuming task in the pre-requirements phase. It often makes more sense if in the first instance boundaries are drawn in terms of responsibilities, because this still leaves open possibilities for change in the way responsibilities are mapped on to work roles.

In this chapter we have presented a model of responsibility and we have shown, through simple models of a health enterprise, how it can be used to express the intentional aspects of a socio-technical system. We have shown that such models may be composed and decomposed in the process of structuring obligations and responsibilities. We have seen, albeit briefly, that these operations support reasoning about conflicts of interest and the contexts of generation and interpretation of information. Such models are created in the context of the development of policy and the exploration of requirements and may be descriptive or normative in nature. They form an essential component of architectural discourse in which organizational requirements are clarified and solution options explored. In this respect, they can be an important part of a soft systems methodology, in which normative and descriptive models are offered up to each other and discrepancies explored.

ACKNOWLEDGEMENTS

This work has been developed over many years with the assistance of many colleagues in many projects. Of particular importance are the contributions of Ros Strens and (especially) Mike Martin.

REFERENCES

1. Axelrod, R. (1984). *The Evolution of Cooperation*, New York, Basic Books.
2. Checkland, P. (1981). *Systems Thinking, Systems Practice*, Chichester, John Wiley.
3. Checkland, P. and Scholes, J. (1990). *Soft Systems Methodology in Action*, Chichester, John Wiley.
4. Lucas, J. R. (1995). *Responsibility*, Oxford, Clarendon Press.
5. Luhmann, N. (1979). *Trust and Power*, Chichester, John Wiley.
6. Parsons, T. (1951). *The Social System*, London, Routledge and Kegan Paul.

Chapter 4

STANDARDIZATION, TRUST AND DEPENDABILITY

Gillian Hardstone, Luciana d'Adderio and Robin Williams
Research Centre for Social Sciences, University of Edinburgh

1. INTRODUCTION

How is an information system made, or how does it become seen as 'trustworthy' and hence dependable? And how trustworthy is the information entered into that system? These questions become particularly acute where users of a system are geographically distant from each other; or where there is cognitive and substantive distance between their domains of knowledge; or where the knowledge and practice of one community have not been fully articulated, and are hence considered less significant or more remote from the everyday concerns of another community. All these situations raise socio-technical issues of trust, or its absence. One answer suggested by the literature (1)(2)(3) to the issues of dependability highlighted above would appear to lie in a certain level of standardization of information structures and organization practice in order to facilitate control and co-ordination at a distance.

However, our empirical material illustrates that standardization intended to increase trust can itself create or reveal system undependabilities, thereby compromising organizational and professional trust and discretion. The questions then concern what level or type of standardization may be deemed workable or desirable, in order to create more dependable products, processes or systems. Since local work groups (communities of practice) tend to articulate their own systems of meaning, including information systems, around their particular context, practices and purposes, does standardization imply or result in the privileging of or support for some groups - and their ways of thinking, doing and recording - over others. Does

K.Clarke, G. Hardstone, M. Rouncefield and I. Sommerville (eds.), Trust in Technology:
A Socio-Technical Perspective, 69–103.

standardization force other groups to align their practices with those embedded in standardized information system procedures, or compel them to perform a continual translation process between domains? This raises questions about the costs as well as the benefits of standardization.

The chapter presents three case studies of moves towards standardization within organizations: two from manufacturing industry (ComputerCo and MotorCo) and one from public sector primary healthcare (NHS Urban). These demonstrate different types and degrees of standardization, whether of products, processes, practice and terminology, forms of knowledge or social relations, to point up a variety of possible organizational approaches and outcomes. Combining insights from the empirical material with sociological studies of standardization we reflect upon the implications for the development and implementation of more dependable computer-based systems.

We conclude that organizational processes of standardization are more negotiable than formalist approaches (4,5) assume. Conversely standardization processes are not as open as many accounts that foreground the contingent nature of local adaptation and translation processes suggest (3). We demonstrate that in practice, levels and types of informational and operational standardi-zation vary widely between and within organizations, and can be related to organizational control and co-ordination strategies.

Standards, trust and the dependability of socio-technical systems

Standardization of organizational procedures and information practices, whilst in theory ensuring the dependability of activities, can also be seen to imply and arise in response to a lack of trust that individuals and organizations, left to their own devices, will think, act or keep records in the manner deemed appropriate by some other party. In short, they cannot be depended upon.

Why then are issues of trust (and of standardization) achieving greater salience? One reason for this increased scrutiny and prescription may lie in the increasing complexity of organizations and their resources. Let us consider the evolution from simple to complex socio-technical systems. The operation and performance of simple socio-technical systems may be subject to direct scrutiny; the actors and technical components are known, their capabilities are accessible in the sense that participants may acquire broadly adequate knowledge to assess and verify the properties and performance of other (human or technical) elements. Where the scale and scope of activity become too large for direct scrutiny, simple forms of communitarian trust may come in to play based upon presumptions of reciprocity, broadly shared norms and established repertoires of behaviour and rooted in experience of repeated performance. This traditional form of trust emerges retrospectively through membership and practice; it is thus not well equipped for dealing with novel and rapidly changing socio-technical settings.

Traditional communitarian trust becomes challenged by the increasing complexity of socio-technical systems and by contemporary requirements for more formalized verification of system dependability, for more explicit accountability and for much higher levels of performance of socio-technical systems in terms of dependability. Contemporary socio-technical systems are larger in scale, more elaborate and more heterogeneous in terms of arrays of knowledge deployed. They raise questions about how we can operate dependably at a distance, when players are separated in spatial, temporal, social, and knowledge terms. How can we ensure that the system and its components will behave in a way that is expected or desired when they are no longer in our direct scrutiny?

Standards seem to provide a solution, holding out the promise of eliminating ambiguity about the performance of distant actors and artefacts; a means of creating what Latour (6) has termed 'immutable mobiles', 'Standards aim at making actions comparable over time and space; they are mobile and stable and can be combined with other resources' (2:273). The paradox is that such reliance upon standards reflects the absence of traditional communitarian forms of trust, and the consequent development of forms of external control and co-ordination. Law (2) has suggested that 'the undistorted communication necessary for long-distance control depends on the generation of a structure of heterogeneous elements containing envoys which are mobile, durable, forceful and able to return' (2:257). However, our three case studies show that the standardization of systems and processes, as part of such a structure, is unable to maintain 'undistorted communication', and hence to guarantee either trust or dependability across communities of practice.

Standardization has been characterized as having both positive and negative aspects. It may make things more manageable and controllable; provide economy in record keeping; reduce ambiguity (7); enable calculation, measurement, comparison, and data manipulation; assist in institutional problem-solving; give activities and entities existence and legitimacy; and provide a tool for co-ordination and accounting for resources. There are also economic and technological incentives to standardization, in that it may trigger the codification of knowledge (8), which can then be 'transmitted over long distances and within complex networks, at a very limited cost and high speed' (9:1354). Standardization can also help create or affirm communities of practice.

However, standardization of information practices can result in loss of meaning for some individuals and groups seeking to make their own distinctions and classifications for different, though equally legitimate purposes. For example, an information system may standardize data in a form relevant to some practitioners, but not others. This may result in incomplete, inaccurate and inconsistent data entry, with knock-on effects for the dependability of the system as a whole. Standardization can also be used for control or co-ordination purposes and to induce or monitor particular behaviours, whether individual or organizational, 'In a sense, the power of normalization imposes homogeneity; but it individualizes by making it possible to measure gaps, to determine levels, to fix specialities and to render the differences useful by fitting them one to another' (1:184). Yet although computer systems record and may make visible some of the activities of an organization, they do not record others, so are not necessarily Panoptic (1) in their operation (10).

Socio-technical approaches to standardization

Standardization can be defined as the activity of establishing provisions for 'common and repeated use, rules, guidelines or characteristics for activities or their results, aimed at the achievement of the optimum degree of order in a given context' (11), or as conformity with 'any set of agreed-upon rules for the production of (textual or material) objects', spanning more than one community of practice and persisting over time (12:13). The concept needs to be considered in context, since there are different levels and types of standardization, including those of product and service, the processes and technologies for their delivery (operational), and administrative or financial procedures (informational), and organizations may practice all or only some of these. Some standards are generated externally to organizations. Some may be in widespread use; some are adhered to (or not) by practitioners operating within particular domains of knowledge and practice. Other standards may be internal to a specific organization. Indeed, it could be suggested that standardization is one of the distinguishing features of current organizational life.

Standardization tends to be premised at least partly on the prior existence or creation of classification systems: apparently simple but significant technologies for ordering the world. Classification appears to be a fundamental human activity enabling us to tame 'the wild profusion of existing things' (1:xv) and make sense of the world's complexity. It is an intensely social undertaking, rooted in communities of practice and contexts (13), and is often domain-specific. It involves ordering entities into groups on the basis of their relationships to establish a classificatory system, the assignation of subsequent instances of such entities to groups in an established classificatory system (14), and using the results of that classification as a basis for future action. Again, classifications can be generated externally to a particular organization, as in the case of the International Classification of Diseases (12), or they may be organization-specific (15).

The design of computer-based systems tends to assume that certain aspects of a user organization's practice and knowledge have been (or will be) standardized, in order for the system to operate effectively. At the very least, there needs to be a decision within the organization about what data should be recorded, and how data should be structured within the system to allow for subsequent retrieval and analysis. There may also be decisions about who may enter or extract data, and how and when this may be done. For example, the classification systems inherent in database fields imply that a shared, standardized way of thinking about and recording (and sometimes doing) activity and information has already been developed, even where this has not actually occurred or been fully adopted. This becomes a particular issue in organizations where several communities of practice interact, each with their own bodies of knowledge and ways of ordering that knowledge. The Motorco case study highlights the translation effort required between different professional domains when an organization attempts to integrate previously separate information systems, and the consequent potential for undependability. Can standardization be seen as both a prerequisite for and a result of the implementation of computer-based systems; a means of enhancing and enforcing dependability?

Formalist accounts of standardization and classification in system design (4,5) that do not take into account their social dimensions (12) suggest that following principles of good practice, such as ensuring consistency, completeness, and mutually exclusive categories in any classification will ensure the usability and dependability of the resultant system. Because it can be argued that standardization enhances system dependability, it is sometimes assumed that increased levels and types of standardization will make systems more dependable. However, Timmermans and Berg (3) suggest that 'a certain looseness' may be needed to achieve workable standardizations that offer users 'local universality', whilst Bowker and Star (12) acknowledge that there are tradeoffs, 'for a classification system to be standardized, it needs to be comparable across sites and leave a margin of control for its users; however, both requirements are difficult to fulfill simultaneously' (12:232). Our case studies show that organizations indeed exhibit considerable variety and latitude in their approaches to standardization, and that over-standardization can in some instances be counter-productive for dependability.

Even the achievement of standardization is not a foregone conclusion. It cannot always be assumed that decisions about data have been made, let alone accepted by all users of a system. Bowker and Star (12:44) suggest that 'the spread or enforcement of categories and standards involves negotiation or force', and this is especially pertinent where packaged ICT applications are being configured to the needs of a specific organization, or where inter-organizational systems are being developed. Here, tensions can arise between standardization and specificity, and between the global and the local, relocating existing foci of conflict and negotiation work to another space. Attempting to fit specific instances into a standard framework does not reduce ambiguity, but awareness of the issues is transformed as users struggle to standardize their lived experience into the system, or to understand what others mean by their choices. Do systems intended to facilitate different groups of professionals working together through standardization in fact make this more problematic by highlighting those differences?

Levels of standardization

One tendency, noted by Timmermans and Berg (3), is for accounts of standardization to simplify and overstate its progress and its positive or negative impacts (12,7), or to assume that standardization will always be imposed rather than negotiated (1,16). Other accounts of system implementation highlight the contingent and contestable nature of all standardization efforts (15), and hence the difficulties in agreeing and implementing standards within and between organizations (17,18). As we argue elsewhere (18) there are dangers both in over- and underestimating the success of standardization efforts.

Much (though not all) depends on the level of investigation and the context in which standardization occurs. What may appear all-encompassing from a top-down viewpoint may on closer inspection prove to be less than totalizing in its everyday practice, and what seems messy and unique at the micro level of individual interactions may well turn out to exhibit more regularity of features when compared with similar instances. These problems can be related to shortcoming in the kinds of study adopted (for example of top-down accounts of standardization that do not pick up local diversity, snap-shot case-studies that highlight short-term barriers to alignment). To address these effectively, a dynamic understanding is needed which encompasses both standards development and implementation, and offers a comparative and historical perspective which explores diversity and alignment across different settings and which is alert to longer-term processes of alignment of systems of practice and meaning.

There are various explanations for why there exist different levels or degrees of standardization. What Douglas terms 'denoting', the assigning of names and their definitions within the wider classification schemes or systems of which they are part, is seen as an essential aspect of 'the making of worlds' (13:248), 'For some purposes, imprecision is acceptable, even desirable. For other purposes, denoting needs to be very exact'. Standardization contributes, in theory, to that kind of exactitude, and thereby produces certain kinds of result, 'the standardized form admits only a limited range of formal, objective and impersonal information, which in some cases is exactly what is needed to solve a particular problem' (7:84). One example would be the translation from individual clinical data to mass epidemiological statistics. Exact parameters for specifying products or components may be necessary in manufacturing systems to avoid ambiguity and to act at a distance. There may also be a link between increased need for precision and the criticality of the task or the knowledge involved in its execution, and it could be suggested that the more critical the activity, the higher the level of control that will be exerted over it in the form of standardization. Other explanations might include the degree to which the system is tightly-coupled, where what happens in one part of the system has rapid and major knock-on effects on other parts (19), or the number of organizations or domains of knowledge that need to work together to create a product, service or process.

Standardization addresses the need for precision and co-ordination, but different professional domains have different, albeit equally precise, languages for specification that reflect the arrangement of their domain knowledge. From this perspective, some worlds, such as the engineering domains of knowledge and practice in Motorco or the specific corporate culture of Computerco, may require exact correspondence between signs and their referents, whereas others such as NHS Urban are (for the present) content to allow variety and imprecision to flourish as a concomitant of standardization because this allows for the initial formation of a new multi-disciplinary, multi-agency world of patient care and the creation of a new and more IT-oriented community of mental healthcare practice. The following case studies reveal some of the perhaps ambiguous implications of standardization for dependability.

2. THE TRANSFER OF DEPENDABLE PRODUCTION PROCESSES: THE CASE OF COMPUTERCO

This case study discusses a transfer project undertaken by a world-leading manufacturer in the high-end electronics sector; the project was aimed at duplicating and transferring the entire production facility for their most advanced and complex server to one of their overseas subsidiaries. The rationale behind the transfer was to sharply increase the manufacturer's production capacity in order to cope with anticipated rapidly escalating demand for one of their high quality and highly customised server products. The move entailed the articulation, codification, validation, selection and transfer of all product-related knowledge as well as the exact replication of all product-related testing, production and manufacturing processes, rules and procedures to the new site. With such complex products it can be difficult to identify, trace back and rectify sources of product failure in the production process. Reliability is a crucial characteristic of the product and is inextricably related to the reliability of the production process. To ensure that the new facility would meet the stringent quality/dependability requirements for this product it was therefore decided to mirror the production processes in the originator facility. However, this strategy of exercising tight control through top down standardisation highlighted differences in approach to dependability assurance between the sites, related to the need to transfer product and processes across two different organisational cultures as well as labour structures; while performing a fundamental coordinating role, the heavy-handed standardisation also highlighted crucial trade-offs between standardisation and development of the production process, or, in other words, innovation and exploitation.

Sources of inter-site heterogeneity

From an organizational viewpoint, the transfer involved the coordination of two different site organizations located across two continents. The two organizations differed substantially in their culture, skills set and knowledge bases, as well as being characterized by radically different control and coordination regimes.

The first site, the 'originator' of the transfer, was a recently acquired, US-based, single product organization, historically renowned for its excellence in the production of highly complex and highly customized server products; this organization's principal focus was on producing the highest quality products while remaining extremely agile and therefore able to quickly adapt to rapidly switching demand. The site was characterized by a strong 'engineering culture' centred around the individual engineer's experience and intuition combined with a strong ability to fulfill goals and resolve problems 'by heroics', which entailed a strong emphasis on local improvisation and adaptation. This was clearly demonstrated by the recognition paid to highly skilled and experienced technical personnel, as well as their intensive use of tacit and local knowledge to support flexible and adaptive practices. Coordination at this site was principally achieved by word of mouth, whereas training and knowledge sharing were procured on the job, by means of tutoring by examples. The low extent replicability of their procedures, which were mostly uncodified and held in the memory of experienced practitioners, were from the outset viewed by the other site as signs of potential process unreliability due to the inability to promote consistency across sites, as well as supporting the full articulation and codification of knowledge and procedures, thus leaving gaps open to individual discretion and local adaptation.

The second site, the recipient of the transfer[6] was the enterprise's European-based manufacturing facility, a multi-product organization renowned for its reliance on validated 'best practices' and its demonstrated ability to align to enterprise-wide standards as well as to global ISO 9000 requirements. While having no previous knowledge about the server product being transferred, this site organization had strong expertise in the production and manufacturing of other similar (if somewhat less complex) artefacts. The site had a strong tradition of codification and proceduralisation of both knowledge and practices. Co-ordination was achieved by articulation, codification and standardization of all relevant knowledge and procedures, as far as it was feasible. Knowledge and routines were selected by gathering the diverse, discipline-specific viewpoints and putting them through a trial process where implications and alternatives were discussed and either accepted or dismissed. Due to its strong accent on standardization and control, this organization was viewed by the US site as being somewhat bureaucratic as well as prone to (and a potential source of) rigidity and therefore unresponsiveness to the external environment.

The sources of heterogeneity, however, were not limited to inter-site differences. Important discrepancies and asymmetries of knowledge, goals, preferences and incentives were also identified within each organization as a result of the differences in each site's specific internal structure and division of labour among different functions (i.e., site engineering, testing, manufacturing, materials, etc.). Repeatedly during the project the objectives of these specific communities (epistemic communities) clashed with the

---

[6] These labels indicate initial conceptions of the role; as we see, both sites contributed to the subsequent innovation of the manufacturing process.

rules or goals set by the overall project rationale (communities of practice) and the global need for alignment and synchronization. The personnel structure of the new production site was created from scratch to mirror the structure at the other site identically, so that each individual at one end would have an exact counterpart at the other; as a consequence, it was a common scenario that sites would agree at the level of the individual counterpart while at the same time disagreeing with the overall level of the project.

Following the transfer, the existing differences between the two sites were further emphasized; this was due to the need for the two organizations to work together in (nearly) perfect synchronization, involving the need to adopt and use identical production processes to create server products of identical looks and, most importantly, of identical quality.

It was perceived that such diversity within and across sites would ultimately undermine the success of the project. A strict standardization process was therefore instigated in order to reduce heterogeneity and promote coordination while at the same time ensuring control. This is consistent with the Economics of standardization literature (Cowan, David and Foray 1998) emphasis on standardization as a means of high level coordination and reduction of bottlenecks. Our evidence, however, highlighted how, while standardization did play a fundamental role, coordination was ultimately made possible by an idiosyncratic mix of standardization and adaptive practices which prevented rigidities and conflicts to grind the process to a halt.

The 'Exception Process' and the reduction of diversity

The differences between the two organizations emerged strongly from the very early stages of the project. The initial stages were characterized by a severe lack of spontaneous knowledge sharing and trust across the two sites. At the same time, full synchronization between the two sites was deemed fundamental to ensure consistency in the quality measured across the products that would eventually emerge out of each individual factory. This led to the set up of a joint committee to manage and harmonise the transfer process; this was named Failure Is Not An Option (FINAO), reflecting strategic importance attached to the need to avoid not simply 'technical' but also of deeper process and organizational forms of failures (cf. Perrow, 1986). The combined influence of a lack of trust and the need for tight synchronization across sites triggered the creation of the 'Exception Approval Process', which was lead by the FINAO team made up of manager representatives for each function and site.

The Exception Process constituted a striking attempt at harnessing technological and organizational diversity. The process was set up as a means to ensure that all the differences between the two sites identified as 'exceptions' were going to be highlighted, brought to the FINAO forum's attention, discussed, acted upon, aligned (or not aligned) and finally closed and published on to a shared live database. Such a strict standardization process together with tightly coupled coordination between sites was aimed at leaving very limited, if no scope at all, for local variation and differentiation. The process involved a strong reduction of diversity through the standardization of data collection, reporting and analysis; it also entailed the set up of coordinated cross-functional Change Management and Audit processes and tools. The transfer process was based also upon the black boxing, or freezing, of both artefact and production process for the entire duration of the transfer; product and process improvements were mostly to be put on hold because seen as a source of uncertainty and variation that could generate misalignment between the two sites. Through the exception process, diversity was made explicit, prosecuted (cf. Bloor, 1978) and finally either accepted (in the few specific cases classified as 'approved exceptions') or fully and permanently eradicated. The second set of tools introduced beside the Exception process was the 'Big Rules'. The Rules were high-level imperatives that played a fundamental role in enforcing control and coordination throughout the duration of the project as well as in the longer term. They consisted of metaphors and strong images (i.e. to 'drag & drop', 'mirror image', 'carbon copy', all referred to the need to transfer the process identically), which were effective in communicating the need for perfect alignment across the two sites.

Standardization and the persistence of diversity

The exception process represented an unprecedented effort to help them maintain control over any request for changes that would have arisen then and in the future. While some changes were indeed allowed in order to introduce some improvements as well as to align both sites together and to the wider global organization, the product and process were eventually transferred almost intact. At the management (and FINAO) level the exceptions retained, and not brought into alignment, were in fact only around 3-5% of total exceptions identified. This is a staggering result when considering the complexity of the artefact, the process and the organizations involved. Further evidence, however, later revealed that, while strong consistency was retained at the highest procedural level, at the lower levels the continuity broke down. The lack of articulation on part of the site from which the transfer originated had left scope for interpretation and 'gap filling' at the other. Detailed practices looked rather different across the two sites. Audits revealed worrying instances of misalignment as well as possible causes for future divergence.

While a potential source of divergence, gaps in lower level process definition played an important role in preventing, in the short term, further conflict from arising. While the gaps were obviously unintentional, they nevertheless served the purpose of delaying further conflict to a stage where the project was more advanced, a trust relationship had been established, and tensions had been addressed and to an extent mitigated. Thanks to those gaps, people were able to bring their knowledge and expertise into the process as well as leaving some scope for local variation. While in the longer term these gaps would place the organization in danger of misalignment, in the short term, for the duration of the transfer project, they allowed engineers and technicians alike a small amount of discretion that allowed them to perform their tasks efficiently and meet their targets. It is important to acknowledge that fundamental progress has been made to close these gaps, but that ultimately it is impossible to close them completely and this may not be desirable as, in relative terms, they allow for some degree of flexibility and adaptation[7].

This triggered a process of further identification and capture of differences to obtain greater alignment. The continued and long-term emphasis on the reduction of heterogeneity suggests that a governance mode involving a strong emphasis on control and standardization is not only compatible but is in fact required for a complex and distributed organization focused on the production of complex, high-quality artefacts. This is consistent to the superior scope for the codification of knowledge and practices that characterizes the high-end electronics sector.

Another force that promoted diversity and misalignment between the sites was the need for product and process improvement. The US 'originator' site had initially instigated the Exception Approval Process to ensure that the other site would adopt exactly the same procedures – allowing them, in this way, to retain ownership and control over the evolution of the product and the related process. Over time, however, the exception process proved to be a double edged sword. It was later used by the 'recipient' organization to ensure that the US site did not implement radical changes they couldn't keep up with or local changes that were not compatible or globally approved. This revealed a trade off between the need for control (via standardization), on one hand, and the need for continuous improvement on the other.

---

[7] On the limits to knowledge and process codification see also D'Adderio (2004).

Standardization and Trust as two different modes of coordination across heterogeneous cultures and organizations

The case study has highlighted the coexistence of two coexisting but contrasting strategies for maintaining coherence and dependability in complex technical organizations: the first is coordination by standardization, involving the formalization and codification of products and organizational practices to ensure visibility and uniformity; the second is coordination by trust, involving the formation of a new 'community of practice' which created a standard process and more or less flexible tools aimed at promoting infra- and inter-site communication and conflict management as well as to encourage a broadly compatible culture. The latter strategy based on trust had provided an effective mechanism for highly dependable processes and outcomes in the originator facility; however, there were problems in extending it to the UK site that was characterized by different organizational, cognitive and governance structures.

The marked lack of trust and familiarity between the originator and recipient sites, on one hand, and strong need for coordination and synchronization in the transfer of the production process, on the other, underpinned the pursuit of a very high level of control over the transfer by enforcing detailed standardization. Such high levels of control and standardization proved very successful in this tightly coupled, very high quality production environment and a highly complex product system. In this type of environment differences are not simply highlighted and made explicit but whenever possible and as far as possible eliminated. While there is an awareness at the management level of the costs/risks that would derive from misalignment, the benefits are considered to be much greater.

While in fact such a strong standardization effort potentially stood in contrast to other goals – notably the desire to improve processes – it did not in the longer term prevent improvement and adaptation; standardization was instead used to channel local innovation, including harnessing opportunities for improvement which typically emerged through local learning, but had potentially widespread, but difficult to predict, ramifications to other parts of the production process. The culture of certification/formalization at later stages allowed the recipient site to exert control over the adhocracy and autonomy of the US site's engineering culture by applying the techniques that were well understood by the European technical staff but which the American team found difficult to abide to and adapt to their own working practices as well integrating into their existing knowledge base.

At the same time as putting a strong emphasis on control, however, we have seen that sufficient flexibility was allowed to prevent the formation of process rigidities and the generation of strong conflict among the different cultures and communities that participated to the project. Rather than preventing coordination, gaps in procedure provided an opportunity for flexible and adaptive behaviour that contributed to ensure the success of the transition.

3. STANDARDISING ACROSS HETEROGENEOUS ORGANISATIONAL DOMAINS AND COGNITIVE STRUCTURES: THE CASE OF MOTORCO[8]

This case study concerns the process of introduction of a standard integrated COTS software system in place of separate systems for the design and manufacturing functions at a leading automotive manufacturer. It analyses the implications of software implementation for the standardization of knowledge and practices across heterogeneous tasks and organizational functions.

Product Data Manager (PDM) software is a state-of-the-art, enterprise-wide application solution, which is widely adopted across the most diverse range of manufacturing sectors, spanning from consumer electronics to the aerospace. PDM is specifically designed to facilitate the integration of processes and knowledge sources along the product life cycle (from product concept, to maintenance) and across the entire organization, including links to OEMs and the extended enterprise. To support these capabilities, PDM stores and controls huge quantities of information generated by engineers and other practitioners throughout the development process; this allows product administrators to control product life across multiple locations. PDM is designed to manage the evolution of a product configuration after its first release (freeze); afterwards, as product definition matures, PDM ensures that the correct design information is distributed to and accepted by the various enterprise organizations responsible for transforming the design into a finished product (i.e. Engineering, Production, Manufacturing, etc.). This is intended to promote better communication across the different functions and disciplines that are involved in development as well as the concurrency and synchronization of actions across multiple tasks and organizational locations. According to the software producer, these capabilities are technically enabled by the software's ability to store knowledge about the systemic

---

[8] A deeper and extended discussion of this case study has been published in D'Adderio (2003) and (2004).

structure of the product (i.e. product parts list) as well as of the processes that are used to make that product, including concurrent knowledge about the input of individuals and functions alike into the design process (i.e. design workflow). This is in turn enabled by the standardization of both product and process structures across the organization as well as the centralization of product and process data repositories in one single central database linked to PDM. Such heavyweight standardization is implemented with the aim to support multi-disciplinary and multi-functional collaboration and work synchronization; our example however shows that, at least in the short-term, it tends to emphasize existing organizational heterogeneities by highlighting cognitive (substantive) differences among different functions having different knowledge bases, objective, incentives and speaking different discipline-specific languages.

The coexistence of two incompatible structures

The introduction of PDM at our automotive organization has generated a strong push towards the codification, or 'inscription', and standardization of local knowledge and practices. As mentioned, such standardization and centralization of knowledge and practices is intended to facilitate co-ordination and cooperation across the different groups and functions involved in product development. Standardization in this case involved the structural reconfiguration of both knowledge and practices as these were progressively codified and embedded in software.

Following PDM implementation at the design end of development, a new standard Engineering Parts List (EPL) was introduced at the Engineering end of development, with the aim to subsequently extend it across the entire organization, thereby providing a unique product definition for anyone or any functions involved in development and beyond. The perceived benefits of implementing a single, PDM-managed, EPL were at the time related not merely to the ability that the new technology provides to visualize and display assembly data; more significantly the act of embedding configurational data into PDM helps to ensure that the assembly data is at all times configured, controlled, synchronized and verified, and can be shared by different organizational functions throughout all stages of the development process, and beyond. In this sense it was intended to support the co-ordination and integration of knowledge and practices that is at the basis of the software implementation philosophy.

The EPL is a structured list that contains all of the items contained in a product's configuration, including their relationships[9]; it is used to generate and maintain the evolving configuration of a product, plus all its variants (product family), over time. The List is used by both Engineering and Production, but with different objectives. Engineering compiles an EPL in order to facilitate the process of vehicle configuration extraction; this is done by extracting those parts that belong to an individual product configuration out of the total list of parts contained in an entire vehicle programme. Production uses the EPL for 'prototype verification' of fully built production vehicles.

While the Engineering and Production EPLs contain the same data, they vary substantially in the way they structure such data (i.e. the way they manage the relationships among the various parts contained in a technology assembly). PDM orders product assembly data in a hierarchical structure, based on 'parent/child' type of relationships. Production's EPL, instead, which is based on Total Modular Statement (TMS) technology, is characterized by a flat file structure whereby the relationships among different items and their exact position into product assemblies are captured by complicated, horizontal, Boolean statements. The more complicated the product structure, and the higher the number of configurational (vehicle) variants, the longer and more complicated are these algebraic statements [fig.1].

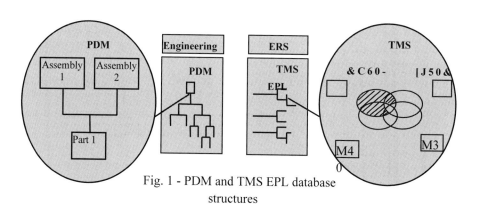

Fig. 1 - PDM and TMS EPL database
structures

In our organization, as a result of PDM introduction, PDM and TMS technologies are brought to coexist side by side. As a consequence, the basic incompatibility between the two different modalities in which PDM and

---

[9] A vehicle's Parts List includes all of its component Systems (i.e. car body), Sub-systems (i.e. a door), Features (i.e. door trim), Assemblies (i.e. gear box), Sub-assemblies (i.e. gear stick), etc., down to the finest configurational details.

TMS technologies organise information and compose product structures is emphasized. PDM implementation has in fact highlighted a mismatch between the way data is acquired and interpreted by two different ends of Product Development: Engineering and Production.

The introduction of a PDM-managed List has created a fracture with the Production (TMS) List, due to the fact that TMS technology is structurally incompatible with PDM's parent/child database morphology. Because of their radical difference in structuring the data, it is not easy to shift between the two technologies. On one hand, Production finds it difficult to understand PDM's EPL because they are not familiar with a parent/child structured List. On the other, only highly experienced practitioners are able to understand the complexities involved in structuring information according to TMS's logic. Before PDM implementation, basic techniques were in place that enabled each department to independently interpret the data in order to adapt it to its own specific information needs. The two different ways of structuring data were allowed to coexist. In order to support the implementation of an integrated software strategy, however, practitioners in Production are now expected to adopt the PDM-structured EPL, which is unfamiliar to them. The PDM-EPL configuration is information for engineering because they have the knowledge required to interpret it. Production instead comes from a different sub-disciplinary background and is unable to make sense of the data contained in the engineering EPL.

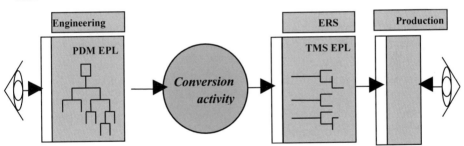

Fig. 2 - PDM and TMS Engineering Parts Lists

Engineering and Production basically spoke two different configurational and database languages, corresponding to two different disciplinary and functional backgrounds. The production engineers' language is based on a hierarchical object-oriented logic, which is also the logic embedded in software. The language spoken by production engineers is instead based on horizontal Boolean algebraic statements. The software-embedded language attempted to substitute itself to local, discipline-specific and task-specific dialects. This generated clashes between organizational groups and functions (or 'communities') speaking different, idiosyncratic languages and holding different knowledge, viewpoints, objectives and incentives. The newly introduced, software supported product structure creates a break in communication and knowledge transfer across upstream and downstream functions. The PDM-embedded parts list turns out to be an inflexible artefact that instead of facilitating prevents the development of a common system of understanding and meaning across the production and manufacturing end of the organizational spectrum.

The introduction of new 'integrated' software and subsequent attempt to standardize across heterogeneous discipline- and task-specific boundaries has at least partially failed due to the persistence of local idiosyncrasies. While some of these idiosyncrasies could be eliminated over time, as PDM implementation and the subsequent standardization progress, some will inevitably persist as they are related to the nature of the internal division of labour and specialisation. This is not necessarily entirely a drawback as such idiosyncrasies, though providing obstacles for coordination, can perform a valuable role as mechanisms by which tacit and local knowledge sources can be brought to bear into the development process.

The persistence of organizational heterogeneity

Software-induced standardization bears important implications for the organization, as it tends to radically reconfigure the very mechanisms by which organizational knowledge is structured, stored, retrieved and reused. In the attempt to impose a new, common, 'language', software generates a push towards greater standardization and reduction of technological and organizational heterogeneity (i.e., local, idiosyncratic 'dialects'). While the newly introduced (standardising) 'language' and routines were aimed at reducing the duplication of efforts and at improving co-ordination by eliminating inconsistencies of data and actions across the organization, they clashed with existing organizational heterogeneities; these took the form of various 'epistemic communities' and 'communities of practice', each having their own knowledge base, culture, objectives, and discipline- or activity-specific languages.

The example of the two (incompatible) product structures shows that the attempt to standardize across such heterogeneous organizational domains has paradoxically emphasized those existing inconsistencies and differences in knowledge bases and cognitive structures across functions. While standardization may eliminate some technological and organizational bottlenecks, as some economists have argued (cf. Cowan & Foray 1997), it also tends to create new ones. This example can therefore be conceptualised as a failure to impose a common, artificial language, due to the persistence of local 'dialects' (i.e. existing database structures, technologies and routines). In other words, it can be argued that the software-embedded product and database structure have failed to perform as a 'boundary object' (Bowker & Star, 1999): the new structure does not in fact possess the interpretive flexibility required to support collaboration among heterogeneous functions; rather, it is more similar to an inflexible 'standardising device' as it lacks the interpretive flexibility required to facilitate coordination across diverse and heterogeneous groups. This demonstrates that achieving shared meanings in a heterogeneous organizational setting therefore requires more than the mere co-ordination of information flows often advocated by economists and technicist literatures alike: it requires the integration of (often) incompatible meaning structures.

The heterogeneous groups and functions that compose an organisation differ significantly in their ability to learn, interpret, know and memorise. These inconsistencies are often heightened by the introduction of software, which tends to disintegrate existing organisational patterns while challenging the stability of existing routines. This leads to a fundamental paradox for the organisation: the need to exploit heterogeneity (of knowledge and practices), therefore fully exploiting the advantages of specialisation, while at the same time reaping the advantages of software-induced standardisation. Heterogeneity must (and indeed does) remain, but needs to be co-ordinated and supported (rather than over-ridden) by software systems.

Achieving dependability across heterogeneous organizational settings

These results bear important implications for dependability understood as the emergent outcome of complex, socio-technical, embedded-embedded and artefact-mediated interactions. The evidence shows how real life dependability decisions are influenced, among other factors, by the socio-economic setting such as the division of labour and knowledge within the user organization. Organizations are characterized by multiple conflicting dependability requirements that are owned and promoted by the diverse groups making up the organization. The mitigation of such conflicts always involves an uneasy compromise around the dependability attributes and mechanisms chosen to realise them. Specifically, we have demonstrated that the ways in which software-embedded structures and meanings operate in an actual heterogeneous implementation environment can produce a major source of undependability. The need for workarounds generated by an inflexible standardized (and standardising) system in our case has highlighted a fracture between embedded product and process models that undermines system effectiveness.

This highlights the need to extend the notion of dependability to the wider techno-organisational setting, which characterised by heterogeneous technologies, practices and communities. The properties of such a system are always evolving and emergent. In our case, the existence of organisation's internal heterogeneity is mirrored in the persistence of multiple data and meaning structures and of coexisting conflicting technologies such as PDM and TMS. Such uncomfortable coexistence of heterogeneous knowledge bases, technologies, and models has hindered the ability of organisational functions to interpret and extract meaning from the data supporting software-embedded product configurations. This has raised the issue of how to understand and identify risks and faults in unbounded (emergent) evolutionary systems, or systems-of-systems (Randell 1998), whereby heterogeneous components such as legacies and standardised software modules come to coexist.

A related observation is that the uneasy coexistence of contrasting data and meanings brought about by standardization has also undermined Production's ability to validate the data embedded in each configuration and therefore has diminished their trust in the reliability of such data. While previously Production had been able to independently verify the validity of data by drawing from its original source (paper and CAD drawings and sketches), after software introduction they had to rely solely on PDM-configured data whose format and integrity they could not verify and therefore trust. In addition, while the informal workaround which was set up to translate between the two functions and databases was partially successful in restoring system effectiveness by 'repairing' local communication flows between the two functions, this had also produced new types of undependabilities including frequent errors and substantial delays in the delivery of data from Engineering to Production and vice-versa, thus contributing to diminish the practitioners' trust in the integrity and validity of the data. This highlights the danger that informal adaptive practices, while effective in repairing local inefficiencies and restoring flexibility, can at the same time generate global, or higher level, systemic undependabilities.

4. NHS URBAN

This case study examines issues of standardization raised by the introduction of an integrated patient information management system (PMS) for primary mental healthcare in a large, predominantly urban, Scottish NHS region (NHS Urban). The NHS is a vast and heterogeneous organization that still provides most of the nation's primary (non-acute) and acute healthcare through the operation of General Practitioner (GP) facilities and local NHS regions. These keep detailed records of each individual patient's symptoms, diagnoses and treatments in the form of case notes, and also generate aggregate data and information about our health in order to plan and make resourcing decisions at local and national level about future healthcare provision. Whilst it might appear desirable that some of the information should be standardized (and perhaps the underlying patient care?), there are many cogent reasons why this has not been achieved, not just on a national scale, but within particular NHS Trusts, and even at team and individual Healthcare Professional (HCP) level. Previous studies have shown the implementation of integrated information systems in the NHS and elsewhere to be problematic. What part do attempts at standardization play in these difficulties, and what were the implications in NHS Urban for everyday practice and for overall system dependability?

Organizational and professional complexity and variety

The organization and delivery of primary mental healthcare services in NHS Urban was complex and distributed. A wide variety of general and specialist Mental Health Services provided for patients' needs from cradle to grave. Services ranged from Child and Adolescent through General Adult to Care of the Elderly, whilst specialist areas included those connected with substance misuse, eating disorders, or post-traumatic stress disorder. Service provision was organized into eight geographical areas, across many sites. Each provided general and some specialist services, with other cases requiring specialist care being referred to the relevant central facility. Locations in which Trust clinical activity occurred included hospitals (day clinics and longer-stay wards), outpatient and other clinics on NHS premises, clinics at GP practices and community health centres, patients' homes and other locations in the community.

The services provided by NHS Urban also exhibited high levels of method, process and outcome variety. They were delivered by multi-disciplinary teams of HCPs, including clinical consultants, community- and hospital-based psychiatric nurses, support workers, social workers, counselors and occupational and other types of therapist. Each of these HCPs belonged to a professional and/or occupational community of knowledge and practice with its own domain-specific language, as well as having a multi-disciplinary team- or specialty-orientation in terms of their every day work. Moreover, the needs of each patient and their trajectories of care were unique and complex: some might require only a specific intervention of limited duration by a single HCP, whilst others with severe and enduring mental health problems might receive continuing care of varying intensity over many years, involving HCPs from many different disciplines.

Old and new systems

In response to government policy changes and a substantial programme of investment in new, integrated information technologies, which it was hoped would lead to a more streamlined (and perhaps standardized) approach to patient care and its administration, NHS Urban began to implement an integrated computer-based Patient Information Management System (PMS) for its Primary Care Mental Health Services in Spring 2001. PMS was a commercial off-the-shelf (COTS) package provided by a specialist application content provider focused on healthcare markets. It was a database-driven, modular system, based on established technologies, claimed by its suppliers to be configurable to the requirements of each user organization. The new system was intended to replace the numerous separate manual and computer-based systems previously developed and used by different parts of the service, with the aim of integrating data and information across the Trust, "so we're all singing from the same hymn sheet" (PMS Project Manager). It was thereby hoped to improve patient care, and the accuracy, timeliness and completeness of mental health information used within NHS Urban for clinical and administrative decision-making, and for the compilation of statistics submitted monthly to the Scottish Executive from which national policy and resourcing decisions were made. It is worth noting here that PMS was not intended to replace the manual case notes maintained for each patient.

It was the first time this NHS Trust had attempted to integrate, and hence to standardize information systems across its services. It was also the first time that administration-related data entry had been devolved from a centralized medical records department to clinicians (as opposed to the handwritten case notes that had always been maintained by HCPs). This removed the previously existing 'buffer zone' between clinical and administrative staff, in which any necessary translations of information between domains had been carried out – a function whose value seems to have been largely unacknowledged. In order to achieve this, PMS was 'sold' to clinical users with the expectation that they would be able to extract from it all kinds of useful data never before so easily available or manipulable, both for research purposes, and to move towards an increasingly evidence-based clinical practice. PMS was to be used for data entry, retrieval and analysis by a variety of professional groups, each of which constituted different communities of knowledge and practice, and had different interests.

Here we shall confine ourselves to one specific and representative example that nicely illustrates some of the standardization issues raised by the introduction of PMS within the Trust. These exhibit interesting similarities with and differences from the other manufacturing and engineering organization case studies in this chapter.

The Contact Purpose menu

Whenever HCPs had face-to-face contact with a patient, details such as date, time, duration and location were to be entered into the system. PMS also required users to select one option from a pull-down menu of 'Contact Purpose' descriptions, whose completion was mandatory within the system, although the data were not utilized for wider statistical purposes. This effectively classified the work done by HCPs trust-wide into standard categories. As PMS was primarily an administrative system and not a fully Electronic Patient Record, 'Contact Purpose' was one of the few fields clinically relevant to HCPs, and one they felt should reflect their practice accurately. The evolution of this classification system reflects the NHS Trust's broad approach to standardization and its relation to system dependability.

The original Contact Purpose menu came with the system, having already been configured for Scotland from the English version of the system, and was initially re-configured to NHS Urban's anticipated requirements prior to roll-out. This included the migration of contact-related (though not exactly equivalent to Contact Purpose) options from several menus in a previous system (CPS). The menu was subsequently reconfigured during the early phases of roll-out in response to feedback from certain specialist teams, and further additions made periodically at the request of other users. Early on, the process was not systematic, but from June 2001, all requests for additions to the system were logged and a procedure put in place for dealing with them. Additions had to be 'owned' by a team, and they had to be defined. From the outset, the PMS Contact Purpose menu was a conflation of incommensurable options from a variety of sources: a heterogeneous instrument for any standardization of recording practice. Only one option could be selected, with the default being 'Not Specified'.

During implementation, two differing views of the Contact Purpose menu emerged; one from clinical users seeking to input their practice-related data into PMS, the other from the perspective of the PMS Implementation and IS Teams which were trying to ensure compliance with system use and quality of data entry. Existing mechanisms for user feedback were not working effectively, which meant that the Implementation Team was largely unaware of clinical users' conceptual and practical difficulties with 'Contact Purpose'

The clinical view

Clinical users reported difficulties deciding which option to select from the Contact Purpose menu, because the categories offered did not fit the way they described the work they did with patients. This could be because the specific practices of their particular professional grouping were not reflected in the menu options: "You've got [what an] Occupational Therapist does and she would have to report that as a 'Follow-Up' [but] it doesn't really describe what goes on". (Area Team Leader, General Adult). It could also be because the menu failed to reflect the work of the team. For example, some teams caring long-term for people with severe and enduring mental illness had on their caseloads patients who needed support to undertake even basic daily activities, such as shopping, socialising and leisure, "Just social contact. … that's recorded as 'Follow-up', which doesn't really describe … it doesn't really accurately describe what we do" (Area Team Leader, General Adult). Whilst some teams felt that the menu options were inadequate to categorize the crisis management and emergency call-out work they did, other teams felt that PMS did not reflect the 'everyday stuff' they did with patients, and that the system was weighted towards activity, "If things are going well for a patient… it doesn't mean you do nothing, it's more a question of ongoing support. There's no menu option for this…PMS assumes you should be doing something to the patient, rather than just being with them" (Community Psychiatric Nurse).

Clear definitions of each menu option did not exist, or were not available in an explicit form. Users picked the option that seemed closest, taking refuge in terminological ambiguities, whilst deploring them, 'the information is [not] truly representative of what we're doing. I suppose we're having to fit what we're doing, round about these 2 or 3 words on a line really' (Specialist Team Leader, General Adult). By contrast, the CPS system had allowed users to select more than one option, which they had found useful for representing their practice more fully, "Now… you monitor their mental health, do their depot, you might give them a bit of support, a bit of counselling, but [in PMS]… you can only identify one thing that you've done" (Area Team Leader, General Adult). Even within teams or occupational groupings with similar caseloads and work practices, there was at first little attempt to reach a consensus on meanings, " … between the five of us, I might say it's problem resolution, but someone else might say it's treatment… Or is it therapy?" (Charge Nurse, General Adult). As a last resort, some PMS users selected the 'Not Specified' default option, because having searched the pull-down list, they failed to find an option they felt adequately reflected their everyday practice, 'they're not relevant. ... rather than recording something that's not true.. I'm not going to specify..." (Area Team Leader, General Adult).

The administrative view

In the first months of roll-out, the Implementation and Information Services (IS) Teams, were most concerned about the validity and dependability of PMS data in terms of its completeness and timeliness, as detailed reports extracted from the system revealed that some HCPs and teams were not using PMS to record data, and others were frequently using the default 'not specified' Contact Purpose option. Administrators saw this as clinical laziness, rather than as a last resort. Remedial action was initially planned on this basis. Each team already received a monthly Error Report, detailing individual user errors, for correction by the user. Since the correction of data already in PMS represented an 'easy win' in terms of data quality improvement - easier, at that point, than compelling non-users to se the system - it was decided to make the use of 'not specified' a correctable error, even though the option remained visible on the Contact Purpose and other similarly contested menus. This offended clinical users' sense of rightness of classification, and veracity, and meant that they viewed PMS as even less accurate and dependable from a clinical perspective.

By early 2002, Implementation and IS also started to question the accuracy and dependability of data entered into the system. Differences between the activities of teams and within multi-disciplinary teams between domains of knowledge and practice had created multiple definitions of work. These were revealed to a previously unsuspected extent when the data in PMS were analyzed centrally. Their concerns were accentuated by the decision to start using PMS data as the main basis for NHS Urban's monthly reports to the Information Services Division (ISD) of the Scottish Executive. At this point, the mismatch of clinical and administrative perspectives was brought to the attention of the Implementation Team, raising the issues of how diverse work practices should be classified in a reasonably standard manner, and the need to produce more or less stable, workable definitions of categories of clinical activity by consultants, nursing staff and therapists. By now, the Contact Purpose menu had acquired 38 options, yet still confused and failed to satisfy users (see Table 1). Neither clinical nor administrative staff viewed PMS as dependable for their purposes.

Assessment	Case conference
Challenging behaviour	Cognitive behavioural therapy
Depot medication	Detox
Discharge	Enabling
Epilepsy	Follow-up
Full assessment	Health promotion
Initial assessment	Lawyer/solicitor report
Maintenance	Management
Mental health assessment	Methadone contract signing
Methadone programme	Methadone review
Not specified	Other report
Palliative and bereavement care	Parole report
PF report (Procurator-Fiscal)	Planning
Problem resolution	Relapse prevention
Restoration	Review
Second opinion	Special needs
Supervised medication	Supervision
Support	Therapy
Tolerance test	Treatment

Table 1. PMS 'Contact Purpose' menu options as at June, 2002

Accommodating diversity: managing standardization?

In May 2002, the Implementation Group agreed that the Contact Purpose menu was 'out of control' and action was needed. The possibility of creating sub-sub-menus reflecting each team's activities in their own terminology that would map to a reduced Contact Purpose sub-menu had finally to be rejected as technically infeasible. The issue was raised at a meeting of the User Group to elicit suggestions for dealing with the situation. One proposal was *"Just cut it down to 10 choices, and let them get on with it"* (medical consultant), which was felt to be unworkable and undesirable, as it would further upset many users. However, making significant changes to existing classifications in the system ran the risk of rendering extracted statistics non-comparable between time periods, hence introducing additional, though temporary, data undependability. It was therefore decided to explore the use, origins and evolution of the menu, and to (re)establish definitions of existing menu terms.

The Systems Administrator produced a report on use of each Contact Purpose category from April 2001 to June 2002. This was illuminating in many respects. Of nearly 200,000 patient contacts during the period, 80%

had been allocated to 6 menu options (representing just 16% of the 38 categories). Fewer than 1% of contacts were described as 'not specified', which strongly suggested that concern over misuse of this category had been overstated, even accounting for reclassification as a result of the Error Reports. It was also likely that some categories were only being used in error. The Implementation Group then examined the menu classification, in order to amalgamate similar options into a slightly smaller number of categories. It was considered that this could be safely undertaken. The Group also experimented unsuccessfully with categorizing the categories.

At the same time, the Group sought and tabulated definitions for every existing contact purpose. Only two, 'follow-up' and 'discharge', had nationally agreed definitions, so it was up to NHS Urban to reflect local practices in the rest. In early 2003, teams were asked to decide which of their activities translated to which contact purposes, to agree team-level definitions of the latter, and to feed these back for inclusion in the definitions list, which was then re-circulated to users. Additions to the menu were still permitted, provided they were defined and 'owned' by a team. The Implementation Group decided that for the time being, it could accommodate this kind of local variety within the system, *"just as long as we know what each team means"* (Data Protection Manager), and could map it back onto a more global classification scheme, for use by the IS Team at Trust-wide and external reporting levels. Hence the work of translation between domains had been passed back to administrators. However, although it appeared in theory that teams' recording practice had stabilised, the reality was not quite so unified in practice, and the lengthy process of rendering PMS data dependable continued.

Over the summer of 2003, a Working Group representing users from different professional groups and from various areas or specialties of the Community Mental Health Service met to refine and work on the definitions. This proved immensely problematic, both in terms of the articulation of tacit practice by experienced HCPs, and in terms of definition disagreements between groups with differing professional allegiances. In the course of these meetings, the view emerged that use of the Contact Purpose menu options had become unwieldy and too difficult to manage, for clinical, nursing and administrative staff alike. A decision was made to reduce the menu at the end of December 2003 to only three choices: 'assessment', 'treatment' and 'support', and to agree how existing options would map to these for comparability with past data, and for future recording practice. This may have become possible because by this time, the PMS system had acquired various clinically-focused 'bolt-on' modules, which satisfied clinical and nursing users' needs to have their practice reflected in and acknowledged by the system. This made the Contact Purpose menu a less significant arena in which to struggle for professional visibility. However, no sooner had the reduction been announced than some specialist teams began (again) to request additions to the Contact Purpose menu to accommodate their information needs - this time for reasons of cost tracking and external billing, rather than clinical accuracy as before. Other similar requests followed. Meanwhile, standardization effort had been transferred to other classifications that were considered to require further definition, such as 'Contact Outcome'. Standardization and differentiation remained salient issues well beyond system design and initial roll-out.

5. DISCUSSION

The point of departure of our analysis was a consideration of how complex socio-technical systems can be established that work reliably across cognitive, functional and geographical distance. This, of course, raises some extremely broad questions about how it is that a complex division of labor and knowledge within an organization can be sustained involving a close interplay between humans, processes and artifacts. We focused specifically on the role and contribution of standardization efforts to working 'at a distance' across different geographical, cognitive and functional domains.

Within this context we have examined the implications of standardization for the dependability of computer-based and wider organizational systems, focusing on its influence on the usability and the resultant trustworthiness of the information generated, stored or reproduced therein. We have therefore highlighted the role of organizational and professional culture and trust in supporting heterogeneities in both practice and culture and emphasized that this may prove difficult to sustain where systems and processes are highly distributed across different groups, functions, communities and physical locations both within an organization, as well as across different organizations that make up an enterprise or a network.

Specifically, we have illustrated three different attempts at standardization, in settings characterized by different levels of organizational heterogeneity and diversity. The MotorCo case provided an example of standardization within the boundary of a single organization; heterogeneity there consisted in the coexistence of different engineering communities collaborating within product development; these communities referred to a discipline-specific 'codebook', held different specialised knowledge and meaning frames, as well as having different incentives and speaking different database languages. The server production transfer case study at ComputerCo concerned instead an attempt to standardize a product and its related production processes across two different organizational units that were distantly located; heterogeneity was due to the fact that the two organizations had very different knowledge and culture as well as being characterized by two different labour structures. Finally, NHS Urban was attempting to standardize the recording of clinical practice across different communities of mental healthcare practitioners each with their own bodies of professional knowledge and practice and were spread across a wide range of institutional locations.

The case studies illustrated three different attempts to manage and reduce organizational complexity and heterogeneity by means of standardization. In the Motor Co case, standardization entailed the introduction a new software-supported product structure (or language) across those diverse communities; this was aimed at eliminating the various local 'dialects' (discipline-specific languages) as well as providing a single database were all product and process related knowledge could be centralised. In the ComputerCo example, standardization entailed the creation and implementation of a series of rules and methodologies aimed at codifying, transferring and exactly reproducing the product and process from one site to the new facility. In the case of NHS Urban, the implementation of a computer-based system that would integrate clinical and administrative information across the region led to an effort to standardize the recording of clinical practice through the development of new ways of classifying activity-related data, such as the purpose of health practitioners contacts with patients.

On one hand, we have seen that in all three cases standardization was partially successful. In the ComputerCo and MotorCo case, standardization and the tools used to enforce it (such as the 'Big Rules' at ComputerCo and PDM software at MotorCo) provided a strong unifying point, coordinating action and helping to enforce control. Similarly, in NHS Urban, the PMS system held out a promise of integrated care delivery, including potential benefits such as access to an updated and consolidated patient record potentially updated in real time, as well as the development of a standardized language for recording and analyzing information about patient care.

On the other, we have also shown how in all three cases standardization partially failed in its initial objectives and new forms of undependability arose. In the case of MotorCo, a procedure had to be set up to translate data from the central database into the individual functional domains (i.e. from PDM in Engineering to Production's TMS database). We have seen that, while a conversion process has been established, this does not allow for the formation of meanings at the Production end of development: what is ordered information for the Engineers, is only disordered data for Production, which is unable to interpret it, or 'decode' it, and therefore attribute meaning to it. In this case, standardization instead of resolving existing incompatibilities as codification economists have argued (20) had created new bottlenecks. While the aim of PDM was to unify data structures so to eliminate data redundancy and ambiguity, there has paradoxically been a reduction in the dependability of the data flows across the two functions; this reflected in an upsurge in errors and in an increased complexity of the configurational tasks than before the introduction of PDM. In the case of ComputerCo., there were limitations in the ability of practitioners to articulate some of the lower level process knowledge that could not therefore be codified and transferred; a related problematic issue was the difficulty of adapting one site's knowledge and labour structure to the other's with the subsequent inability to transfer some of the expertise across from one site to the other. In the NHS Urban case, the achievement of a standardized, dependable and universally accepted classification system was highly problematic, even after a lengthy process of negotiation with the various stakeholders. Clinical users of the computer system were unable to fit some of their activities to the new system's pull-down menu options. The resultant data undependabilities led administrators to realize just how much translation work had always been needed to render data dependable.

The standardization effort in all our cases has had the effect of throwing up new organizational conflicts, and/or focusing attention upon existing divisions. The attempt to improve coordination and organizational performance by pulling hitherto relatively separate groups into closer and more immediate, and computer-mediates collaboration has removed the buffers and the organizational spaces in which differing local cultures and practices had been mediated. In the MotorCo case, the software-related standardization has emphasized an underlying incompatibility in understandings and practice between an upstream (Engineering) and a downstream function (Production). This incompatibility, which until the software was introduced was only latent, as both functions could draw their information from paper drawings and spreadsheets, degenerated into a clash as the two functions were forced to share the same software-embedded data structure. While aiming to coordinate the work and the views of different organizational communities more tightly to enhance overall flexibility, the software-embedded configuration was revealed to be an inflexible 'standardising device' (22). In the case of ComputerCo, conflicts were generated by the need to transfer data across two organizations having very different cultures, one a 'heroic engineering' culture based on a strong tacit tradition and one a 'scientific management' tradition based on codification and the reproducibility of standardized knowledge and processes. Evidence showed that conflict there was attenuated and temporarily deferred by allowing rules to be interpreted flexibly and change their meaning as they evolved over time. In the case of NHS Urban, the new computer system highlighted and created a lack of common understandings, and was the subject of conflict and tension between various clinical and administrative groups, following the removal of the 'buffer' domain of Medical Records, which had previously performed the necessary translations. In this case standardization was hindered as the many professional groups involved took a long time to buy into a new vocabulary/domain of practice, and to undertake the necessary translation themselves. As with the PDM system, PMS failed to incorporate the informational needs of the many groups involved.

All our cases have shown therefore that standardization has partially failed to eliminate heterogeneities and that sources of diversity tend to persist through the continuation of local communities having different knowledge, viewpoints and objectives and exercising a degree of local autonomy. Even if the complete elimination of heterogeneity in both knowledge and practice was indeed achievable, our cases show that it would not be desirable. While a potential source of disruption, in fact, such heterogeneities may facilitate innovation, as in the MotorCo example, where they allowed tacit and local knowledge to be incorporated into the development process (22); they facilitated adaptation, as in the server transfer example where heterogeneity supported continuous product improvement; and they contained the viewpoint as well as expressing the requirements of different categories of practitioners, as in the case of NHS Urban. We have found that in all three cases ambiguity, rather than being eliminated was only partially displaced, or transferred to more subtle niches (for example, in NHS Urban, from classification development to categorization work, and from the Contact Purpose Menu to other classifications in the system such as Contact Outcome; in the case of MotorCo in the translation between databases; and in the server transfer case, in lower levels procedures).

We have also emphasized that the level of standardization that an organization will tolerate can vary significantly across domains. In the MotorCo and ComputerCo examples, diversity and standardization were prosecuted and reduced or eliminated wherever possible. The faster pace of technical change as well as the extent of customization in these sectors, related to the design and production of increasingly complex artefacts subjected to increasingly stringent quality requirements has brought about a strong emphasis on formalization, certification and standardization of procedures within each as well as across multiple product platforms. The result was very immediate interdependencies (tight coupling) between different specialist and technical functions. In the NHS Urban case, diversity was tolerated. The health services exhibit sharply contrasting culture and traditions – the historical emphasis has been on the promotion and regulation of health and related professions. Their person-centred activities show much less tradition of formalization. In the first two cases there was an objective attempt to standardize meanings; with PDM, there was pressure to adopt the same database language; in the server transfer case, to clarify and unify descriptions of procedures as well as concepts, such as the notion of 'failure'; in the case of Urban Trust different meanings and definitions were instead allowed to coexist (whilst being made increasingly explicit). We suggest that organizations adopt deliberate strategies that allow them to achieve the desired level of coupling and reduction of heterogeneity that best fits their sectoral and idiosyncratic characteristics. These differences are partly due to different demands and exigencies facing engineering and health service organizations; different traditions of work re-organization and technological change as well as different requirements for control and coordination. For example, the need in manufacturing for different functions, groups and organizations to collaborate in a concurrent manner often leads to the need for stronger control regimes and reduced scope for local autonomy; the health sector, instead, is characterized by the presence of specialist groups, such as consultants, which often demand (and deploy arguments to support) a higher degree of autonomy and discretion for their operation.

Our empirical material has therefore illustrated that standardization intended to increase trust can itself create or reveal system undependabilities. In particular, standardization may result in the privileging of one group or community over another, which may thereby be forced to align their practices with those embedded in and supported by the standard information system procedures or compelled to perform a continual translation process between domains[10].

This shows that determining the benefits of standardization may be elusive as there are hidden organizational costs, which might in some cases outweigh the perceived benefits, at least in the shorter term. A longitudinal analysis would allow us to verify the validity of these finding over time. We maintain however that, while some of the obstacles encountered may reduce over time due to ongoing learning and adaptation, heterogeneities that can be attributable to cognitive and functional specialisation tend to, and indeed must, persist (23,24). We therefore take issue with two of the main currents of analysis of standardization. On the one hand, we differ with those

---

[10]. For a deeper analysis of the dynamics of organizational translation processes or 'translation routines' see D'Adderio (2001).

accounts that have taken as their starting point the effectiveness of standardization efforts, pointing instead to the constraints upon the adoption of standardization and the negotiability of outcomes where standardized procedures are adopted (for example where existing heterogeneities in information/information practice are translated into categorization work to 'repair' the gap between standard classification schema and local contexts). On the other hand, we see these outcomes as less contingent than those accounts that foreground the local nature of adaptation and translation processes, but which may underplay processes of incremental alignment (15).

6. CONCLUSIONS

We conclude by considering the implications for theory and for practice. The theoretical challenge emerging from this paper concerns the need to address the dynamics of standardization (encompassing both the formation and implementation of standardization). Our analysis has drawn the attention to the contradictory implications of standardization efforts. The visible alignment process thus initiated may, at least in the short term, encounter or set into play resistance and obduracy in the organization's socio-technical systems. Discrepancies between standard schema and local practice (rooted in existing heterogeneities in information structures and practices) mean that the introduction of standardization which can yield a sense of increasing general accountability, scrutiny and control over distant activities may also be accompanied by a loss of local focus and detail oversight. This may be a source of new undependabilities. The contradictory effects of standardization efforts go to the heart of questions of trust and in particular the notion that standardized information structures and practices can resolve the problems of trust in complex and (spatially and culturally) dispersed organizational settings. The impossibility of guaranteeing the trustworthiness of elements outside direct scrutiny (the fact that intended immutable mobiles are neither wholly immutable or mobile) does not mean that standardization is doomed to failure. Indeed comparing the very different organizational settings of health care and high technology industry highlighted the influence of sustained efforts geared towards 'informatisation', formalization and standardization efforts in the latter cases. The outcomes of past alignment attempts provide the foundations for current standardization. We also note, as the MotorCo case illustrates, that differences in approach, entrenched in earlier local standardizations, may constitute a barrier to subsequent alignment. This again points to the double-edged character of standardization.

Two sets of recommendations can be drawn for practice. The first is for Information Systems designers. Once we acknowledge that local meanings and practice matter, the challenge becomes how to cater for diversity/heterogeneity in culture and practice and design systems that allow for local flexibility whilst at the same time continuing to perform a strong coordinating function. A corollary is that designers also need to conceive systems that enable an organization to align with change over time. The second set of recommendations concerns management practice; the challenge in this case is the need to enforce standards while taking into account the different levels and types of heterogeneities and need for differentiation that are specific to each individual organizational context. The principal challenge for managers remains how to decide, on an ad-hoc basis, what form of coordination (i.e. high level coordination by enforcing a standard interface vs. emergent local coordination by groups of practitioners) as well as what extent of coupling (strong coupling, or elimination of diversity vs. loose coupling or the coordination of diversity) can be appropriate to an organization, in relation to the complexity of its environment, the nature of its cognitive and governance structures and the quality and type of its outputs. This is an interesting - and challenging - issue that deserves to be systematically explored in future work.

ACKNOWLEDGEMENTS

The authors would like to acknowledge the financial support of the EPSRC, through the Interdisciplinary Research Collaboration on Dependability (DIRC)

REFERENCES

1. Foucault, M. (1977) (trans. A. Sheridan), *Discipline and Punish*, Penguin : London.
2. Law, J. (1986), 'On the methods of long-distance control: vessels, navigation and the Portuguese route to India', in Law, J. (ed), *Power, Action and Belief: A New Sociology of Knowledge?*, Sociological Review Monograph 32, Routledge, Henley, pp. 234-263.
3. Timmermans, S. and Berg, M. (1997), Standardization in action: achieving universalism and localization in medical protocols, *Social Studies of Science*, vol. 27, pp. 273–305.
4. Formal ref.
5. Formal ref.

6. Latour, B. (1986), Visualization and cognition : thinking with eyes and hands', *Knowledge and Society : Studies in the Sociology of Culture Past and Present*, 6:1-40.

7. Postman, N. (1993), *Technopoly : the surrender of culture to technology*, Vintage Books : New York.

8. Cowan, R. and Foray, D.(1997), The economics of codification and the diffusion of knowledge, *Industrial and Corporate Change*, Vol. 6: 595-622.

9. Cohendet, P. and F. Meyer-Krahmer (2001), Editorial, *Research Policy*, Vol. 30 (9) : 1353-1354.

10. Bain, P. and Taylor, P.(2000) 'Entrapped by the 'electronic panopticon'? Worker resistance in the call centre' , *New Technology, Work and Employment*, Vol. 15 (1):2-18.

11. European Standard, EN 45020, 1998.

12. Bowker, G. C, and Star, S.L., (1999) *Sorting things out : classification and its consequences,* Cambridge, Mass./London : MIT Press

13. Douglas M. and Hull D.(eds) (1992), *How Classification Works : Nelson Goodman Among the Social Sciences*, Edinburgh University Press : Edinburgh.

14. Starr, P. (1992), ''Social Categories and Claims in the Liberal State', p. 154-179, in Douglas M. and Hull D.(eds) (1992), *How Classification Works : Nelson Goodman Among the Social Sciences*, Edinburgh University Press : Edinburgh.

15. Anderson, S., G. Hardstone, R. Procter and R. Williams (forthcoming), Down in the (Data)base(ment) : Supporting Configuration in Organizational Information Systems.

16. Sewell, G. and Wilkinson, B.(1992), 'Human Resource Management in "Surveillance Companies"', in Clark, J. (ed) (1992) *Human Resource Management and Technical Change*, Sage : London.

17. Graham, Ian, G. Spinardi, and R. Williams, (1996)'Diversity in the emergence of electronic commerce'*Journal of Information Technology*, Vol. 11 No. 1 pp. 161-172.

18. Williams, Robin 'Universal solutions or local contingencies? Tensions contradictions in the mutual shaping of technology and work organization' (1997) Chap. 8, pp. 170-185, in McLoughlin, I and D. Mason (eds), *Innovation, Organizational Change and Technology*, London: International Thompson Business Press.

19. Perrow, C (1999), *Normal Accidents: Living with High-Risk Technologies*, Princeton, NJ : Princeton University Press.

20. Cowan R., P.A. David & D. Foray (2000), "The Explicit Economics of Knowledge Codification and Tacitness", *Industrial and Corporate Change*, Vol. 9 (2) pp. 211-53.

21. Pickering, A. (1992), *Science as Practice and Culture*, Chicago : Chicago University Press.

22. D'Adderio, L. (2001), Crafting the virtual prototype: how firms integrate knowledge and capabilities across organizational boundaries', *Research Policy* 30(9):1409-1424.

23. D'Adderio, L. (2003), 'Configuring software, reconfiguring memories : the influence of integrated systems on the reproduction of knowledge and routines', *Industrial and Corporate Change* 12(2):321-350.

24. D'Adderio, L. (2004), *Inside the Virtual Product : How Organizations Create Knowledge through Software*, Cheltenham : Edward Elgar.

Chapter 5

'ITS ABOUT TIME': TEMPORAL FEATURES OF DEPENDABILITY

Karen Clarke[2], John Hughes[2], Dave Martin[2], Mark Rouncefield[2], Ian Sommerville[2]; Alexander Voß[1], Rob Procter[1], Roger Slack[1] and Mark Hartswood[1]

[1]*School of Informatics, The University of Edinburgh*
[2]*Departments of Computing and Sociology, University of Lancaster*

" ..man is nothing; he is, at most, the carcase of time" (Marx and Engels 1976: 127)

"All human action occurs in time, drawing upon a past which cannot be undone and facing a future which cannot be known" (Barbalet 1996: 82)

1. INTRODUCTION: TIME

Issues of time and timeliness are pervasive in all aspects of the design and deployment of computer-based systems. This chapter uses our empirical ethnographic studies on organizational culture and trust to examine issues of timeliness as a feature of dependability. In 'Technics and Civilisation', Mumford (1963) suggests that *"The first characteristic of modern machine civilization is its temporal regularity"* (Mumford 1963: 269) involving the structuring of social life by forcing activities into fairly rigid temporal patterns. Mumford identifies four major forms of temporal regularity – regular patterns of associating social events and activities – rigid sequential structures, fixed durations, standard temporal locations, and uniform rates of recurrence, stressing the fact that these often constitute binding normative prescriptions. Similar arguments have been advanced more recently by Bolter (1984) who compares the computer with the clock in terms of its

K. Clarke, G. Hardstone, M. Rouncefield and I. Sommerville (eds.), Trust in Technology:
A Socio-Technical Perspective, 105–121.
© 2006 *Springer. Printed in the Netherlands.*

massive social impact – not just on time itself but every aspect of social life and our ways of thinking about the world.

Issues of and arguments about time have long occupied sociologists who have endlessly theorized about (if rather less investigated) its social character – and little more than a brief (and ineffective) sketch can be offered here. Durkheim (1947) in 'Elementary Forms of Religious Life' pointed to the intimate connection between social and temporal issues, that time is in modern sociological parlance (though he would not have used the phrase) 'socially constructed': "it is the rhythm of social life which is at the basis of the category time." For Marx the orientation to and regulation of time – in particular labour time – was a central feature of industrial capitalism and part of the inherent logic of capitalism involved attempts to devise means to squeeze more time out of the proletariat either by extending the working day or, in the long run more productively through the denser forms of work supported by technology. The impact of these new forms of working and people's new orientations and responses to time, and what amounted to the discipline of time, are outlined in Weber's treatment of the Protestant ethic and Franklin's epigram "time is money". More recently, (Lash and Urry 1994; Adam 1990) sociologists have proffered a range of different understandings of time. Giddens (1981), for example, drawing on Heidegger (1978) outlines a number of concepts for understanding the social impact of temporal change: regionalization, presence-availability, time-space distantiation, time-space edges, power-containers and the disembedding of time and space from social activities. While there is insufficient space to give these even a cursory treatment the important point is that, whilst acknowledging the social character of time, as Adam (1990) comments, these sociological accounts have rarely reached much agreement about time – associating it, for example, with death, with order and structure and treating it as a measure, as a parameter and as an idea.

2. TIME AND TECHNOLOGY

Sociologists have also identified a number of different and changing forms of temporal organization that reflect and contribute to wider social features and how technology – the clock, the steam engine, the computer – has acted to mediate a range of 'natural' rhythms and cycles. According to Castells (1996) the dominant temporality of contemporary society is what he terms 'timeless time' – this occurs because computer systems can disorder the sequence of events and make them simultaneous and thereby time is dissolved and past present and future mingled. At the organizational level ICT supposedly generates new patterns of working and new forms of organizations – the most remarked upon, and the most hyped, being the 'virtual organization'. Such an organizational form supposedly heralds massive changes in temporal and spatial aspects of work and organization as the 'time discipline' associated with industrial capitalism is challenged and transformed by new technologies that supposedly overcome spatial and temporal constraints. In a similar fashion Nowotny (1994) argues that the immediacy presented and produced by ICT produce an experience of 'instantaneous time' and, with specific reference to issues of trust Adam (1990) would suggest that such experiences of 'instant time' could lead to a distrust of the future. We are, however, a little sceptical of many of these claims (Hughes et al 2002), a reliance on notions of 'virtuality' too often obscures rather than illuminates the very real issues associated with the relationship between ICT and everyday working practices within changing organizational contexts. Much of the work is also theoretical rather than empirical – focusing on providing explanations for these changing temporal frames rather than an understanding based on real world explication (Thrift 1996).

The focus of this chapter is on issues of time and timeliness as instantiated in our empirical studies of everyday work – how time is woven into organizational culture. As Failla and Bagnara (1992) argue the relationship between technology and time should be considered in the context of organizational culture. Our interest is in discovering and demonstrating how temporal patterns – rhythms and trajectories – provide individuals with a resource for seeking, providing, and managing information in the course of their everyday work and the implications these findings have for the design and deployment of dependable socio-technical systems. The material on which this chapter is based upon is from long-term ethnographic studies, and as such temporal issues are at the heart of the research enterprise. As we have said in more detail elsewhere, the point of ethnography is to provide a detailed exposition of 'real world, real time' activities in their natural setting (Hughes et al 1994; Lebbon et al 2003). The aim is to provide details of the everyday practices through which the work is accomplished, identifying the contingencies that can arise, how they are overcome and accommodated, how the interdependencies of a division of labour are actually achieved, how technology does or does not get to be incorporated into work activities, and so on. The focus is a social one emphasizing the 'situated' character of work and the related judgments and discretion routinely employed in response to everyday work and its inevitable contingencies. It is 'being there' which enables the ethnographer to identify the cooperative aspects of 'real time, real world' work, such as the small-scale constellations of assistance, the deployment of local knowledge of how the organization works, the awareness of others, etc., which support the actual performance of work activities. The method is directed toward producing a rich portrayal of work activities on the grounds that theoretical categorization is likely to prematurely 'construct' a picture of the work which is likely to bear only a superficial relationship to the work as actually done in 'real time'.

Our empirical, ethnographic studies of organizational work in DIRC have highlighted a number of facets of timeliness that we will draw upon in our analysis. In our studies of road safety engineers, for example, aspects of time – such as the time of day, the day of the week and the month of the year were all seen as crucial in both understanding and providing viable solutions to road traffic accidents (Harper et al 2001). Or in steelmaking and the rolling of steel plate – where speed of rolling is vital in maintaining the heat within the slab and thus ease of rolling – timeliness becomes a central feature of awareness and coordination of the working division of labour (Clarke et al 2003). Or in our studies of mammography, where the consideration of mammograms over time afford consideration of the identification (and treatment) of cancers (Hartswood et al 2001).

Our studies of engine manufacture highlight mundane issues of timeliness within 'just-in-time' production. The ethnographic study of work in a manufacturing plant 'ENGINECO' (Voss et al 2001 and see Chapter 10 this volume) producing mass-customised diesel engines provides some interesting insights into coping with temporal features of 'just-in-time' production and the contingencies and 'local logics' of day-to-day production management. Here computer systems are an integral feature of 'just-in-time' production; reducing stock and work in progress, improving flexibility and avoiding late deliveries. At ENGINECO the precondition for 'just-in-time' production is that all parts are available in time for production – called 'buildability'. This requires that all component parts and information are available before production starts. Assembly planners download assembly packages (collections of production orders) into the Assembly Control Host. These production packages are supposed to be compiled with a lead time of one or two working days, enabling the timely scheduling of material and creating a buffer of spare orders for production in case some orders cannot be built because of breakdowns. At ENGINECO, and other companies employing just-in-time production methods, software systems have often failed to deliver expected outcomes since the technology carried assumptions about the organizational setting that did not match the temporal and spatial realities of everyday working life – or, more simply, fail to cope when things go wrong (and things always go wrong). The temporal aspect is particularly relevant here because, of course, decisions are made in real time. Workable solutions to everyday production problems manifested themselves in the form of 'local logics', organizational and temporal 'workarounds' that attend to the incompleteness of knowledge on both organizational and spatial-temporal levels. This included ideas about where items are or should be, the timeliness of activities as well as what actions were organizationally acceptable, what was acceptable solution just here and just now. As an example of the worldly, temporal contingencies that routinely arise, Voss et al (2001) describe how when a material storage tower went offline so that no messages to the Assembly Control Host were generated when boxes were emptied (and thus no new parts would be ordered) Control Room workers solved this problem by marking all material in the tower "faulty" which resulted in new material being ordered from the logistics provider. Consequently, supporting production work in all its contingent aspects requires that planning systems pay attention to the occasioned character of the logic of production. Thus successful long-term IT development critically depends on the day-to-day interaction (and trust) between use and development, between users and developers as they collaboratively track down troubles with the system and work to come up with solutions, as temporary fixes, changed working practices (e.g., stable work-arounds) or changes to the IT system.

3. TIME IN MEDICAL SETTINGS - ILLNESS TRAJECTORY AND RHYTHM

The bulk of this chapter will be concerned with temporal issues arising from our ethnographic studies of everyday hospital work such as staff handover, bed management, process modeling and mapping and developing and deploying new IT systems, to illustrate some of the temporal features of everyday work in medical settings. Healthcare informatics is a rich source of dependability issues. Healthcare also represents a domain in which dependability is of considerable public concern and policy importance. It thus represents a site that is of considerable strategic importance to DIRC and our efforts to demonstrate the relevance of our achievements.

Time features heavily in sociological analyses of the experience of illness. The concept of Illness Trajectory (Glaser and Strauss 1967) refers to: "not only to the physiological unfolding of a patient's disease but to the total organization of work done over that course of illness plus the impact on those involved with that work and its organization. ...we shall occasionally refer to "trajectory work", simply meaning the various kinds of work done in managing the course of the illness and in handling the interrelationships involved in that task". In this view trajectory replaces the singular notion of process with a more complex, multi-dimensional flow of events and situations. Illness trajectory has four aspects or facets; the physiological, the temporal, the sentimental and the social. The physiological involves disease and disease processes. The temporal facet reflects the consequences of time in illness and the schedules of the day-to-day activities of nursing care. The sentimental focuses on carer-patient interaction and the intensity of sentiment associated with confronting illness and its consequences. The social aspect pays attention to the social consequences of illness, of dependency and so on.

The 'temporal order' refers to, and provides a means of understanding, the meanings that use of time introduces to medical events or situations. So, for example, the daily round structures medical staff's view of a day and its likely sequence of activities. For nursing staff the daily shift is structured into a temporal sequence by regularly scheduled events like meal times or periodic observations on patients. Particular days, operating days or admission days for example, will possess and achieve a temporal order that is noticeably different:

> "But time as a facet of the illness trajectory is only a reflection of the established or re-negotiated temporal order. Time passing is experienced by the patient and by the nurse. Some days are slow and tedious; some weeks seem to pass by unnoticed. The common experience of visitors to a patient is that visits pass uncommonly slowly. While for the patient who has eagerly anticipated visiting time for much of the day, visits pass all too fast. To the busy nurse, a minute or two at the bedside seems costly time; to the patient the interaction was hurried and, in consequence, uncaring. How medical staff, nursing staff, patients and others experience time-passing, how they cooperate with or fight against someone's proposed schedule and what that schedule means for these various participants fills in the temporal facet of that trajectory" (Kelly nd).

The notion of recurrence of temporal patterns is a particular feature of Zerubavel's (1985) work on 'temporal rhythms' in hospital settings: "The world in which we live is a fairly structured place. Even the most casual glance at our environment would already reveal a certain degree of orderliness. One of the fundamental parameters of this orderliness is time – there are numerous temporal patterns around us" (Zerubavel 1985: 1) In his classic study of social rhythms in a hospital, Zerubavel described the cyclical nature of work in order to emphasize its temporal features- helping us understand the work of an organization by foregrounding its intrinsically temporal and cyclic nature. Zerubavel's (1985) discussion of schedules and cultural calendars presents an intriguing picture of the pervasiveness of social rhythms, of how rhythms are socially created and manifest themselves in various ways as a facet of our everyday lives. Although these rhythms are a feature of the daily work they are not unchanging or unchangeable but are affected by unexpected occurrences. As Reddy and Dourish (2002) suggest, while work rhythms provide information to help people accomplish their work and guide future activities, they can also pose challenges to the coordination of work. "Medical practitioners must continually balance and integrate medical and organizational information in decision-making; that the processes of seeking and providing information are seamlessly interwoven with other working activities; and that they are coordinated in part through the set of working rhythms that provide a resource to interpret and manage work". The relevance of rhythms in everyday working life is that they orient members towards likely future activities and information needs in the course of doing their work. Current activities are crafted with an orientation towards expectations of future events. Different work rhythms can conflict with each other – nurses and physicians for example – and can produce different expectations about the availability of information.

Reddy and Dourish (2002) use the concept of rhythms to highlight how temporal patterns or rhythms provide individuals with a resource for seeking and providing information. These rhythms can be more or less regular, and operate on a large or a small scale, though clearly rhythms can be disrupted by unexpected occurrences. Dourish and Reddy distinguish between 'large scale rhythms' and 'fine-grained rhythms'. Large scale rhythms refer to the broad pattern of daily work such as shift changes, doctors' rounds, patient changeover and so on. Fine-grained rhythms refer to patterns of medication administration, the arrival of lab or test results. These working rhythms orient staff, patients and others towards likely future activities and information needs in the course of doing their work.

One example of these temporal rhythms comes from our ethnographic studies of everyday work in a toxicology ward, a specialised inpatient service that allows for joint medical and psychiatric assessment of patients who have been referred following a suspected self-harm incident. Of particular interest is temporal features of access to and use of patient notes as a feature of mundane work. Record folders for each patient are kept in a trolley that follows the cycle of activity within the ward. During the morning ward round (usually held between 8.30 and 9.00am) it is wheeled from bed to bed and each of the record folders are accessed in turn. At the 9.00am meeting two handovers are given to the Psychiatric Assessment Team. Typically the consultant toxicologist runs through the medical status of each of the patients, and a nurse gives a 'psychosocial' handover. The records trolley is wheeled into the ward at the beginning of this meeting, allowing sequential access to the records as each patient is discussed. A nurse produces each of the records in turn, referring to the progress notes to give a brief synopsis of salient factors of each presentation. The sequential structures of the activities lend themselves to a similar sequential access to the notes. At the end of the morning meeting the patients are allocated to team members for assessment, who then avail themselves of the relevant notes. Team members will typically read through these notes prior to seeing the patient. After the assessment is complete it is the nurses who make the final entries in the notes when the patient is discharged. This is typically done at the nurses' station in the ward. The pages comprising the completed notes are removed from the record folder and placed in the wire basket on top of the filing cabinet in the doctors' room and collected routinely by the secretaries. Thus there is a tie between the location of the records as a collection, and the particular activities carried out on the ward, and variations in the organization of the records as a collection depending on the activity.

Although these activities were not always as neatly temporally organized as portrayed, such common patterns – and the process described is not unusual – illustrate the role that rhythms play in knowledge work, in particular in information seeking. Examining information seeking in the light of an understanding of work rhythms indicates that people want information – in this case the patient records – when it will be the most beneficial to them in their work. The rhythms of their work guide their need for, and likelihood of getting, information. Taking rhythms into consideration therefore affects notions of information seeking and how we might think about providing such information – for example through electronic patient record systems. Of particular relevance is some form of situated understanding of the extent to which the request for and the provision of information is couple or 'decoupled' to any particular work rhythm. But different work rhythms can produce different expectations about the availability and timeliness of information and problems may occur when the information needs of different types of work – for example, medical and administrative – conflict. Clinical notions of exactly what information is time critical and exactly what timeliness might entail are often very different from administrative considerations of these issues.

4. "IMPROVING KNIFE TO SKIN TIME": TIME, PROCESS MODELLING AND NEW TECHNOLOGY

As modern healthcare institutions have become increasingly information intensive technology increasingly plays an important role in healthcare delivery and management. When 'time is money' healthcare information systems are intended to supply cost effective improvements in managing patient care; in information gathering and dissemination; and in coordinating distributed organizational work (Doherty et al 1999). One organizationally popular approach to ensuring time, resources, staff and systems are allocated and used efficiently is process modeling. Process modeling is fundamentally about time allocation and time awareness – it requires knowing appropriate sequences of activity and the likely or preferred time each activity will take. This section presents some findings from our observational research shadowing hospital managers documenting their everyday activities as they dealt with the creation and implementation of process models. The intention was to standardize as many processes as possible to ensure an identity of service and practise across the distributed operations of the hospital. At the time of the fieldwork the production of process maps was being used to identify "bottlenecks" in the 'processing' of patients which, in the words of one manager, delayed "knife to skin" time.

One initial and obvious problem with process modeling in a distributed organization was that despite the increasing investment in new technology managerial work often involved working with various kinds of 'legacy' system. A legacy system is one which, having been introduced with the best of intentions as an 'all singing, all dancing' solution has not been maintained, modified or developed to accommodate organizational or technological change. This has a temporal relevance in that the system is unlikely to do all that is required or even 'talk' to more recent applications resulting in various time consuming 'workarounds'; workarounds that may well defeat some of the central objectives of process modeling. So, for example, the Pharmacy system, crucial for process models in terms of the costing of drugs and treatment, was unable to 'talk' to any of the other databases or management information systems, necessitating time consuming 'workarounds' in the form of the printing of documents and multiple entry of data. The paradox of such legacy systems is that, despite their outdated and time-consuming character, they are often trusted. Such systems are adhered to long after their usefulness has become limited, precisely because of the way in which they are embedded in longstanding social and organizational processes.

One particularly important observation of the development of process models in the hospital is the ways in which process modeling becomes centrally implicated in activities of working towards achieving mutual relevances and co-ordination. Members frequently drew upon ad hoc and wholly contingent interpretations and activities in order to arrive at an adequate representation of a particular flow of work. It is just these kinds of fine-grained, situated practices that are often 'missing' from the ultimate process model. This recognition of what a process model will inevitably miss is not intended as a suggestion that process modeling is somehow without any efficacy. On the contrary, despite the ironies and the quips and the griping exhibited while doing it, members clearly did find some kind of purpose in doing all of this. A paramount achievement was, however, arrival at some kind of shared local appreciation, 'knowledge' of what a particular division of labour or process amounted to, and the implicativeness of that. That is, process modeling in the hospital was noteworthy for the way in which it promoted 'knowledge' through co-ordination and arrival at a sense of mutual relevances, and understanding of 'how a place like this works'. The actual achievement of any process map makes it clear that all versions of 'best practice' are negotiated products. The formulation of 'best practice' is a situated affair – and process maps are, at heart, locally sensible versions of best practice and problems may arise where such locally sensible versions are exported throughout an organization to other settings where other relevances may apply. One significant finding here, then, is that process maps are not systematic, rational, scientific deductions of the most efficient process. Rather they are contingent objects of negotiation and experimentation amongst members who primarily attend to local, situated concerns and understandings.

5. TIME AND PROJECT WORK: TEMPORAL ASPECTS IN DEVELOPING A DEPENDABLE EPR

In this final section of the chapter we focus on some temporal aspects of an associated feature of much of the process modeling reported earlier – moves to provide comprehensive, integrated computer support through developing and deploying electronic patient records (EPRs) that all NHS Trusts are required to develop in the next 5-10 year period. We present some very early findings from a DIRC research project that has been investigating some of the everyday practicalities of delivering an EPR project within a hospital Trust. The EPR presents a means to provide timely and location-independent access to comprehensive patient data that can be integrated with respect both to type (clinicians' notes, medical imaging, charts etc.) and time (a single patient-centred record of each and every interaction between patient and healthcare providers). The EPR is seen as providing the conditions for the imposition of greater discipline and structure on record-keeping practices, and has also become a major factor in the drive for the standardization of medical record formats and ontologies. The intention is to design and deploy systems that support and facilitate clinical work as well as administrative and reporting functions and thereby provide integrated working as a means to more coordinated and, importantly, cost-effective healthcare. In examining temporal features of this work – and it is work that is ongoing in many NHS hospital trusts – the emphasis is on the EPR as a project, a project that needs to be managed in order to be successful. Our focus is on the everyday work of the project, of the mundane and routine concern with addressing organizational contingencies and constraints, documenting how and in what ways the orderly character of such project work is achieved and delivered.

System design in a large NHS Trust (and the associated processes of analysis, configuration, testing, integration, evolution etc) is a complex, messy business, but, given national, governmental targets and priorities there is a sense in which this is a project that cannot afford to fail, despite the long history of IT failures within the NHS. Implementation Team Meetings are the arena in which practical project activities are reported, discussed, negotiated, planned, and decisions made. These team meetings provide an opportunity for people to orient to the project as a totality and provide some correspondence between what project members should be and are doing. At the same time the project manager uses team meetings to keep people informed, thereby keeping any progress or problems visible. A key feature of this concerns temporal aspects of project work and is evident in the debates about 'roll-out' time:

"...News has come from XCo that the dates they've given us for rolling out the .. database and the interface are months behind ... it doesn't look like they can give us lot the interface when we need it, ... there's no guarantee that we're not going to have a microbiology interface up and running for the beginning of phase one

...Well the fact is that they're not doing it until September ....we won't have it for Phase One I can assure you of that.. .. the fact that only two of the pathology systems will be linked .. people will lose faith in the EPR system and in a sense this one isn't our issue... "

Our observations indicate a number of ways by which the contingencies and uncertainties of organizational and project life can be handled. As Button and Sharrock (1994) note, organizing a project into 'phases', for example, is intended to ensure that tasks are worked on until completed, to achieve for the work a paced sequential progression and provide for the recognition of uncompleted steps. All phases are planned in advance in terms of what they consist of and when they will take place – identifiable major phases in this project include: procurement, award and signing of contract, 'data collection', 'database build and configuration', 'application testing', 'integration testing', and finally 'go-live and transition management'. Phasing exhibits some sensitivity to timelines of practical decision-making – by specifying considerations relevant to a decision prior to any deliberation on that decision. Phases may be (almost certainly will be) delayed, tasks reallocated, items of the contract and hence the phasing re-negotiated and re-defined. Nevertheless phasing remains a key resource for the on-going practical management of the project – enabling the distribution and coordination of work, allocating responsibilities, keeping track of activities, measuring work progress.

Phasing also relates to another aspect of practical project management, the methodic handling of tasks (or at least maintaining the semblance of method) and some way of measuring progression – how they are doing, how much has been done, where they are, what remains to be done. This involves maintaining the agenda of tasks, ordering, sequencing, allocating, managing and keeping track of progress and problems through the issues and risks logs. In this fashion the project manager can determine where they are relative to the project schedule, and whether the work, going at the pace it is now being conducted at, will be done by the scheduled date. The field note below, from a project meeting, illustrates just such an attempt to keep a project 'up-to-speed':

"And if I can just ask everyone to keep doing that I think we have to be very pro-active and keep emailing your analyst and say what do you want me to work on what d'you want me to do ..-I'm getting nervous for a variety of reasons .. I'm just not sure what they're going to throw back at me .. just want to make sure we're .. covering our bases as well."..

Of course, 'slippage' from the plan is a 'normal, natural trouble' and its importance or magnitude is measured against the schedule:

"...there was fifty three days where we were looking at database configuration and I've said that now there's, not to scare anyone, twenty eight days left ... twenty eight business days left before .. its in the plan its identified that we're going to start testing, we've not done any configuration"

Where 'slippage' does occur, contingency plans are made by reference to possible implications:

"...it may be that we'll we'll have to go with the idea that they don't interface in phase one... but we'll carry on in discussing it um, further just to sort of look at all of the implications around it and I'm hoping that its not as. Its more annoying than anything right now if the truth be told, but in term of the scope of the overall project I think there's ways we can get around it without making it um too ..too specific too.. too much of an impact on the end user"

Such solutions often involve considering various workarounds.

6. CONCLUSION: DESIGNING SYSTEMS IN TIME

Our particular interest in the DIRC project has been in time as a feature of the background expectancies of trust in organizational life - how technology influences the temporality, the temporal organization, of our social and organizational activities – does it allow us to work faster, alter our background expectancies about how long tasks might or should take? Temporality encompasses a variety of aspects that reflexively influences the introduction and use of technology. The spatial and temporal aspects of mobility in human interaction have been researched in various ways. Within CSCW, for example, temporal aspects of everyday work have been discussed in relation to technological innovations such as the internet applications, groupware and various information systems (e.g. Ellis et al., 1991) as well as mobile ICT applications (Bellotti and Bly, 1996; Dix and Beale, 1996;) that supposedly make the work environment flexible and independent from geographical and temporal constraints. Time is especially relevant to IT systems since efforts to invent new technologies and introduce them into existing work settings are frequently motivated by temporal issues: accelerating the speed of work and saving time. Negroponte (1995) for example, documents the impact of email on work time, its effect on the rhythm of work and notions of the working day and week.

But speeding-up and saving time are not the only temporal transformation of social activities induced by new technologies, nor should temporal changes be misconstrued as being merely 'about time'. As Barley (1988) argues the temporal order of the workplace serves as a template for organizing behaviour as well as an interpretive framework for rendering action in the setting meaningful. Barley diffentiates between structural and interpretive aspects of temporal change. Structural aspects include notions such as sequence, duration, temporal location and recurrence Interpretive aspects of temporality are concerned with how people in the work place interpret the change of the structural parameters. He argues that such an approach lends meaning to events in the everyday world of work – as reflected in everyday comments such as "isn't X (person, process, document etc) a bit late?" "You should have done that already", and so on. Barley's study of temporal order and its change in hospital radiology departments further distinguishes between monochronic (single task) and polychromic (multi-task) approaches to organizing temporality. He suggests that the newly introduced technology increased the monochronicity of actors' activities by restructuring structural and interpretive framework of temporality. In a similar fashion Lee and Liebenau (2000) found that a new EDI system restructured the temporal order of the companies' business operations, increasing monochronicity. Perhaps reflecting the wider scale and diversity of our research no such simple conclusions have been reached. Our studies of hospital managers, for example, have showed that by using email or other asynchronous ICT applications, managers deal with multiple tasks simultaneously; ICT permits information and ideas to be instantaneously transmitted and accessed contributing therefore to what Barley would term polychronicity. As Dix (1996) argues in 'Natural Time' what matters is not absolute timing, but the match, the relationship between the pace of interaction and the pace of the task that we are performing. "The problem is usually not so much that the computer is too fast for you, but more the often erratic delays which break the flow of your work. The mismatch is between the speeds at which the computer works and the paces of activity that seem natural for you. So, what exactly is a natural timescale? "As he suggests, to answer this question, we need to know about the sort of jobs we are doing – and, we would suggest we need to know about this in real world, real time as opposed to laboratory, conditions. Hence the attractiveness to DIRC of, for want of a better word, ethnomethodologically informed ethnographic approaches, particularly as this leads to the design of systems for people engaged in real world, real time, work rather than, as Dix (1996) playfully suggests, building computers for cavemen.

This chapter reiterates a more general message emanating from DIRC's research that we have outlined on a number of occasions (Hartswood et al 2003). This is a timely, but not a simple or even optimistic, message. When design for dependability is taken seriously, as when, in this instance, the temporal features of everyday work and design are foregrounded and design relevant; when IT systems and artefacts become ubiquitous at work, and design becomes more entwined with the complexities of organizational working, then the challenges facing systems designers correspondingly increase. The 'design problem' becomes not so much concerned with the simple creation of new technical artefacts or the 'computerization' and replacement of work practices as it is with the effective integration of computer systems with existing and developing localised work practises. This thereby effectively takes the 'design problem', and the various temporal issues associated with it, beyond the design phase to implementation and deployment, where users must try and apply any new system to their work and its temporal rhythms, its interruptions, slow downs and moments of frenetic activity, in order for these systems to be useful, trustable and dependable.

REFERENCES

1. Adam, B. (1990) *Time and Social Theory*. Cambridge. Polity.
2. Barbalet, J. (1996) 'Social Emotions, Confidence, Trust and Loyalty.' *International Journal of Sociology and Social Policy* 16 (9/10): 75-96.
3. Barley, S.R. (1988). On Technology, Time, and Social Order: Technically Induced Change in the Temporal Organization of Radiological Work. In Making Time: Ethnographies of High-Technology Organizations. (Dubinskas, F.A. ed.) Temple University Press, Philadelphia, PA.
4. Bellotti, V. and Bly, S. (1996). Walking Away from the Desktop Computer: Distributed Collaboration and Mobility in a Product Design Team. In *Proceedings of CSCW '96,* Cambridge, MA, USA. 209-18.
5. Button, G.& Sharrock, W. (1994) Occasioned practices in the work of software engineers. In *Requirements Engineering Social & Technical Issues* eds M. Jirotka & J. Goguen. London. Academic Press.
6. Castells, M. (1996) *The rise of the network society*. Cambridge: MA. Blackwell.
7. Clarke, K., Hartswood, M., Procter, R., and Rouncefield, M (2001). Hospital Managers Closely Observed: Some Features of New Technology and Everyday Managerial Work. *Journal of New Technology in the Human Services*, vol. 14 (1/2), pp 48-57, 2001.
8. Clarke, K., Hartswood, M., Hughes, J., Martin, D., Nicholls, R., Procter, R., Rouncefield, M., Slack, R., Sommerville, I. and Voss, A. Dependable Red Hot Action. *In Proceedings of the 1st DIRC Conference on Dependable Computing Systems*, London, November 20th-21st, 2002.
9. Dix, A. (1996) 'Natural Time' Position Paper for CHI 96 Basic Research Symposium (April 13-14, 1996, Vancouver, BC).
10. Dix, A. and Beale, R. (1996). Information Requirements of Distributed Workers. In Remote Cooperation. CSCW Issues for Mobile and Teleworkers. (Dix, A. and Beale., R. eds.) 113-44, Springer-Verlag, London.
11. Doherty, N. F., King, M. and Marples, C. G., 'The Impact of the Hospital Information Support Systems Initiative on the operation and Performance of Acute Hospitals', in *Proceedings of the 4th UKAIS Conference,* York, pp 645-655, 7-9 April 1999.
12. Durkheim, E. (1947) *The Elementary Forms of Religious Life.* London. Allen and Unwin.
13. Ellis, C.A., Gibbs, S.J. and Rein, G.L. (1991). Groupware: Some issues and experiences. Communications of the ACM, 34(1), 38-58.
14. Failla, A. and Bagnara, S. (1992) Information Technology, decision, time. *Social Science Information* 31 (4): 669-681.
15. Garfinkel, H. Studies in Ethnomethodology. Englewood Cliffs, New Jersey. Prentice Hall, 1967.
16. Giddens, A. (1981) *A Contemporary Critique of Historical Materialism.* London. Macmillan.
17. Glaser, B., and Strauss, A. (1967) *The Discovery of Grounded Theory: Strategies for Qualitative Research*. Chicago. Aldine. REF.
18. Harper, R., Procter, R., Randall, D. and Rouncefield, M. (2001) 'Safety in Numbers: Calculation and Document Re-Use in Knowledge Work'. In *Proceedings of the International Conference on Supporting Group Work*, Boulder, Colorado, October, 2001. pp 242-251.
19. Hartswood, M. and Procter, R. (2000) Design guidelines for dealing with breakdowns and repairs in collaborative work settings. Inter-national Journal of Human-Computer Studies, 53:91-120, 2000.
20. Hartswood, M., Procter, R., Rouncefield, M. and Sharpe, M. (2001). Making a Case in Medical Work: Implications for the Electronic Medical Record *CSCW Journal*.

21. Hartswood, M., Procter, R., Rouncefield, M. And Slack, R. (2001) Performance Management in Breast Screening: A Case Study of Professional Vision and Ecologies of Practice in Johnson, C. (ed.) Special edition on Human Error and Medical Work, *Journal of Cognition, Technology and Work*, Springer, 2001.

22. Hartswood, M., Procter, R., Rouncefield, M., Slack, R., Voss, A., Williams, R. (2002) Building Information Systems as Universalised Locals. *Journal of Knowledge, Technology and Policy* 14(3), Fall, 2002.

23. Hartswood, M., Procter, R., Slack, R., Voss, A and Rouncefield M (2002) Information Systems and Workplace Studies: Observing the Contingencies of 'Just-in-Time' Production. In Bhattacharjee, A and Paul, R.J. (eds) Proceedings of the First International Workshop on 'Interpretive' Approaches to Information Systems and Computing research. Brunel University ISBN 1 902316 27 4 pp 67-69.

24. Hartswood, M., Procter, R.N., Rouncefield, M., Slack, R. (2003). 'Making a Case in Medical Work: Implications for the Electronic Medical Record'. – in *Computer-Supported Cooperative Work (CSCW) Journal.* Vol 12, Issue 3, pp 241-266.

25. Heidegger, M (1978) *Being and Time*. Oxford. Blackwell.

26. Hughes, J., King, V., Rodden, T. and Andersen, H. (1995) The role of ethnography in interactive systems design. Interactions, pages 56-65, April 1995.

27. Hughes, J., King, V., Rodden, T., Andersen, H. (1994). Moving out of the control room: ethnography in system design, in *Proceedings of CSCW'94* (Chapel Hill NC), ACM Press, pp 429-438.

28. Hughes, J., Rouncefield, M and Tolmie, P. (2002) The Day-to-Day Work of Standardization: A Sceptical Note on the Reliance on IT in a Retail Bank – in Woolgar, S. (ed) (2002) Virtual Society? Technology, cyberbole, reality. Oxford. OUP. pp 247-263.

29. Kelly, R. The Illness Trajectory: understanding being ill as a sociological phenomenon. http:// ethnomethodologist.tripod.com/ethnomethodology atwork/ id3.html

30. Lash, S. and Urry, J. (1994) *Economies of Signs and Space*. London. Sage.

31. Lebbon, C. Rouncefield M and S. Viller, (2003) 'Observation for Innovation' In John Clarkson, Simeon Keates; Roger Coleman, Cherie Lebbon (eds) *Inclusive Design*: *Design for the whole population*. Helen Hamlyn Research Centre, Royal College of Art.

32. Lee, H., and Liebenau, J. (2000) Time in organizational studies: towards a new research direction. Organization Studies 20(2): 1035-1058.

33. Martin, D., Mariani, J., and Rouncefield, M. (2004) Implementing an HIS Project: Everyday Features and Practicalities of NHS Project Work – *Health Informatics Journal* Vol 10, No 4. pp 303-313. Norwich. Sage.

34. Marx, K and Engels, F. (1976) *Collected Works,* Vol 6. London. Lawrence and Wishart.

35. Mumford, L. (1963) *Technics and Civilization*. Harcourt Brace and Co. New York.

36. Negroponte, N. (1995) *Being Digital*. Hodder and Stoughton. London.

37. Nowotny, H. (1994) *Time: The modern and postmodern experience*. Cambridge. Polity.

38. Reddy, M. and Dourish, P. (2002) A Finger on the Pulse: Temporal Rhythms and Information Seeking in Medical Work. *Proceedings of CSCW 2002.* New York. ACM.

39. Sawyer, S., and Southwick, R. (2002) Temporal Issues in Information and Communication Technology-Enabled Organizational Change: Evidence From an Enterprise Systems Implementation. The Information Society, 18: 263-280.

40. Suchman, L. (1987) *Plans and situated actions: the problem of human-machine communication*. Cambridge U.P.

41. Thrift, N. (1996) *Spatial Formations.* London. Sage.

42   Voß, A., Slack, R., Procter, R., Williams, R., Hartswood, M., and Rouncefield, M
     (2002) Dependability as Ordinary Action. In: Stuart Anderson, Sandro Bologna,
     Massimo Felici *Computer Safety, Reliability and Security: Proceedings of the 21st
     International Conference, SAFECOMP 2002.* Catania, Italy, September, 2002.
     Lecture Notes in Computer Science 2434. Springer Verlag, pages 32 - 43.
43. Voß, A, Procter, R. and Williams, R. (2000) Innovation in use: Interleaving day-to-
     day operation and systems development. In T. Cherkasky, J. Greenbaum, P.
     Mambrey, and J. K. Pors, editors, PDC'2000 Proceedings of the Participatory
     Design Conference, pages 192-201, 2000.
44. Voss, A., Procter, R., Slack, R., Hartswood, M., Williams, R. And Rouncefield, M
     (2001). Production Management as Ordinary Action: An Investigation of Situated,
     Resourceful Action in Production Planning and Control. In Levine, J. (ed.)
     Proceedings of 20th UK Planning and Scheduling (SIG) Workshop, Edinburgh,
     December 13th-14th, 2001, pp 230-243.
45. Zerubavel, E. 1979. Patterns of time in hospital life: a sociological perspective.
     Chicago: University of Chicago Press.
46. Zerubavel, E. 1985. Hidden rhythms: schedules and calendars in social life.
     Berkeley: University of California Press.

Chapter 6

EXPLICATING FAILURE

Karen Clarke[2], Dave Martin[2], Mark Rouncefield[2], Ian Sommerville[2];
Alexander Voß[1], Corin Gurr[1], Rob Procter[1], Roger Slack[1], Mark Hartswood[1]

[1]*School of Informatics, The University of Edinburgh*
[2]*Department of Computing, University of Lancaster*

"...how important it is to accept the reality of human fallibility and frailty, both in the design and the use of computer systems...all too often, the latest information technology research and development ideas and plans are described in a style which would not seem out of place in an advertisement for hair restorer." (Randell 2000)

1. INTRODUCTION: EXPLICATING FAILURE

This chapter examines issues of 'failure' and organizational culture by outlining and documenting some of the problems involved in defining and measuring 'failure'. When defined as "the ability to deliver service that can justifiably be trusted" – dependability has a number of attributes. These include: availability (readiness for correct service); reliability (continuity of correct service); safety (absence of catastrophic consequences); integrity (absence of improper system state alterations); maintainability (ability to undergo repairs) and more. But as we consider broader, socio-technical, notions of "system", the ability to achieve a clear and documented understanding of the intended service of the system – and hence some view of dependability – becomes increasingly difficult. Once we start taking into account the actual practice of a socio-technical system rather than any

K. Clarke, G. Hardstone, M. Rouncefield and I. Sommerville (eds.), Trust in Technology:
A Socio-Technical Perspective, 123 –145.

idealisation of it, it seems increasingly difficult to determine with sufficient precision what is meant by the "service" the system offers. Thus it also becomes difficult to determine what is meant by a "failure" of that service, and thus what is meant by "dependability" in this broader context. In these circumstances we may need to broaden our understanding of what dependability means beyond the simple "absence of failure", particularly if we consider 'quality of service' to develop a more nuanced notion of 'dependable systems'. As Randell suggests: "Dependability is defined as that property of a computer system such that reliance can justifiably be placed on the service it delivers." (Randell, 2000)

As computer-based systems become more complex and organizationally embedded, so the challenges of dependability – of building systems involving complex interactions amongst computers and humans – increase. In these systems, failure, or lack of dependability, can result in financial or human loss and, consequently, improved means of specifying, designing, assessing, deploying and maintaining complex computer-based systems would seem of crucial importance. Much of the work on dependability has necessarily, and naturally, focused on massive, extraordinary, public failures such as the London Ambulance Service failure of 1992, the space shuttle catastrophe of 1986, or the Ladbroke Grove train disaster of 1999. This paper begins however, by being concerned with rather more ordinary, everyday instances of dependability and failure. Instances of undependability in many settings are not normally catastrophic, but are rather mundane events that occasion situated practical (as opposed to legal) inquiry and repair. Dependability can then be seen as being the outcome of people's *everyday, coordinated, practical actions*. Workers draw on more or less dependable artefacts and structures as resources for their work of achieving overall dependable results in the work they are doing (Voß et al., 2002; Clarke et al., 2002).

To improve system dependability, we can reduce the number of human errors made, include system facilities that recognise and correct erroneous states, and so on. But when we start considering people using a computer-based system, the notion of failure becomes rather more complex. In a situation where computer-based systems are used by groups or teams of people, usually in conjunction with other systems, then recognising failure becomes even more difficult because different users may have different models of how the system is supposed to behave. Unexpected behaviour to one user is normal behaviour to another. Some users may have learned how to work-round problems in the system, others may not have. We use our fieldwork observations to detail some aspects of 'failure', to examine the everyday 'workarounds' developed to deal with 'failure', the lay conceptions of dependability and the relationship between failure and 'normal' troubles.

This chapter examines the different aspects of failure and dependability in socio-technical systems through the examination of two very different case studies - observations of everyday work in a steel rolling mill and an analysis of the transcripts of the inquiry into the Ladbroke Grove train crash. The first study directs our attention to the means whereby people cope with, and overcome, the possibility of 'everyday failure' through routine workarounds. Our research points to elements of a framework within which everyday work and normal natural troubles in socio-technical systems can be understood. The second study highlights organizational responses to massive failure and raises and contextualizes organizational issues concerning management, scoping, coordination, timing, selection, prioritization, enforcement and agreement suggesting a need to study how these are dealt with as organizational features of everyday work in safety critical settings.

2. 'RED HOT' FAILURE

In this initial section, we wish to consider failure and dependability through explicating dependability in the everyday operations of a steel rolling mill, considering how dependability issues of timeliness, responsibility, security etc can arise, and need to be resolved, in the interaction between computer systems and human skills. Our research consists of a brief observational, 'ethnographic', study (Hughes et al., 1992; 1994) of the Roughing Mill in a steel plant. We offer 'illustrative vignettes' of everyday work and failure in the Roughing Mill as an example of a more 'bottom up' method for developing a richer, situated view of the practical problems of dependability (Suchman, 1995). This provides us with an opportunity to respecify the problem of dependability, and hence the lessons for IT systems design, by documenting 'real world, real time' practices whereby dependability is rooted within the practical ongoing social organization of work. Any abstract 'rules for dependability' – such as procedures, models, proscriptions, prescriptions, etc. – have to be applied within the context of some socially organized work setting in which those who have to apply such rules have to deal with all the contingencies and other demands on their attention and effort. Our interest in the social organization of work is in how the work activities (which are often glossed and idealised) are actually carried out and accomplished as day-to-day activities with whatever resources are to hand, facing up to whatever contingencies arise. As far as dependability is concerned, we seek to understand the work so that any innovation to make systems more dependable resonates with the work as actually done, noting that many systems fail because they simply do not resonate with the work as a 'real world, real time' phenomenon.

The research reported upon in this chapter was motivated by several observed 'problems' or 'routine failures' in the Roughing Mill, many of which may be viewed as relevant to more general issues of dependability in socio-technical systems. These everyday failures or 'normal, natural troubles' included:

'Cobbles' or 'turn-up' of the part rolled slab that made it difficult, and sometimes impossible, to manipulate the slab through the Mill.

Badly shaped slabs coming into the Mill, that produce, for example, 'fishtails' or other defects in the finished slab.

Slab defects produced by the furnace, for example, 'thermic shock' requiring the Mill operator to make adjustments in how the slab is rolled and that might mean the final rolled plate would not yield all the ordered plates.

Various kinds of marking etc. on the slab produced by difficulties in rolling that might influence the quality of the final plate.

A variety of computer problems related to the identification, measurement and sequencing of the slabs.

As in any tightly structured sequence of interdependent activities, such 'troubles', even though they are often regular and routine, are 'troubles' which detract from the dependability of the system by producing waste, slowing production, creating frustration and increasing overall costs. However, and again as with most systems of high interdependency, achieving 'smooth' operation day in and day out is extremely difficult and requires a great deal of experienced skill on the part of the operators of the technology. Our analysis attempts to highlight the grounding of failure and dependability on the social organized skill and competences of those involved in the work setting. To begin, we describe the work of the Rolling Mill and the rolling process in a rather idealised fashion. In this way we can begin to bring out the situated actual activities of the operators as routines of daily work.

The roughing process

The process of rolling a slab of steel into steel plate, ideally, is simple enough. The process begins with the available steel slabs being assembled in the slabyard and moved to furnaces. When the slab has reached the required temperature it is pushed from the furnace, through the wash boxes to remove scale and then aligned and centred on the rollers in the Roughing Mill, a large structure supporting two steel rollers turned by two large electric motors. Slabs are transported on roller tables and can be turned on the 'turning table' that consists of rollers, thinned on alternate sides, which can rotate in opposite directions. Moving side guides are used to centralise the slab for passage through the Mill. The mill uses reversing mills or rollers. The slab is reduced in thickness by a series of 'passes' back and forth through the mill until the desired thickness is reached. The thickness of the slab can, at any stage, be inferred from the screw position – available via various monitors and the Mill 'clock'. The length and width of the slab can be measured by an optical gauge known as the 'Kelk' or 'Accuplan'. The entire process is problematic since the whole mill is significantly elastic under the enormous forces generated by rolling, combined with the fact that the rolls themselves change shape – expand as they heat and wear as more steel is rolled.

The computer calculates the sequence of screw settings and turns which are reset automatically after each pass. The computer requires a width reading when necessary, corrects to achieve an acceptable width, and keeps track of what has been rolled. The operator is responsible for manipulating the slab to turn it and enter it through the Mill centrally and squarely after the screws have been automatically set. This involves hand and foot controls. If necessary the operator can also take control of the screws. At each 'pass' through the mill the steel is reduced in thickness by the 'draft'. As the volume remains the same, the other dimensions must increase. Most of this increase appears as extra length in the rolling direction and is quite easy to predict. The first target is to elongate one of the slab's dimensions until it reaches the width of the final product. It is then turned through 90% and rolled in the same orientation from then on. The drafts from then on will, ideally, be the maximum possible in order to reduce rolling time and minimise heat loss.

Information on the monitor in the 'pulpit' – the control room where the operator works – tells the operator the slab quality, its present width and length, the width and length required, the orientation, the 'turning point' (the measured point at which the operator should turn the slab to roll for final length), and the 'finish point' (the point at which the operator should send the slab through to the Finishing Mill). The rolling operation itself begins with 'pre-broadside passes' through the Mill and the slab is sprayed to remove scale. The operator then 'goes for width' by rolling the slab to produce the desired width up to the 'turning point'. Measurement of the slab through the Accuplan is displayed in the 'pulpit'. As the operator puts the slab through the mill he turns and aligns it. The scheduler reduces the gauge at each pass – displayed on the overhead monitor and the Mill 'clock') until finish point is achieved. The final pass is a reverse pass. The rollers are then lifted and the plate sprayed on its way to the Finishing Mill.

Of course, in actuality the process rarely goes as smoothly as this. 'Troubles' of various kinds are a regular feature. One prominent trouble is when the part rolled slab 'turns up' to form a U or W shape that makes it impossible to manipulate. There are a number of techniques, all involving heavy manual labour, to recover from such events, but they cause delays and do not always succeed. Although the process is not fully understood, the cure is straightforward. The screw settings should ensure heavy drafting at critical points in the process but this requires considerable experience on the part of the controller. Indeed, many of the more experienced operators will go into manual mode for the last few passes. A related problem is when the plan view of the plate is not the ideal rectangle. If the problem is severe the final rolled plate will not yield all the plates required. The operator does have a degree of control over this but the automatic controller gives no help.

3. ENSURING DEPENDABLE PRODUCTION: COORDINATION, PLANNING AND AWARENESS

This section employs a framework for presenting and highlighting issues of everyday failure and dependability in socio-technical settings, looking at aspects of coordination, plans and procedures, and awareness of work. The framework provides a means for explicating the accomplishment of everyday work, working to ensure the routine character of work by responding to contingencies as they arise, for understanding failure as an everyday phenomenon and how routine troubles can become catastrophic.

Coordination:

Work tasks are performed as coordinated activities, that is, as activities that have interdependence with activities done by others who may not be co-located. The activities and the persons who perform them are interconnected as part of some organization of activities and persons that has to be coordinated in order to 'get the work done'. As Popitz et al. remark in their much earlier study:

"It is not sufficient to remark that the individual work activities are embedded within a larger work context. One must be more concrete and with each individual work activity demonstrate how and to what extent cooperation with other work activities is a requirement." (Popitz et al. 1957, in Schmidt, 1994)

There are, of course, some important differences from the steel rolling mill studied by Popitz et al.; ours is predominantly computer controlled; operators have far greater overview of the whole process and facilities for communicating and coordinating work.

The rolling process is designed from the outset to coordinate the various activities of men and machines involved in turning a slab of steel into a plate. The Roughing Mill is part of a series of work activities beginning with the Furnace, the Roughing Mill itself, the Finishing Mill and the Shear Lines where the 'mother plate' is cut into the various 'daughter plates' ordered by customers. (This series could, of course, be linked to other aspects of the organization – producing the slab itself, loading, invoicing the customers, etc.) Further, the process of reducing a slab of hot metal to a plate has to be done in 'real time'. Communication and coordinating between the various stages of the process has to be dependable, reliable and unequivocal. Further, processing the slabs into plate is subject to various and not always controllable inconsistencies in the quality of the material being worked with: slabs are not always the right size or shape, not always at a workable temperature, cannot always be 'roughed' satisfactorily, and so on. Yet contingencies such as these need to be dealt with by the operators, and in a way which keeps the process running as smoothly as it can under the circumstances. Accordingly, communication and coordination between the processes needs to be as simple and as quick as possible.

For the Roughing Mill operator, coordination with the Finishing Mill (the next stage in the production process) is important and was achieved in a number of ways. The rolling process is not always smooth and, accordingly, coordination in this case between two closely connected processes is essential to regulating the pace of the process in 'real time'. Recourse was often made to the RT link (a microphone) in the Pulpit to alert the Finishing Mill to any problems with the roughed plate. This two-way link also functioned to alert the Roughing Mill operator to anything – such as particularly long slabs or the imminence of 'turn-up' – that might affect his work.

"he was letting me know that the front end was up ... so he was bringing it back just to knock it down ... That's another thing we look for ... this (slab) finished length is 12 metres long ... I notice that (pointing at one in Finishing Mill) was 24 metres (that's) why I'm waiting for him to finish."

Coordination with the Furnace was done mainly through the microphone, a monitor and the Mill 'light' which was used to control the supply of slabs to the Roughing Mill.

"I turned my light off because ...\if I'd had problems with it I'd have had another one standing there getting cold and I'd have the same problems again"

What we see here is some of the everyday work that goes into achieving coordination dependably in the process of rolling slabs into plates.

Dependability, plans and procedures

"Despite our attempts to automate an ever larger set of control functions, and to build-in forms of automated reasoning and intelligence into these computerised control systems, there is still a crucial need for human agency to monitor and, if necessary, to over-ride computerised systems under special circumstances or unusual conditions." (Rognin and Bannon 1997)

Plans are designed to ensure success – but of course on their own they do no such thing – instead plans have to be applied, worked through and worked out in real time real world work. Project plans and schedules, manuals of instructions, procedures, workflow diagrams are all ways of enabling persons to use as resources for co-ordinating work activities. There is no implication here that any particular set of plans, etc., is successful at coordination, or conforms to some ideal standard. The explicit point of plans is to coordinate the work of different persons so that separate work activities, either in parallel or serially, have a coherence and, typically, through this meet other goals such as dependability, efficiency, meeting time constraints, beating the enemy, growing the company, and so on (Schmidt, 1997). Although 'plans and procedures' are, of course, about coordination – and often an important resource in its achievement – 'plans' are abstract constructions that require implementation within the specifics of the circumstances in which it is to be followed (Suchman, 1987; Dant and Francis, 1998). The accomplishment of a 'plan' is dependent upon the practical understanding of what the plan specifies in these circumstances, using these resources, and facing up to these contingencies. In many cases of 'real time, real world work', accomplishing the plan often involves using local knowledge, 'cutting corners', 'bending the rules', even revising the plan in order to meet its overall objective.

As the idealised description of the process suggests, transforming a slab of hot metal into a plate is designed as a linear, step-by-step process moving from the Furnace to the Roughing Mill, to the Finishing Mill and, finally, to the Shear Mill where the plate is cut into sizes for the eventual customer. Being a step-by-step process certain conditions have to be met before moving onto the next stage and key to the whole process is scheduling and pacing. But, scheduling and pacing were not always straightforwardly achievable. A number of problems inevitably arose when the computer and automatic systems went awry. In one case, for example, computer problems in the Finishing Mill produced wrong readings for number of passes and wrong measures on every pass. In another instance, the computer lost its reference point and the operator had to take over manually. In another case an operator noticed that the computer was failing to update:

"it's not been giving us first draft reference ... it's brought up the plate draft but kept it at whatever we sent the last plate at ... it's not updating on the screen at all...for some reason it's not updating ...so there's obviously a fault somewhere ... that's why I'm in manual ... I don't trust it now because I don't know what it's doing ... and the computer hasn't pushed now (provided another slab) because it thinks I'm still at 230 (the initial draft of the plate – 230)."

The successful accomplishment of a 'plan' or a 'procedure' is dependent on the practical understandings about what the plan specifies in these circumstances, using these resources, and so on, not least when things 'do not go according to plan'. In such cases it means adapting to the situation at hand as in the following example.

"... if a slab comes down and its all got thermal cracking ... then we'd roll it the other way ... tell them ... make a note ... they'll say ... why did you roll it that way".

That is, if a slab appears with a thermal crack on one side, rather than following the computer's instructions and rolling the slab so that the crack appears at the side of the plate and effectively ruins the quality of all the 'daughter' plates that are cut from it, the operator will override the computer and roll the slab so that the crack appears at the end of the plate and may be discarded in the waste. Indeed, there were a number of occasions where operators used their own judgments rather than the computer in order to realise the aims of the procedure. The operators were aware that different slab qualities are liable to various defects, such as 'fishtails' and 'tongues' and the work adjusted accordingly. For example, the work of the Roughing Mill critically depends upon slab quality, that is, the metallic composition of the slab and the relative proneness to 'turn up'.

"I shan't give this a lot of water as it's 269 quality and liable to turn up ... with 269 quality a lot of drivers drive with barrel water off to keep the heat in the slab."

"going for manganese ... real hard stuff ... we don't use any water ... you just have to work real fast."

Dependability and Awareness:

'Awareness of Work' refers to the way in which work tasks are made available to others and constitutes a major aspect of the means through which co-ordination of work tasks in any setting is achieved as a practical matter. As Popitz argues:

"An operator only operates the system rationally and effectively if each operation is carried out with a view to the necessary cooperation with others ... he has to take into account the preceding, concurrent and immediately ensuing operations. (Schmidt 1994: 26)

This does not point to some psychological property but, rather, to those visible features of the work and its setting by which those involved can make judgments about the 'state of the work'. So, for instance, scheduling and pacing are not simply about doing one's job in isolation from how it might impact on others further down the process. While the Roughing Mill operator ideally, and in theory, concludes his task when the slab has been 'finished at measure', that is, rolled to a specified thickness, length and width, occasionally operators were observed to ignore their 'finish at' measure – instigating an alarm – in order to send the plate through to the Finishing Mill in an adequate state.

"If I send that at 49 ... it's going to shoot up *(turn up in the Finishing Mill)*...it's 233 quality which is the worst one for turn-up ... you need a minimum of 3 metres in length ... because if you get less than that there's a good chance it could turn-up in the Finishing Mill."

"instead of finishing at 35 I'll drive it down and put a bit more length on it ... less chance of it turning-up then."

'Real time, real world' work often involves the utilization of just such 'local knowledge' and 'local logics', even if commonly interpreted as 'cutting corners' or 'bending the rules', in order to support the overall objectives of the plan and produce dependable steel plates. This clearly involves knowledge of the work of the Finishing Mill on the part of the Roughing Mill operator as well as knowledge of the Finishing Mill (that plates need to be over 3 metres to roll easily) and the relative capacities of the two mills:

"... it wants to send it at 60 ... but it's a bit short ... so I take over manually and knock it down a bit (alarm) ... gone to manual ... it wanted to send it away at 50 ... it makes it difficult for the other (FM) drivers ... it'll take him 2-3 passes to get it down to that."

'Awareness' also involves some kind of judgment and comparison between what the computer 'said' and the operator's experience and skill. This was most obvious where the operator went into manual or over rode the scheduler in some way. So, for example, it was common for the most experienced operators to go into manual for the last few passes – because their experience was that:

"... because the computer at less than 45 pisses about ... does 4-5 passes ... that's what causes turn-up.. "

"because it says 45 the computer tries to do it in 3-4 passes when you can do it in 2 ... it's to do with the pacing of the mill ... we're rolling plates quicker than the computer thinks we are.."

In some ways the end product of this was a healthy suspicion of what the computer was 'telling them' or asking them to do. This was heightened by cases of the computer providing wrong slab sizes or instructions and often resulted in a reliance on the (inaccurate) Mill 'clock' rather than the head display for an understanding of what the Mill is doing:

(watching the clock) "the clock is out but only by about 3mm ... we use the clock because its easier to read ... we can anticipate the speed of the screw ... (compared with head display) ... if it's going down in a pattern ... and it suddenly puts 15 on you know something's wrong."

4. BLINDED BY THE LIGHT: ORGANISATIONAL RESPONSES TO FAILURE

"The evidence will show that a multitude of failings together brought about this crash. Probably every one of them was foreseeable and avoidable. Our clients want each of them exposed and remedied for the future. In the course of the enquiry failings will be demonstrated which it will be argued were not causative of the collision. Our clients are naturally concerned to find out which factors were causative and which were not. But they are much more concerned that every factor exposed in this Inquiry which might lead to an accident in the future will be remedied than in any abtruse debate about whether particular factor was or was not a causative of this crash." (Mr. Hendy, acting on behalf of the families of the victims) (2,5,23)

This second section considers how organizations investigate and understand failure – using the case of the Ladbroke Grove Inquiry. Generally, the focus of research in these settings has been technical in nature – looking to learn from technical failures of systems or to improve technical dependability. More recently, research has drawn attention to the social components of such systems – the interaction of people with and around such systems that is vital to their effective operation and sometimes implicated in their failure. It is important, however to broaden our understanding of the range of relevant 'social' elements in the socio-technical system. Systems are produced, implemented, maintained and altered within a wider organizational context where guidelines, procedures, standards and so on affect their production, testing and use. There is an array of safety practices intended to ensure that work practice is safely carried out. Committees are convened to discuss them, consultants and experts are employed to evaluate them, aid in their design and so forth. This section considers these organizational issues to expand our understanding of organizationally embedded socio-technical safety critical systems. How is work related to written procedure, review, and failure investigated? While the idea of 'failure', and its avoidance, is crucial in the design of safety-critical systems, we consider how an understanding of the realities of organizational structures may feed into the articulation of design and urge a re-examination of the idea of 'failure' in complex socio-technical systems. This approach goes beyond current debates on organizational context and safety-culture (Perrow; Sagan)[1] where emphasis remains on providing explanatory accounts of organizational failure rather than describing the complexities of everyday inter and intra-organizational working within which both 'failure' and ' success' are accomplished[2]. The inquiry into the fatal rail crash at Ladbroke Grove provides a platform in which these organizational issues are discussed to expand our understanding of organizationally embedded socio-technical safety critical systems. We consider statements to the Inquiry concentrating on the critical issue of SPADs (signals passed at danger) and the organizational provision for dealing with this issue.

Ethnomethodological studies of safety critical settings Luff, Hindmarsh and Heath 2000) emphasize that systems involved in such settings are thoroughly socio-technical i.e. people are undoubtedly critical to ensuring safe operation of the system. People make decisions, input information into systems, operate them, interpret them, and override them. This further involves the practical 'management' of relations between organizational units, and between different roles and responsibilities. In the case of the Ladbroke Grove disaster the *"immediate"* cause of the accident can be thought of as a failure in the interface between social and technical aspects of the system. Discounting the possibility of malicious intent, stupidity or distraction the Inquiry is confronted with the possibility that the key feature that contributed to the collision was a problem with either the visibility or the working of the signal. This expands the remit of the Inquiry into the organizational practices and procedures enacted in and supporting signal design, placing and testing. What is interesting about the case of Ladbroke Grove, as revealed in the inquiry, is that catastrophic failure is examined as a product of complex intra and inter-organizational features. For many parties at the Inquiry, not only is the tragedy a result of driver error, signal malfunction, poor design or placement but a complex of other, more organizational aspects. Thames Trains are implicated and scrutinized as employers and as owners of the train. As employers, their procedures of selection, training and support are questioned. As owners of the train their level of technical safety measures is questioned. Railtrack is questioned on the design and maintenance of the infrastructure, particularly signal design, placing, maintenance and evaluation and the attendant procedures. Both companies are also scrutinized on their organizational ethos – were their priorities profit or safety, how were these attended to, was the balance right?

Crucially, ethos is seen as something that has a real organizational manifestation in the everyday running of the organizations.

Workaday and catastrophic failures

'Failure' identification and remedy in catastrophic cases generally identify specific failures that can be shown to have caused the disaster. What can also often be identified in such cases are the procedures or technologies that could have stopped the tragedy. Often, such a retrospective analysis simplifies the safety case. In a complex organization, involving socio-technical systems, there may be multiple minor everyday failures. Organizations and those working within them are abundantly aware of this. This is shown in the workarounds, 'usual rituals' and so forth and in the working groups, standards, committees, procedural documents, checklists etc. designed to deal with such problems. This is our focus, the ways in which the management and operation of safety systems is exhibited in the Inquiry as an environment within which everyday issues are managed.

We don't suggest a hard distinction between 'workaday failures' and 'catastrophic' ones, for – as at Ladbroke Grove – one may be transformed into the other. A critical difference is the public character of catastrophic failure. 'Mundane' failures are characteristically locally, organizationally, contained, whilst catastrophes suffer public review. The Ladbroke Grove Inquiry was one-in-a-series of rail crash inquiries, perhaps identifying a general safety problem in the organization of the railways. It is a matter of contestation between the various parties as to whether this occurrence is to be treated as unique or as a symptom of widespread organizational problems in safety management. The public character of the inquiry involves parties questioning whether railway safety management was following the right standards. The setting of the inquiry is one in which many of the proprieties of organizational dealings may be scrutinized and overruled.

Safety Strategies

The character of the inquiry is strongly shaped by the fatalities. Existing safety practices are demonstrably inadequate – they failed to prevent a catastrophe, the question is whether anything could have been done to prevent it. This involves a very different orientation. From the point of view of the existing safety practices, such an incident was an unlikely occurrence. Safety measures, based on risk evaluation, were directed toward minimizing the likelihood of any such incident rather than eliminating its possibility.

The railway organizations were asked if things could have been done to prevent the accident. This depends importantly upon whether these were things that could have been done regardless of the railway companies' safety practices, or whether they could have been done in terms of current risk bearing strategies. Assuredly there were things that could conceivably have been done in terms of introducing new technologies, or reconstructing the railway approach and signaling that would have prevented this occurrence. However, these were not, in the real time environment of current safety management practices, something that could have been done[3]. Existing safety practices involved living with the risk of a collision, and the objective of those practices was to reduce, not to eliminate, that risk. Measures were taken to minimize the risk of collision as a result of SPADs, to render such an occurrence highly unlikely, possible only as an outcome of an unlikely sequence of exigencies. The inquiry highlights the contrast between what seemed – at the time – like reasonable organizational practice and what in retrospect and in these circumstances, looks bad. In the context of the inquiry organizational responses seem an engagement in distasteful practices – making monetary calculations of the value of human lives, being more concerned with traffic than with passenger safety.

SPADs: Different Perspectives

SPADs were a pivotal consideration for the Inquiry, especially signal SN109 (the one passed in the lead up to the collision). SPADs were recognized as what Garfinkel (1967) terms a '*normal trouble.*' They are a 'trouble' in the sense that they should not occur and measures have been taken to inhibit their occurrence, but they are also a 'normal trouble' in that even though measures are taken to prevent them nonetheless they will continue to occur. But SPADs had been identified as an organizational problem because they were occurring *too frequently*. The problem had thus become that of reducing the rate of their occurrence, a task to be addressed given the understandings of the conditions that precipitated SPADs. This was to be achieved by the reconstruction of *organizational policy and practice*, not merely by local engineering adjustments. Action had been taken by Railtrack and, in their estimation, success achieved. However, Railtrack acknowledged that SPAD's were not a one-off problem, but a much more extensive concern.

Whilst Railtrack had taken the problem of SPADs seriously three methodological and organizational inadequacies are identified: the lack of a root cause analysis, the failure to make a '*SPAD mitigation study*' and '*the making of less than adequate risk assessments*'. A different approach should have been taken – '*treating GK/RT0078 (a signal design standard) as a minimum'.* This approach had not been adopted because it seemed unnecessary. It was assumed that the problem of SPAD's was a driver problem, compensated for by 'run ons' at SPAD prone signals: *'in the case of SN109 particularly, a 700 yard run on before a point of collision ... was the opportunity for drivers to bring their trains to a halt even if traveling at line speed.'*

Mr Owen (State representative Counsel for the Inquiry) provided a history of SPADs at signal SN109. He recounted the build up of SPADs, their reporting and the actions or lack of action by Railtrack to deal with them. A number of different 'working groups' were set up to deal with the problems but there were disputes as to the best remedies. Although it was known to be a problem, Railtrack were slow in responding and placed more importance on maintaining traffic movement over a safer configuration (including infrastructure and schedules).

The location of SN109 was recognized as problematic, being (potentially) hard to see in the approach to the station owing to its position in the midst of a complex tangle of overhead constructions, the state of the light, and so on. This problem had been identified in a report on a previous crash, where the number of signals on the gantries in the approach to Paddington, their raised location, their placement relative to curves in the line, and the high line speed were all specified. An HSE (Health and Safety Executive) report had also complained that the signal was partially obscured by overhead lines, that a nearby bridge could produce dazzle, and that the signal was *'susceptible to swamping from bright sunlight'*. The signal design team from Railtrack had *'visited the site on a number of occasions'* due to the complexity of the scheme to re-site that signal. However, the re-siting of the signal had not been undertaken in (official) consultation with HMRI (Her Majesty's Rail Inspectorate) and had been in operation for eighteen months before inspection. HMRI inspection identified the location of the signal as a trouble suggesting the signal was placed in a configuration that *'was highly unusual, if not unique; and it is appears to have been acknowledged that it did not comply with the existing signaling standards'*. However, the HMRI report found that the visibility of the signal on approach was *'borderline acceptable'* recommending a reduction in the line speed at the approach. The Inquiry also highlights train operator worries about the situation. First Great Western's Operations and Safety Director wrote to Railtrack on a number of occasions complaining:

"It is clear from all the SPADs in the Paddington area that there is a serious problem with drivers misreading signals. This has been known for some time and very little action has been taken by Railtrack to date"

This means discounting the possibility of driver error alone. Though Driver Hodder made the error, explanation does not lie just with the driver, but in the organizational background, in the ways in which the system had been prepared to manage occasions of this kind[4].

However, while Railtrack's representative admits to failures, these are minor and mitigated and do not manifest a generalized problem in the responsible management of safety. Railtrack admitted the situation at Ladbroke grove was "complex", but denied that it presented drivers with a situation that was too complex for them to handle. An experienced driver should know that SN109 was a problematic signal, that there had been previous SPADs:

"Any driver driving out of Paddington should know that the gantry lies just beyond Goldbourne Bridge at the locations of SN105, which being lower, is visible over a considerable distance. He or she should be looking for the signal. It does not suddenly appear without warning or without prior knowledge. SN109 should be known to all drivers driving out of Paddington as a multi SPADed signal....etc.....It is not so complex it cannot be taught, learnt, tested and applied." (2,46,6)

It would not, either, have been a matter of mistaking a danger signal for another signal, since all the signals visible were at red. In addition:

"Phantom images of a proceed aspect or aspects in lieu of a red aspect at 109 were not to be seen in the almost identical conditions of the following morning by the HMRI expert Mr Wilkins...Nor was the red light swamped into invisibility ....by the sunshine…"

Thus, the driver should have known that the signal required him to stop the train, and 'all contextual indications should have led him to believe that this was so'. The identification of SPADs as a problem of driver error, to be resolved by training and fail safe mechanisms was the same kind of understanding which resulted in the critical 20 second delay in the reaction of a signalman to the incident. The signalman recognized that a SPAD had occurred, but, based on experience and for good organizational reasons, anticipated the driver would correct it.[5] It was only after the expected adjustment failed to materialize – the 20 seconds delay – that the signalman took belated action.

5. DISCUSSION: EXPLICATING FAILURE AND DEPENDABILITY

This chapter has documented some features of dependability and failure in two very different settings – the situated actions aimed at ensuring everyday dependable production in a steel mill and the plethora of organizational issues that arise in the case of massive, public failure in the complex intra-organizational setting of the Ladbroke Grove disaster. In both cases failure, success and dependability is not simply a product of following or failing to follow agreed rules and procedures – quite the opposite. Not only have procedures to practically implemented; their applicability, their timescales etc are topics of dispute. The issues of reconciliation and coordination suggest a number of issues for dependability in safety-critical socio-technical systems. Even defining the scope of a problem in such complex settings is difficult. What should be taken into account as relating to a problem, how matters should be dealt with, whether solutions are good enough are matters for discussion, negotiation and prioritization.

There is not even, or necessarily any congruence in understanding whether and in what ways a problem should be prioritised. In the steel mill, for example, routine troubles in the form of 'turn-up' or 'cobbles' could be traced to a number of sources – the furnace, the monitors, operator skills, the scheduler or pacing etc. Similarly SPADs were individual problems amongst the many routinely worked on within Railtrack. Decisions had to be made about how pressing particular problems might be and whether finding a solution to that problem pre-empts work on others. Railtrack's approach was to resolve the problem through routine organisational methods – reducing train speeds, raising driver awareness, re-organising train schedules – whilst the issues could be worked through in accord with routine procedures. Perhaps this was a problem that could not be optimally resolved given the need to keep within budgets, avoid major re-engineering and 'keep the traffic moving' and that any short-term practicable solution would necessarily involve trade-offs amongst the requirements for a fully satisfactory solution.

Identification of acceptable solutions is often a matter of achieving sufficient consensus amongst various parties but there may not be any straightforward way to manage this *within the operating routines, the distribution of powers, and the existing burden of workloads within the organization.* So, again for example, in the steel mill, one aspect of improving awareness and consequently dependable production relates to the setting of the controls and the information provided (Andersen, 1999). While this may appear an essentially ergonomic problem in terms of the best positioning of the available controls, modifying the pulpit controls raises a number of interesting, though different, issues. Some operators would prefer the measurement gauges to be on or nearer the monitor (so that they did not need to turn their head); others appeared to have incorporated the head turning seamlessly into their work. Others felt that the mill load gauges should be more easily visible to the operator. This highlights the topic of generating displays that are appropriate to the right people at the right time and in the right place. This may also be related to dependability issues of 'diversity' – of providing a range of measures by which operators can obtain relevant information. In practice this issue of diversity rarely arose as an everyday concern but it became important when things began to go wrong, when the computer started giving the wrong measure or the wrong slab or the wrong dimensions.

In terms of manifest problems with the plates in the form of cobbles, or faults, or quality - the observations revealed an interesting tension and trade-off in terms of dependable production between human skill and computer scheduling. The problem of cobbles was seen by the operators as a product of particular steel features – such as high manganese, no washes, poor sizing etc. that were exacerbated by scheduler problems. This meant that the more experienced operators routinely and regularly over rode the scheduler and went into manual to drive down faster and prevent turn-up. Consequently, despite the desire for 'dependable production', any changes need to be carefully considered in terms of their interactional effect – for example changes in the scheduler may make greater demands on the operators skill and may thereby impact on the quality of the finished product.

The extent to which organizational members have autonomy and discretion in determining the force of requirements originating from other organizations is questionable, as is the capacity of supervisory and co-operating organizations to monitor progress. The situation is incredibly complex, inter and intra-organizational, involving different companies, different technologies, practices, standards, committees, etc. A narrow view of safety focusing only on technology or even a socio-technical perspective focusing on human-technology interaction does not capture the organizational features that are important in selecting, implementing, maintaining, testing, supervising and reconfiguring and upgrading technologies and systems.

Our fieldwork observations suggest that 'problems' were an everyday, commonplace feature of work – mundane, generally low consequence failures, often remedied by skilful 'work-arounds'. When we consider such problems or 'failure' as an everyday fact of life, we begin to modify ideas about problems, failure and dependability. As we suggested at the outset, once we begin to consider the actual practice, the 'real world, real time' work of a socio-technical system, issues of dependability and failure become increasingly difficult. In these circumstances, dependability would, for example, include the quality of the eventual 'daughter' plates that could be cut from the plate; the amount of waste; the timeliness with which the plate is presented to the next stage in the rolling process and so on. One of the most obvious dependability issues to have emerged from this research concerns various forms of awareness and its impact on dependability – in particular a lack of awareness in several, perhaps crucial instances. So, for example, while the computer system is configured to ensure the manager knows the composition of the slabs in the furnace and the order in which they may appear, none of this information is conveyed to the Roughing Mill operators who actually have to work with the slabs. Operators simply respond to whatever slab appears in front of them. Such an awareness – of what's coming out of the furnace – may prove useful both for pacing and teamwork in the Roughing Mill. At the same time, there appears to be little in the way of form of 'reverse awareness' – from the Shear Lines to the Roughing Mill, for instance, in terms of information about the quality of finished plates. This might, for example, enable a mill operator to decide that a plate should be scrapped before it goes through the Finishing Mill because the defects in it – such as lines – make it worthless.

Observations suggest that problems are an everyday, commonplace feature of work and when we consider problems or 'failure' as an everyday fact of life, we shift our ideas of problems, failure and dependability. Dependability becomes one of *dynamically responding in the best way* to problems as they arise and achieving dependable production – in the steel mill for example – involves far more than simply reconfiguring the system but attending to the complexities of collaborative working. Similarly, those involved in dependable socio-technical systems need to take interest in the relationship between organizational 'features' and 'structures' and the activity of the people carrying out everyday work. Through doing so we can hope to better understand how organizational structures as a whole, including people and their interaction with others, systems, plans, procedures etc. are actually constructed, reconstructed, adhered to, violated, worked around. This should begin to broaden our understanding of issues for systems design in complex intra-organizational contexts.

In the case of Ladbroke Grove this involves considering ways in which failures are constituted through organizational practice, are categorized, sized, scoped and evaluated, how they allocated to parties responsible for problem solving, how closely and in what ways the activities of those involved in the problem solving are integrated. SPADs were handled by an array of measures addressed to the problem, *as it was understood*. Organizational constraints shaped what was practicable. Organizational matters of *coordination* and *cooperation* were of great importance. These included the responsiveness (or lack of it) of one organization to another; articulating the procedures and responsibilities of different organizations; controlling distributed problem solving; interpreting the implications and effecting the implementation of recommendations from independent supervisory bodies; and depending on and trusting in the competence of sub- contracted experts. When we consider failure as an everyday fact of life, we shift our ideas of failure, dependability and safety critical settings. We are drawn away from thinking about creating *failsafe* systems for such complex environments. Indeed it may be, as Law (2000) suggests that imperfection is *necessary* to effective system functioning. Instead, the problem becomes one of *dynamically responding in the best way* to failures as they arise.

Complex organizations involving socio-technical systems may experience multiple minor failures on a day-by-day basis. Awareness of such failures is shown not only in the workarounds, 'usual rituals' and so forth, but also in the working groups, standards, committees, procedural documents, checklists etc. that are convened and employed to deal with such issues. Within computer science 'safety critical' is generally used to indicate settings where a computer system is used in which there is the potential risk to the health of individuals through the failure or malfunction of the *technical system*. There has also been a tendency in case studies of safety critical settings (e.g. The London Ambulance Dispatching System (Finkelstein, 1993), Therac-25 (Leveson, 199), Ladbroke Grove (Law, 2001) to focus on situations where a clear loss of life has occurred due to a failure in the system. While this technical orientation provides useful information and analysis there is a need to complement this with an understanding of *dependability* and *failure* issues that relate to the wider *socio-technical system* in which specific technologies are embedded.

In many, broadly speaking, safety critical settings it makes little sense to separate the technical system from the social practices that surround its use for those who do the work are undoubtedly critical in ensuring the operation of the system as a whole. It is people who input information into the systems, operate them, interpret them, make decisions based on them, override them, discount them and so on. No matter how full the specification of the system, no matter how good the code how *dependable* the computer system, if there is a *failure* to take account of and attempt to understand the users and their work there can be problems in the interaction between users and the technology. That is, failures in the socio-technical system. Although technical solutions to failure or for dependability may be of obvious benefit the challenge is to recognize broader socio-technical failure in significant contexts. It could be argued that in many cases the technology involved did not *fail* but was not *dependable* given the broader socio-technical context of its operation.

Our fieldwork studies point to the fact that 'failure' (in a broad sense, covering many minor difficulties) is an organizational 'fact of life'. These mundane failures routinely or occasionally arise in the everyday business of accomplishing work. That they can be routine and unremarkable or occasional but easily fixed is apparent in the way they are dealt with, for example, established procedures, workarounds or basic ameliorative actions. The key point here is that such mundane failures are recognised by the actors in the socio-technical system. Further, because they are recognised they can be acted upon. These are not unrecognised, potentially catastrophic failures. Our approach differs from the focus of failure identification and remedy that inevitably seems to stem from studies of failure leading to catastrophe. This research always comes after-the-fact, where specific failures are identified, focused on, pulled apart and reified. Undoubtedly they can be shown to have caused the disaster and what also can often be easily identified in such cases are the procedures or technologies that could have stopped such a tragedy. Such analysis inevitably leads to simplification. In a complex organization, involving socio-technical systems there may be multiple minor failures on a day-by-day basis. Indeed, organizations and those working within them are often abundantly aware of this. Not only is this shown in the workarounds, 'usual rituals' and so forth but in the working groups, standards, committees, procedural documents, check-lists and so on that are used to deal with such issues. For instance, in the case of Ladbroke Grove, it is not as if Railtrack were unaware of the dangers of trains passing signals at danger nor that they had not instituted a whole range of technical and procedural solutions for dealing with such eventualities. The crucial difficulty here is that when such mundane failures are naturally treated as such it is incredibly difficult, if not impossible to identify and make the failure prescient as one that requires immediate attention or *this time* it will lead to a serious outcome. It is also important to acknowledge that often failure comes about through an unexpected interaction between (maybe many) different parts of the socio-technical system. This brings us to one of the contradictions in design for such systems- that design inevitably involves trying to imagine or evaluate for the unexpected. This is clearly difficult to do, but then, as Rittel and Webber remind us, design is a 'wicked problem'.

REFERENCES

1. Andersen, P.B. (1999): 'Elastic Interfaces: Maritime instrumentation as an example', in *Proceedings of CSAPC'99*, Valenciennes, France, pp. 35-41.
2. Axelrod, R. (1997): *Complexity of Co-operation: agent based models of competition and collaboration*. Princeton. NJ. Princeton University Press.
3. Blumer, H. (1954): 'What Is Wrong with Social Theory?'. *American Sociological Review*, vol. 19, pp. 3-10.
4. Blythin, S., Hughes, J., O'Brien, J., Rodden, T. and Rouncefield. M. (1997): 'Designing with Ethnography: A presentation Framework for Design', in *Proceedings of Designing Interactive Systems '97*, ACM Press, Amsterdam.

5. Clarke, K., Hartswood, M., Procter, R., Rouncefield, M. and Slack, R. (2002): 'Minus nine beds: some practical problems of integrating and interpreting information technology in a hospital trust' in *Proceedings of the BCS Conference on Healthcare Computing*, Harrogate, March 18-20.
6. Clarke, K., Martin, D., Rouncefield, M., Sommerville, S. (2002). "Going Through The Usual Rituals": coping with system failure in a hospital setting. *Submitted to SAFECOMP 2002.*
7. Dant T. and Francis, D. (1998): 'Planning in organizations: Rational control or contingent activity?', *Sociological Research Online*, vol. 3, no. 2.
8. Fogg, B. J. and Tseng, H. (1999): 'The elements of computer credibility', *Proceedings of CHI '99*, New York, NY: ACM, pp. 80-87.
9. Garfinkel, H. (1967): *Studies in Ethnomethodology*, Englewood Cliffs, New Jersey, Prentice Hall.
10. Goodwin, C. (1994): 'Professional Vision', *American Anthropologist*, Vol. 96, no. 3, pp. 606-633
11. Harper, R. & Hughes, J. (1992). 'What a f-ing system! Send 'em all to the same place and then expect us to stop 'em hitting':making technology work in air traffic control, in G. Button, ed., *Technology in Working Order*, Routledge, 1992.
12. Heath, C., Luff, P. (1991). 'Collaborative activity and technological design: task coordination in London Underground control rooms'. *Proceedings of ECSCW '91.* Dordrecht: Kluwer: pp. 65-80.
13. Hughes, J,. King, V., Rodden. T. and Andersen, H. (1994): 'Moving out of the control room: ethnography in systems design', *Proceedings CSCW '94*, North Carolina, ACM Press, pp. 429-438.
14. Hughes, J., Randall, D. and Shapiro, D. (1992): 'Faltering from Ethnography to Design', *Proceedings of CSCW'92*, North Carolina, ACM Press.
15. Hughes, J., Randall, D., Shapiro, D. (1992) Faltering from Ethnography to Design. *In Proceedings of CSCW'92.* ACM.
16. Kipnis, D. (1996): 'Trust and Technology', in R. M. Kramer and T. R. Tyler (eds.): *Trust in Organizations: Frontiers of Theory and Research*, London: Sage, pp. 39-50.
17. Ladbroke Grove Rail Inquiry. http://www.lgri.org.uk
18. Ladbroke Grove Train Inquiry. http://www.hse.gov.uk/railway/paddrail/lgri1.pdf
19. Laprie, J-C. (1995): 'Dependable Computing, Concepts, Limits, Challenges', Invited paper to *FTCS-25 25th IEEE International Symposium on Fault-Tolerant Computing*, Pasedena, USA.
20. Law, J. (2000) 'Ladbroke Grove, or How To Think about Failing Systems'— published by the Centre for Science Studies and the Department of Sociology, Lancaster University at http://www.comp.lancs.ac.uk/sociology/soc055jl.html
21. Luff, P., Hindmarsh, J. and Heath, C. C. (eds.) (2000) Workplace Studies: Recovering work practice and informing system design. Cambridge: CUP
22. Luhmann, N. (1990): 'Familiarity, Confidence, Trust: Problems and Alternatives', in Gambetta, D, (ed.): *Trust: Making and Breaking Cooperative Relations*, Oxford. Basil Blackwell. Available online at www.sociology.ox.ac.uk/trustbook.html
23. Luhmann, N. (1979): *Trust and Power*, Chichester Wiley.
24. Martin, D., Bowers, J., Wastell, D. (1997) The Interactional Affordances of Technology: An Ethnography of Human-Computer Interaction in an Ambulance Control Centre. *Proceedings of HCI '97.*
25. Perrow, V. (1984) Normal Accidents. Basic Books. New York .
26. Popitz, H., Bahrdt, H., Jures, E. and Kesting, H. (1957): 'Technic und Industriearbeit', *Soziologische Untersuchungen in der Huttenindistrie*, J.C.B. Mohr, Tubingen.
27. Randell, B. (2000): 'Facing Up to Faults', Turing Lecture, January 31st.

28. Rogers, W.F. (1986): *Report of the Presidential Commission on the Space Shuttle Challenger Accident.* http://science.ksc.nasa.gov/shuttle/missions/51-l/docs/rogers-commission/table-of-contents.html

29. Rognin, L. and Bannon, L. (1997): 'Sharing Information: The Role of Teams in contributing to Systems Dependability Constructing Shared Workspaces through Interpersonal Communication', *Proceedings of Allocation of Functions (ALLFN'97)*, October 1-3, Galway, Ireland.

30. Sagan, S.D. The Limits of Safety: Organizations, Accidents, and Nuclear Weapons. Princeton University Press, Princeton, NJ.

31. Schmidt, K. (1994): 'Modes and Mechanisms of Interaction in Cooperative Work: Outline of a Conceptual Framework'. Riso National Laboratory.

32. Schmidt, K. (1997): 'Of maps and scripts: the status of formal constructs in cooperative work', *Proceedings of GROUP'97*, ACM Press.

33. Suchman, L. (1995): 'Making Work Visible', *CACM*, vol. 38, no. 9, pp. 56-64.

34. Suchman, L. A. (1987): *Plans and Situated Actions: The Problem of Human-Machine Communication.*, Cambridge. Cambridge University Press.

35. Voß, A., Slack, R., Procter, R., Williams, R., Hartswood, M. and Rouncefield, M. (2002): 'Dependability as Ordinary Action', *Computer Safety, Reliability and Security: Proceedings of the 21st International Conference, SAFECOMP 2002*, Catania, Italy, September. Reprinted in S. Anderson, S, Bologna, M. Felici (eds.): *Lecture Notes in Computer Science* vol. 2434, Springer Verlag, pp. 32-43.

---

[11] For an illuminating example of this approach applied to the Ladbroke Grove disaster see John Law (2000)[7]

[12] And in such a way - through a theoretical matrix - that the details of lived organizational work are obscured. Instead research seems reduced to a 'pick-and-mix' approach to analysis (sic) where apparent details of organizational life are opportunistically mapped to various characteristics of, for example, tight or loose coupling, complex or linear organization and so on.

[13] " Railtrack had a conflict between safety and the need to make a profit. But Railtrack should not be blamed for that, it is a company which has a duty to make profits to its shareholders and this is exactly what happens when you privatise a public service."

[14] "When it comes to the action or inaction within the Great Western Zone of Railtrack, there stand out from all the detail perhaps four simple facts: no Signal Sighting Committee was convened for this signal, as was required; no overall review of Paddington signalling was carried out, although more than once intended and even instructed; no measure was implemented to the signal itself at 109 from 1994 with the exception of the prior yellows being removed; and the gantry remailed where it was without mitigation" (Counsel for Thames Trains)

[15] Based on prevailing practice at the Slough signal box and his previous experience of SPADS (and this only amounted to three) and the fact that most SPADs are 'technical' (the driver passing the signal by only a few metres), the signalman waited for a phone call from the train driver. The organizational features of this situation were that if the signalman had followed strict procedure and pressed the 'signals on' button - causing all signals in the area to go red - disruption (in the morning rush hour) would have been enormous. There may have been other possible SPADs; passenger injuries caused by drivers applying emergency brakes; and, in the last resort, possible financial penalties for both Railtrack and the train operating companies. As John Law writes "..if it is the case that the signalmen didn t quite work to rule, ..they failed to do so for very good reasons .. if the prevailing practice of the signalmen across the network was in fact to wait and see then this was a system imperfection which actually helped to keep the wheels turning almost all of the time" Law 200:15)

Chapter 7

PATTERNS FOR DEPENDABLE DESIGN

David Martin, Mark Rouncefield and Ian Sommerville
Department of Computing, University of Lancaster

1. INTRODUCTION: DESIGN AND THE SOCIAL SCIENCES

The argument for the involvement of social scientists in dependable socio-technical systems design reasons is that, to be dependable, systems need to be appropriate both for the application domain and potential users. Before designers can solve a design problem they need to understand some basics - such as what they are designing, who should use it, how often and in what circumstances (Scherer 2002); social analysis of settings where systems are deployed can expose subtle interactions and practices that are crucial to achieving this understanding but which are not revealed by a more structured, technical analysis.

This 'turn to the social' recognises a new kind of end-user, a 'real time, real world' human and social scientists can provide designers with insights and sensitivities, to inform design. The use of observational or ethnographic studies has been a feature of our work over the past 10 or so years as we have attempted to inform the requirements and design of dependable, cooperative socio-technical systems through studies of 'real world, real time' work. (Hughes et al 1997) Over the years, we have generated a considerable corpus of workplace studies in a range of settings from control rooms to local government offices. As this corpus continues to develop, the issue becomes one of how this material can contribute to the formation of general concepts and principles of systems design. Despite being strong advocates and supporters of ethnographic methods, (Hughes et al 1994) we

K. Clarke, G. Hardstone, M. Rouncefield and I. Sommerville (eds.), Trust in Technology:
A Socio-Technical Perspective, 147–168.

acknowledge persistent problems in determining how these particular studies, and the growing corpus of ethnographic work, can best be utilized, or made useful, for design. As Bannon argues;

".. a critical issue for research lies in determining ways of transforming the ethnographic material in such a way that remains sensitive to the practices of designers themselves and thus can readily be used by them in the design process." (Bannon 2000: 250)

We also acknowledge that, given the pressure on time and resources in the system design process, it is unlikely that prolonged ethnographies will become a standard part of design practice. We therefore need ways of allowing the results of workplace studies to be reused in new and different situations. This requires a balance to be struck between the need for the emergence of general principles and the central importance in ethnographic studies of detailing everyday situated practice. If we are to provide more general design principles, we need techniques to facilitate generalization from ethnographic studies and to allow the results of such studies to be married with more general statements of design.

This chapter proposes the use of patterns of interaction as a partial solution to the problem of designing systems that can seamlessly integrate with the practices and activities of the workplace. We suggest that patterns provide a way of representing knowledge about the workplace so that it is accessible to the diverse, multi-disciplinary team that is involved in design. Patterns provide a framework within which work and design issues can be discussed and generalized. If dependability is a product of careful design then patterns may provide a method whereby designers may come to understand something about how work gets done. They attempt to provide some sense of, and some sensitivity to the activities that occur within the workplace, and the problems, and workarounds of everyday working life, with which any new design may have to be aligned.

Furthermore, As Erickson notes: "Design is becoming increasingly interdisciplinary. Neither 'designers' nor 'end users' are homogenous groups; they lack common disciplines, practices, and conceptual frameworks. All that we can realistically expect those involved in design to share is access to the situation for which they are designing. As a consequence, pattern languages, with their emphasis on embodying design knowledge as a network of concrete prototypes, have the potential to serve as a lingua franca for workplace design". Our Patterns of Cooperative Interaction highlight similarities in research findings across ethnographic studies related to particular socio-technical configurations. They begin to address the question of how we might generalize from ethnographic studies to provide guidance for system designers and other users.

2. DESIGN AND THE PROBLEM OF GENERALISATION

Our observational research studies within the DIRC project, such as a long-term study of hospital managers, document, describe and analyse work and activity as it actually occurs. The general conception is, therefore, a focus on the everyday accomplishment of work, concerned with how the order of work is socially produced – i.e. how this order is achieved, maintained and repaired. They are concerned with the role that action and interaction, between personnel, and with technology, have in the production of order, and how the ecology of settings and the design of artefacts relate to the way work is carried out. We have now reached a stage where it is important to reflect on what the collection of studies tells us as a body of knowledge, going beyond topics that serve as orienting and organizing devices (which are described below), to discuss how the actual details of work in particular settings relate to one another. For instance, are certain work configurations similar, and do they lead to similar activities?

Furthermore, we need to present this knowledge in a manner that is useful and usable for a variety of professionals working in the field and with an interest in the findings of such studies. As experienced researchers, we are aware that our widespread knowledge and experience benefits us when describing and analysing work in new settings. Furthermore, it helps in making what we find and document useful for software engineers or systems designers. We are also aware that to others, as a corpus, these studies can appear like a disparate collection, united by method and orientation but with findings peculiar to each particular setting. The designers' or software engineers' problem, here, has therefore been one of seeing how particular findings in diverse settings may provide useful background for characterising and understanding work in different settings.

3. PATTERNS AND PATTERN LANGUAGES

Recent emphasis on patterns in design can be traced to the work of the architect *Christopher Alexander* outlined in two books, A Timeless Way of Building and A Pattern Language (Alexander 1979; Alexander et al 1977). Patterns are attempts to marry the relevant aspects of the physical and social characteristics of a setting into a design; they provide a facility to share knowledge about design solutions and the setting in which such a solution is applied –

"..every pattern we define must be formulated in the form of a rule which establishes a relationship between a context, a system of forces which arises in that context, and a configuration which allows these forces to resolve themselves in that context"(Alexander 1977)

Patterns are then a way of conveying to designers some sense of the application domain. They are,

"..ways of allowing the results of workplace studies to be reused in new and different situations. .. ways of representing knowledge about the workplace so that it is accessible to the increasingly diverse set of people involved in design.."(Erickson 2000)

While inspired from Alexander's original work, the notion of design patterns has moved from the original conception suggested by Alexander to something that is more prescriptive. We wish to exploit patterns in the much looser spirit suggested by Alexander's original work where familiar situations were used to convey potential architectural solutions. In fact, the observed recurrence of familiar situations lies at the core of our argument for patterns. Designers often encounter similar situations and one justification for this focus on patterns is a particular take on notions of re-use - where the emphasis is on drawing from previous experience to support the collection and generalization of successful solutions to common problems. As Alexander suggests;

"each pattern describes a problem which occurs over and over again in our environment, and then describes the core of the solution to that problem, in such a way that you can use this solution a million times over, without ever doing it the same way twice".

Another rationale behind patterns is Alexander's notion of 'quality' ('The Quality Without A Name') and the idea that "a pattern is a solution to a problem in a context".   Here 'quality' refers not to some mystical characteristic but to features of systems that ensure that they 'really work', that they fit with the social circumstances of use. Interestingly this is also part of the rationale for the turn to ethnography in systems design (Crabtree et al 2000) and is also clearly intrinsic to dependable socio-technical design.

The discovery and presentation of patterns provide a way by which the important findings of different studies are highlighted and presented in a manner that is more accessible to designers. In the following sections we outline our own efforts to uncover and present patterns of cooperative interaction derived from the growing corpus of ethnographic studies. In identifying patterns we were describing grossly observable phenomena in ethnographic studies with reference to their context of production and seeking a way to present them using a standard framework.

Principles of Pattern Generation

Patterns, as we have said, encapsulate commonalities that occur in different settings and a fundamental criterion in identifying patterns is that these should come from practice. That is, they are not academic abstractions but we have drawn them from field observations taken from our corpus of ethnographic studies. Trying to uncover descriptive patterns within the field studies soon highlighted the need for some set of guidance. Although we were focusing on grossly observable features as the core of the genesis of the pattern it was unclear what sorts of features provided a set of readily understood patterns and what features were of most significance. To provide a focus on the issues of importance to designers, we turned to our previous work in outlining a presentation framework for ethnographic studies in order to develop a set of generative principles (Hughes et al, 1997a) These principles are based around three main workplace characteristics.

Spatially oriented features that focus on the physical nature of the work and the observable arrangements within the workplace.

Work oriented features that focus on the principles of social organization used to structure and manage the cooperative work.

Temporally oriented features that focus on the temporal nature of the work and observable sequential arrangements within the workplace.

Focusing on these concerns is a means of highlighting aspects of work that seem important in considering dependability as a feature of design.

Spatially oriented features

These concerns seek to emphasize the observable arrangement of work and physical nature of the work setting. Three key features are of particular importance and can be expressed as key questions

- **Resources** – what are the various resources in the setting used to support the work taking place and how are they shared.
- **Actors** – who is involved in the cooperative work taking place and how do they orientate to each other.
- **Activities** – what are the main observable techniques for structuring activities and how are these represented?

Work oriented features

These concerns seek to emphasize the socially organized nature of work and how these is manifest in practice within particular settings. For simplicity we have again focused on three key features drawn from previous work on a framework for presenting fieldwork.

- **Awareness of work** – how and through what means are those involved in work aware of the work of others, how do they exploit this awareness and how do they make others aware of their work?
- **Distributed Coordination** – how do those involved in the work coordinate their activities and what practical techniques do they use to do this?
- **Plans and procedures** – what techniques do those involved in the workplace use to orient their work in practice to the formal plans, procedures, representations and artefacts of work?

Temporally oriented features

These concerns seek to emphasize the observable temporal arrangements of work settings, how aspects of timeliness and sequentiality enter into the accomplishment of work. Two key features are of particular importance and can be expressed as key questions

- **Sequentiality** – is work accomplished in a particular order or sequence? How do actions relate to previous actions and preface future activities?
- **Routines and rhythms** – is the observed orderliness of work and interaction a product of and productive of observable routines and rhythms of activity?

Developing a Descriptive Pattern Language

These basic concerns provide a key set of concepts to drive the identification and highlighting of descriptive patterns. Our framework for presenting the patterns combines their different features to produce an agreed pattern language:

Cooperative Arrangement: The cooperative arrangement details, in very basic terms, the *actors* and *resources* that are involved in the pattern of interaction: the people, the number and type of computers and artefacts, the communication medium(s) employed and the basic *activity*.

Representation of Activity: This describes how the activity is represented, for example, on a technology or as a plan and may address the relationship between the activity and the representation. This is related to *plans and procedures.*

Ecological Arrangement: This has the form of one or more pictorial representations of the pattern. For example this may include *abstract representations, plan views, information flows, copies of paper forms, screen* *shots or photographs.* There may be good reason for these to be fairly abstract as the real detail may be found in the referenced studies themselves if this is desired. This explicitly addresses the *spatial* characteristics.

Coordination Techniques: This details the type of practices, procedures and techniques employed in carrying out the activity/interaction and how, and in what way, coordination is achieved. This is related to *awareness and distributed co-ordination.*

Community of Use: This is related to an idea of domain, but instead seeks to capture something about the user group. For example, is it customer-customer or a small team of co-workers in a control room?

For each identified pattern a set of illustrative examples drawn from the field studies is presented. This arrangement is designed to promote comparison across pattern examples drawn from different field sites.

4. PATTERNS OF COOPERATIVE INTERACTION

Patterns of Cooperative Interaction provide a basis for abstraction and generalization of findings from ethnographic studies, for the purposes of comparison and re-use in new design situations. They are descriptive in nature but can be put to generative use. By thinking about how the patterns relate to a current design situation the researcher can gain analytic leverage on systems design problems.

Patterns were discovered through studying the fieldwork corpus, and looking for examples of phenomena that were similar across at least two different studies. We now have a collection of ten patterns each presented with a front-page summary description, with access to further pages in which specific instantiations of the pattern are documented. These are presented as 'vignettes' that show details of the pattern from specific studies. Thus, the pattern as a whole is composed of specific vignettes as well as an abstracted 'front page' description that unites the vignettes.

On the front page, we provide an abstract description that pulls together the vignette examples, discussing what makes them similar and what differentiates them. It also contains hyperlinks to access the specific vignettes, a short paragraph on why we drew attention to the pattern ('Why useful') and some design and dependability considerations that arise from the pattern (in a section termed 'Design for Dependability')[6]

At the 'deeper' level of vignette, each vignette has two major components. The first component is a textual description (and sometimes a pictorial representation) of a socio-technical configuration of people and artefacts in a particular setting. The second component is a description of the social practices by which work is achieved given that configuration.

The Patterns Collection

Our Patterns collection, presented via a series of web pages, provides access to the corpus of ethnographic studies by placing *findings* as the entry point into the material rather than through the studies themselves. The full list is currently as follows:

1.   Artefact as an audit trail
2.   Multiple representations of information
3.   Public artefact
4.   Accounting for an unseen artefact
5.   Working with Interruptions
6.   Collaboration in Small Groups
7.   Receptionist as a hub
8.   Doing a walkabout
9.   Overlapping Responsibilities
10.   Assistance Through Experience

Each pattern name is a hypertext link that takes the user to a front page for the pattern in question. This includes the high level description under the heading 'The Essence of the Pattern'. Below this, there are three more sections entitled 'Why Useful?' 'Where Used?' and 'Dependability Implications?'. These detail why we have chosen to draw attention to the pattern; the specific fieldwork settings where we have found examples of the pattern; and some comments about what the identification of the pattern may mean for certain questions concerning 'good', usable, dependable design. The specific examples on screen serve as hypertext links to the vignettes and a greater level of detail.

All of our patterns focus on work practices and interactions and how various work and technology configurations give rise to these, facilitate or constrain them. Some patterns focus particularly on different *artefact* designs and placements and their relationship to work practices and interactions (Public Artefact, Multiple Representations of Information, Artefact as an Audit Trail, Accounting for an Unseen Artefact). Other patterns are less focused on specific artefacts but on how 'work' and 'job' design are related to actual practices and interactions given certain configurations (Working with Interruptions, Collaboration in Small Groups, Receptionist as a Hub, Doing a walkabout, Overlapping Responsibilities, Assistance Through Experience). We present an example from each 'sub-group'. The first is "Working with Interruptions".

Pattern: "Working with Interruptions"

This pattern is concerned with the commonplace situation where personnel have to interleave computer and paper based work in the face of multiple interruptions. How staff deal practically with interruptions, what the problems are and what works well is detailed. Such workplace arrangements are familiar and the pattern and vignettes provide a resource for thinking about design in situations where similar issues are pertinent.

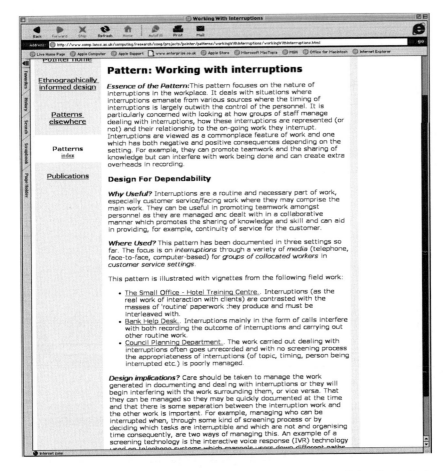

Figure 1: Front page for 'Working with interruptions' (small detail missing)

The first vignette comes from Rouncefield et al (1994). It focused on how frontline reception work (face-to-face and over the phone) became a set of 'interruptions' that had to be managed skillfully in order that organizational paper work could be successfully completed.

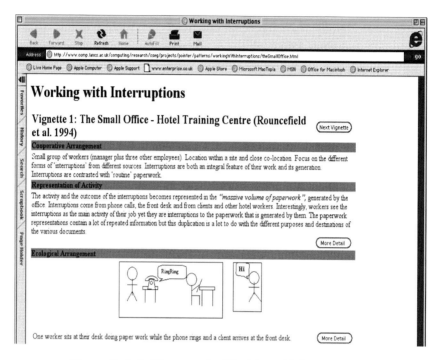

Figures 2. & 3. Vignettes for 'Working with interruptions

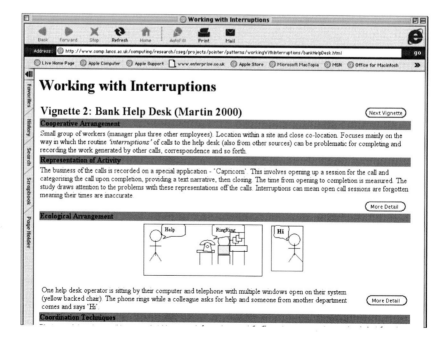

The second study focuses on the work of a software help desk in a bank. Again the concern was with the management between the work required to deal with the interruption and the work it produced. Here, however there was quite a strong focus on the call recording system and the requirement to record calls in various ways.

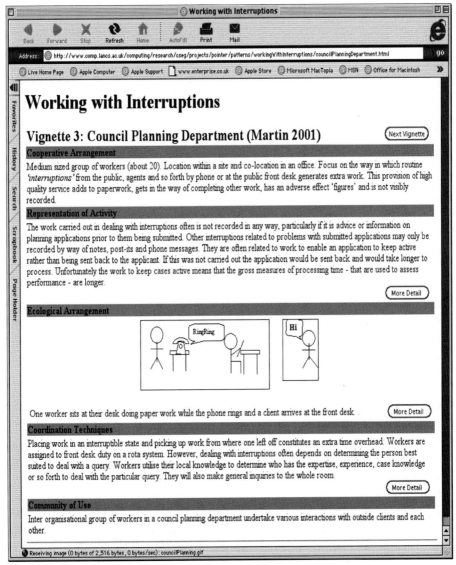

Figure 4. Third vignette for 'Working with interruptions'

The third vignette is derived from a UK local government council planning department. Here there was a contrast between interruptions from an inside source and those that were external. Inside source interruptions were often positive in that they could be negotiated and often were about sharing knowledge and expertise. External interruptions were unpredictable, often inappropriate or directed to wrong staff member but still had to be dealt with.

Taken as a whole the pattern provides design and dependability considerations for such service work settings. For example, designers should concern themselves with the separation or interleaving of other work (e.g. paperwork) with the work of dealing with interruptions - what is interruptible, what needs to be separated, should there be a separation of jobs, or by shift or whatever? Furthermore, it raises questions on the utility of rigorous interruption (call) recording procedures and suggests organizations may gain from screening and filtering interruptions. With this pattern we have tried to provide a flavour of what we are trying to achieve - building up a collection of findings where similar phenomena are grouped together, certain issues and problems are highlighted; providing a useful design resource when encountering a novel situation with similar features.

Pattern: "Accounting for an Unseen Artefact "

Our second example is "Accounting for an Unseen Artefact" (figure 5). Here we only provide the front page for reasons of space. This pattern deals with the now fairly familiar set up where an operator interacts with a system while dealing with a customer or client over the phone. Such a set up is routine in call centre work across various service industries as well as control centre work.

The pattern focuses on the 'role' of the system in the interactions between operator and client, considering the ways in which it guides the interaction, how operators communicate aspects of the system, its informational requirements and so forth. It also details how the caller orients to the system and system use. The two vignettes present contrasting cases. The first provides examples where system use is skillfully embedded within the interaction between operator and caller in telephone banking. It is not that difficulties never occur, but rather that operators employ techniques to orient callers to aspects of the system and its required interactional sequencing such that over repeated contacts callers are seen to configure their talk to achieve business smoothly. Here operators reconcile diverse customer perspectives with the required organizational process. This situation is contrasted with Whalen and colleagues (1998) analysis of a call to a 911 emergency line where the operator is seen to orient more to the requirements of the system to the detriment of managing the business of the call - providing a swift response to a medical emergency. This leads to a tragic outcome as the call is prolonged. By contrasting a dependable socio-technical system with a more problematic arrangement the pattern provokes issues concerning support system design, operator skills and training (e.g. concerning how the system is made accountable (visible and reportable) within interaction) and the need to understand caller characteristics.

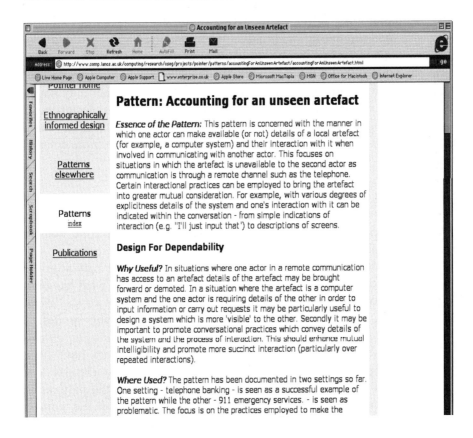

Figure 5. Front page for "Accounting for an unseen artefact"

5. THE PATTERNS COLLECTION: SCENARIOS OF USE

Researchers and practitioners may use our collection of patterns as an aid to understanding socio-technical considerations for dependable design. As such, reading through them should provide a good background understanding of some of the social design issues that arise. In this section, we expand on our remarks about use by providing a scenario to show how patterns might be used in a specific situation of design.

In describing these potential scenarios of use we have envisaged situations where an ethnographer, or socially oriented researcher may not be present. Here, we are thinking more about use by systems designers or requirements engineers. In these cases the patterns, to some extent, serve as a surrogate for not having an ethnographer available to carry out more detailed field studies.

Specific Use: scenarios and reflections

We envisage three possible scenarios of use of the patterns collection for specific design projects by requirements engineers or system designers.

- At the start of a project, the engineer or designer may scan the patterns collection to get an overall impression of what has been important in previous projects and hence what he or she might look out for during the requirements engineering or design process.
- During a project after some observations of work have been made, the engineer or designer may attempt to classify and organize these observations by 'fitting' them to the patterns in the collection. He or she is then prompted by the pattern language for the other relevant information about the situation (the representation of the activity, ecological arrangement, etc) that may be relevant to that situation.
- After a pattern has been discovered and located within the patterns collection, the general pattern information and the vignettes associated with the pattern tell the engineer or designer how the pattern is manifested in other settings and hence provide some clues as to the requirements that might be generated in this case

We will now illustrate the potential for use by engineers and designers with a small scenario that makes use of the *Working with Interruptions* pattern. Consider a situation where we are developing the requirements for a student information system. This system will manage confidential student information, collects information from a range of sources and is used by different users who cooperate synchronously and asynchronously. Many of these users work in public offices and have regular contact with faculty staff and students.

We always recommend that designers visit the setting where the system will be used and let us assume that a short period of observation has shown that interruptions are common. The *Working with Interruptions* pattern is consulted to discover the commonalities with other comparable situations and the questions that should be answered for that specific setting. From the vignettes associated with the pattern, the following questions emerge:

- What is the cooperative arrangement in the setting where the system is used?
- How is the activity represented so that users can 'start where they left off' when an interruption occurs?
- What is the physical arrangement of the office and how does it contribute to supporting the working practice?
- How do different users coordinate their work?
- Who are the users?

The answers to these questions do not generate requirements in themselves but provide an effective starting point for discussions with users and other stakeholders about the system.

Further examination of the patterns reveals that an important issue when dealing with interruptions is often finding the best person to deal with that interruption. This can be difficult when people work in physically separate areas and may generate a system requirement as follows:

- The system shall include a facility that allows users to discover other users who are making use of the system.
- The system shall support a 'query broadcast' facility that allows a user to broadcast a query to all other connected users and to receive responses from them.

While these requirements could be derived by a sensitive analyst, an approach that is simply based on work tasks (that is, the use cases of the system) is likely to miss this type of social requirement that can be identified through the use of patterns.

6. PATTERNS FOR DEPENDABILITY

The notion of organizational cultures of safety or dependability is widely recognised. In such organizations, safety or dependability issues are paramount and the everyday work practices have evolved to ensure that safety and dependability issues are given the highest priority. Our patterns are related to organizational culture in a fairly straightforward manner – they represent (partial) instantiations of organizational culture. Patterns of Cooperative Interaction have components that explicitly deal with these issues of system dependability. Since they are concerned with socio-technical configurations and attendant practices, the emphasis is on system dependability in a broad sense, not merely confined to technical system reliability but to the operation of the system as a whole, involving social and technical 'components' and the interactions between these.

The basic contribution of ethnographic research has been to furnish designers with an in-depth understanding of current socio-technical system operation. It highlights problem areas in socio-technical system operation, particularly in the interface between social and technical 'components'. This understanding helps avoid design errors that may come from considering work abstractly or hypothetically. Patterns orient to dependability in a similar fashion but serve as short-cuts, as examples of dependable operations can be compared against others that do not operate so well. Trade-offs in dependability can be examined by comparing and contrasting vignette examples. In this way the patterns are meant to serve as a resource for thinking about dependability issues in design.

Achieving dependability relies on both formal structures and informal working practices that have evolved in response to specific problems or weaknesses in the procedures or technology. Formal structures may be defined processes for cross-checking work, procedures and rules to be followed, sanctions against errors, etc. Informal practices or 'workarounds' are the everyday coping mechanisms that develop to deal with inadequacies or inconsistencies in the formal structures or the workplace technology. Patterns must consider both formal structures and informal practices, related to ensuring dependability and making issues of dependability visible. As part of the patterns project we have added a section 'Dependability Implications' to the front-page overview of each pattern. In this section we pick up on various aspects of the socio-technical configuration and attendant practices and discuss how they impact on dependable system operation, how they promote or inhibit dependability, and how such dependability might be maintained or altered by changes in the socio-technical configuration. Thus, for example, in the case of pattern 2: *Multiple Representations of Information* we state:

"In a situation, particularly involving a complex, real-time, dynamic task such as handled in a control room it is useful to employ multiple, different, representations of that unfolding task which may be both textual and visual. These can be designed to focus on different aspects of the activity or to present them in different ways.

This provides a resource for managing the different tasks involved in achieving the activity and builds necessary redundancy into the system making it more likely that failures will be spotted early or avoided. When these are made available to a small, collocated group as in the documented settings this allows for the tasks to be solved collaboratively and builds in an extra level of redundancy in the personnel."

Multiple Representations of Information are therefore described as a way to promote collaborative work amongst small groups of personnel in control room type settings. Different views on the same information or problem assist in breaking down complex tasks and facilitate the identification of problems. Items and objects are replicated and can be viewed in different ways – one view may be useful for identifying certain problems while another, other potential failures.

The two specific examples come from control room settings – one from air traffic control (Hughes et al. 1992) and one from ambulance control (Martin et al. 1996). In both settings *Multiple Representations of Information* are presented in such a way as to try and promote dependability. However, in these cases, these (and other measures) do not seem to have been instituted specifically to counteract system failures that have occurred – that personnel, procedures, practices or technology could not be trusted. Rather we have two situations where individual failures can easily take on catastrophic proportions, where the organizational culture that is instantiated is one of high reliability. It is less that the systems are distrusted, more that procedures need to ensure no failures take place, hence the measures designed to provide redundancy, checking, overseeing and so forth.

Pattern 8: *Doing a Walkabout*, illustrates other features of dependability:

"In the consultancy firm doing a walkabout has specific benefits in the achievement of work. For individuals working closely together on a project it facilitates integration of the group, allowing collaboration and the sharing of expertise and knowledge. The small size of the group and the site is important, and notably collaboration with workers at a different site is less and has to be more structured.

In a hospital it is a necessary response to system information that is often not necessarily up to date and accurate for the purposes of the directorate manager. Where possible, design for such activities and collaboration can seek to design office layout and group constituency to facilitate such activities. In considering distributed settings one can consider a number of solutions for technical support of the activities of doing a walkabout. Shared access to computer systems that for example, allow access to other's work, local environment and so forth can be thought of as possible solutions, particularly when supported by different communications technologies. For example, the directorate manager is particularly interested in talking to the ward managers in relation to the public artefacts that are the bed boards (indicate bed allocation status) located in each ward.

Another important component is the face-to-face contact with the ward managers. Therefore any solution might seek to make a version of the bed boards available electronically in distributed locations as a shared application. This might be achieved through video snapshots of the wards and videoconferencing technology or by providing an electronic version of the boards along with some kind of audio communication channel."

With the examples contained in the *Multiple Representations of Information* pattern we can see that dependability is high on the agenda for both the organization and the workforce. Trust seems less of a salient issue here apart from the fact that they need to trust the system such that as close to zero failures occur. *Doing a Walkabout* illustrates how these issues play out differently in other situations.

The pattern is illustrated with examples from a consultancy firm and a directorate manager in a hospital. In the consultancy firm example, we note that the activity of doing a walkabout facilitates various types of *ad hoc* collaboration that is fruitful for the achievement of work. The walkabouts do not seem to make the system more dependable or to promote trust (except through personal bonding). We can contrast this with the walkabout of the directorate manager that is occasioned by a situation in which the bed occupancy figures cannot be trusted. The bed occupancy figures that the hospital directorate manager receives every day are known to be 'approximate' or 'inaccurate within certain limits' yet the fact that they cannot be trusted to be accurate is unproblematic unless they reveal a shortage of beds, in which case the manager needs more precise figures to reveal whether there is a 'real' shortage and if so more accurately what this is, where it is and so forth. The walkabout is specifically occasioned for clarification in specific instances.

In the case of pattern 9: *Overlapping Responsibilities* we state:

"Designing a work organization in settings such as this, where workers in tightly inter-linked roles have overlapping responsibilities, attempts to build in dependability to the socio-technical system. For work design this seeks to promote supervision, redundancy and the ability of the group to respond to various dynamic contingencies within their environment. As with the related pattern, *Career Trajectory through Different Roles*, we may firstly consider how such a work organization design might promote dependability in similar situations. Clearly there may be a concern with designating in which ways responsibilities may overlap, however, the point to note, is that in the situations described here, the demarcation or delineation of these is always an on-going accomplishment. For technical design, the consideration could be one or a number of the following:

Can technology be designed to enhance the monitoring/supervision possibilities created by such work organization? For example, by providing access to other's work, sounding/showing warnings concerning other's tasks.

Can technology be used to provide cooperative opportunities where face-to-face access is not possible? Clearly audio channels already provide links but can we enhance this with other, e.g. CMC technology.

Can technological support be provided for enhancing/facilitating fluidity of roles, group organization, doing two things at once? For example in the naval navigation case, can instruments be accessed remotely and their readings be relayed to the charthouse electronically, allowing easy access to carry out different tasks from one location?

Can technical support be provided to help deal with complexity, ambiguity, failure recovery and so forth that characterises these systems when problems or crises occur, the situations that require more intense cooperation, fluidity of roles and so forth?"

The two studies from which this pattern is drawn are the ambulance control room and a case study of naval navigation (Hutchins, 1991). In both these cases we focus on a workplace design whereby co-workers have responsibilities, job descriptions and skills that overlap. The contention is that such 'formal' organizational design is specifically instituted to promote a more dependable system in safety critical situations.

7. CONCLUSION

"If pattern languages can assist design teams in communicating effectively with their users, noticing connections between activities and artefacts that would have been otherwise missed, or simply decrease the time between encountering a workplace and being able to ask useful questions, they will be a boon to design". (Erickson)

In this chapter we have introduced our collection of Patterns of Cooperative Interaction. These Patterns are derived from ethnomethodologically-informed studies of work and technology and focus on extracting comparable socio-technical configurations and the work practices that exist given those configurations.

Design teams faced with all the usual constraints and contingencies of 'real world, real time' design have pragmatic needs. They need information that can be mastered quickly, applied to new situations, and used as a basis for creating a dialogue with their users. We believe that patterns provide some of the information that design teams need if they are to take a socio-technical and not merely a technical perspective on complex systems.

Our patterns are designed for a multidisciplinary design audience, provide concrete instances of socio-technical systems in use and are intended to facilitate communication and generalization across settings. As Erickson notes, the modularization of workplace knowledge instantiated in patterns, makes it easier to apply to new domains. They serve as a resource for analysis and design that focus on social aspects of design. They can act as intermediary tools for a variety of practitioners to bridge the gap between 'rich descriptions' of current work practice and the design considerations that may arise from them. We have provided a number of examples that seek to demonstrate how these descriptive Patterns may be used in a generative fashion – to think about various design considerations in new settings and how they may be used to generate considerations for dependable design.

ACKNOWLEDGEMENTS

This research was supported by the UK Engineering and Physical Sciences Research Council: Dependability Interdisciplinary Research Collaboration (DIRC), grant no. GR/N13999/01 and Patterns of Interaction project, grant no. GR/M54650. Thanks to all the attendants of the patterns workshop held at Lancaster on 11th June 2002.

REFERENCES

1.   Alexander, C., Ishikawa, S., Silverstein, M., Jacobson, M., Fiksdahl-King I., Angel, S. (1977). A Pattern Language. New York: Oxford University Press.
2.   Alexander, C.(1979). The Timeless Way Of Building. New York: Oxford University Press.

3. Anderson, R., Hughes, J., and Sharrock, W. (1989). Working for profit; The Social Organization of Calculation in an Entrepreneurial Firm. Aldershot: Avebury.

4. Belloti, V. and Bly, S. (1996) Walking Away from the Desktop Computer: Distributed Collaboration in a Product Design Team. In Proceedings of CSCW'96.

5. Bentley, R., Hughes, J., Randall, D., Rodden, T., Sawyer, P., Shapiro, D., Sommerville, I. (1992). Ethnographically-Informed Systems Design for Air Traffic Control. Proceedings of ACM CSCW'92 Conference on Computer-Supported Cooperative Work. pp.123-129, © Copyright 1992 Association for Computing Machinery.

6. Brighton Usability Pattern Collection   http://www.cmis.brighton.ac.uk/research/patterns/home.html

7. Button, G., Dourish, P. (1996) Technomethodology: Paradoxes and Possibilities. In Proceedings of ACM CHI 96 Conference on Human Factors in Computing Systems 1996, v.1, pp.19-26 © Copyright 1996 ACM.

8. Cooper, J.W. (2000). Java Design Patterns. Longman.

9. Crabtree, A., Nichols, D. M., O'Brien, J., Rouncefield, M. And. Twidale, M. B. (2000) Ethnomethodologically-Informed Ethnography and Information System Design. In Journal of the American Society for Information Science, 51(7), pp.666-682.

10. Crabtree, A., Hemmings, T. And Rodden, T. (2002). Pattern-based support for interactive design in domestic settings. Proceedings of the 2002 Symposium on Designing Interactive Systems. London: ACM Press.

11. Erickson T. (2000a) "Supporting interdisciplinary design: towards pattern languages for workplaces", ' In Luff, P., Hindmarsh, J. and Heath, Christian. (eds) Workplace Studies: Recovering Work Practice and Informing System Design. Cambridge, CUP.

12. Erickson, T. (2000b) "Lingua Francas for design: sacred places and pattern languages". In proceedings of Designing interactive systems: processes, practices, methods, and techniques August 17 - 19, 2000, Brooklyn, NY United States, pp. 357-368.

13. Gamma, E., Helm, R., Johnson, R. & Vlissides, J. (1995). "Design Patterns: Elements of Reusable Object-Oriented Software." Reading, MA: Addison-Wesley.

14. Garfinkel, H., (1967) Studies in ethnomethodology. Englewood Cliffs, N.J.: Prentice-Hall

15. Gibson, J. J. (1979). The ecological approach to visual perception. Boston, Houghton Mifflin.

16. Grudin, J. (1990). The Computer Reaches Out: The Historical Continuity of Interface Design. In proceedings of ACM Conference on Human Factors in Computing Systems. CHI'90: Seattle, Wv.1, pp.19-26 © Copyright 1996 ACM.

17. Hughes, J., Randall, D., Shapiro, D. (1992). Faltering from ethnography to design. Proceedings of ACM CSCW '92, Conference on Computer-Supported Cooperative Work, pp. 115-122. © Copyright 1992 ACM.

18. Hughes, J., King, V., Rodden, T., Andersen, H. (1994). Moving Out from the Control Room: Ethnography in System Design. Proceedings of ACM CSCW '94, Conference on Computer-Supported Cooperative Work, pp. 429-439. © Copyright 1994 ACM.

19. Hughes, J., O'Brien, J., Rodden, T., Sommerville, I. (1995). Presenting Ethnography in the Requirements Process. Proceedings of RE '95. IEEE Press.

20. Hughes, J., O'Brien, J., Rodden, J., Rouncefield, M., Blythin, S., (1997a) Designing with Ethnography: A Presentation Framework for Design. Proceedings of DIS'97: Designing Interactive Systems: Processes, Practices, Methods, & Techniques 1997, pp.147-158 © Copyright 1997 ACM.

21. Hughes, J., O'Brien, J., Rodden, T. And Rouncefield, M. (1997b). Ethnography, Communication and Support for Design. CSEG Technical Report Ref: CSEG/24/1997.
22. http://www.comp.lancs.ac.uk/computing/research/cseg/97_rep.html
23. Luff, P., Hindmarsh, J. and Heath, C. C. (eds.) (2000) Workplace Studies: Recovering work practice and informing system design. Cambridge: Cambridge University Press.
24. Mackenzie, A., Monk, S. & Lewis, P. (2002). From cards to code: how Extreme Programming re-embodies programming as a collective practice. In…
25. Martin, D., Bowers, J., Wastell, D. (1997) The Interactional Affordances of Technology: An Ethnography of Human-Computer Interaction in an Ambulance Control Centre. Proceedings of the HCI'97 Conference on People and Computers XII 1997, pp.263-281.
26. Martin, D., Wastell, D., Bowers, J. (1998). Ethnographically Informed Systems Design: The development and evaluation of an Internet-based electronic banking application. In Proceedings of ECIS '98.
27. Martin, D., Rodden, T., Rouncefield, M., Sommerville, I And Viller, S. (2001) Finding Pattern in the Fieldwork. In Proceedings of ECSCW '01.
28. Martin, D., Rouncefield, M. And Somerville, I. (2002). Applying Patterns of Cooperative Interaction to Work (Re)Design: E-government and planning. In Proceedings of CHI 2002. Minneapolis, Minnesota. © ACM press.
29. Reddy, M. And Dourish, P. (2002). A Finger on the Pulse: Temporal Rhythms amd Information Seeking In Medical Work. In Proceedings of CSCW 2002. New Orleans, Louisiana. © ACM press.
30. Rouncefield, M., Hughes, J., Rodden, T., Viller, S. (1994). Working with "Constant Interruption": Proceedings of ACM CSCW'94 Conference on Computer-Supported Cooperative Work. pp.275-286 © Copyright 1994 Association for Computing Machinery.
31. Rouncefield, M., Hughes, J., O'Brien, J. (1997). Ethnography: Some Practicalities of Ethnographic Analysis. CSEG Technical Report Ref: CSEG/27/1997.
32. http://www.comp.lancs.ac.uk/computing/research/cseg/97_rep.html
33. Sacks, H., Shegloff, E. And Jefferson, G. (1974). A Simplest Systematics for the Organization of Turn Taking for Conversation. Language, 50, 4, pp. 696-735.
34. Sharrock, W. And Anderson, R. (1992). Can organizations afford knowledge? Computer Supported Cooperative Work, 1, 143-162.
35. Sommerville, I., Rodden, T., Sawyer, P., Twidale, M., Bentley, R. (1993). Incorporating Ethnographic Data into the Systems Design Process. In Proceedings of RE 93: International Symposium on Requirements Engineering, January 4-6, San Diego, IEEE Press: 165-174.
36. Tolmie, P., Pycock, J., Diggins, T., Maclean, A. And Karsenty, A. (2002). Unremarkable Computing. In Proceedings of CHI 2002. Minneapolis, Minnesota. © ACM press.
37. Viller, S. And Sommerville, I. (1999). Coherence: an Approach to Representing Ethnographic Analyses in Systems Design. Human-Computer Interaction 14: 9-41
38. Whalen, J., Zimmermann, D., Whalen, M. (1988). When Words Fail: A Single Case Analysis. Social Problems. Vol. 35, 4, pp. 335-363.

---

[16] Now that our collection is of a reasonable size we are keen for our resource to be more widely used and contributed to. As part of this we have cloned the main website onto wiki web pages http://polo.lancs.ac.uk/patterns)

Chapter 8

DEPENDABILITY AND TRUST IN ORGANISATIONAL AND DOMESTIC COMPUTER SYSTEMS

Ian Sommerville, Guy Dewsbury, Karen Clarke, Mark Rouncefield
Department of Computing, University of Lancaster

1. INTRODUCTION: DEPENDABILITY AND DOMESTIC SYSTEMS

Our economy and national infrastructures are dependent on a range of socio-technical systems and, by and large, these systems can be trusted to provide a dependable service. For example, electricity and telecommunication systems are generally reliable, the bank ATM network can usually deliver cash to authorised customers and automated stock control systems have meant that large stores and supermarkets rarely run out of specific products.

In essence, at least in Western societies, the vast majority of people trust the services that are provided through the physical and economic infrastructure. This trust is engendered because these services almost always meet the expectations of their external users. In order to meet these expectations, complex socio-technical systems have to be put in place by the service providers and these now, universally, rely on computer-based information systems. These information systems are essential elements of the socio-technical systems so both the organizations running these systems and the system users depend on them.

The information systems that support the socio-technical systems that run the national and business infrastructure have two important characteristics:

K. Clarke, G. Hardstone, M. Rouncefield and I. Sommerville (eds.), Trust in Technology:
A Socio-Technical Perspective, 169–193.
© 2006 *Springer. Printed in the Netherlands.*

- They are situated in organisations (banks, telephone companies, electricity generators) that have a history of service provision and that have well-established processes for managing the delivery of these services. External users of organisational systems trust these organisations to use their best endeavours to ensure that their computer systems deliver correct information. Furthermore, it can be assumed that the people in these organisations follow the defined operational processes when it is appropriate to do so and react in a contingent way when they are faced with exceptional situations not covered by these processes.

- They are essential for the effective provision of organisational services and the people within the organisation who are involved in the process do not have the authority to decide whether or not the automated systems should be used. It can be assumed that the operators have received some training in the use of the software and also that, whatever the flaws in the software system, they do not have the discretion to simply discard that system and replace it with an alternative.

Organizational systems are designed for a specific purpose, support known and defined processes and their use is controlled by the organization. In this context, when we consider the issue of what is meant by a 'trusted' computer system, we argue that a technical view of trust is appropriate. A system is trusted if it correctly provides the services that it has been designed to deliver and is available for service when required. Because both the operators and the computer system are within the organization then issues such as the provenance of the system are disregarded in assessing its trustworthiness. Furthermore, as far as external users of the system are concerned, their access is mediated by a human operator so there is no direct trust relationship between the external user and the computer system.

Therefore, for systems that have a clear role in organizational socio-technical processes, the primary trust relationship is between the operator and the computer system and the dominant factor in that trust is the *dependability* of the system. We discuss the notion of dependability in the following section but, essentially, you can think of it as an amalgam of other system properties such as system availability, security, reliability, etc.

More broadly, however, when we consider socio-technical systems that are not entirely situated within an organization then trust is, of course, far more than a technical issue. It reflects the user's confidence that the system will do what they want (whether or not this has been specified by the system designers) and that it will not cause damage that results in losses of time, information, money, etc. to the user.

The degree of trust that an external user has in a system depends on factors such as previous experience with comparable systems, the provider's reputation, the existence of external sanctions on the system provider if they fail to deliver services and the price paid. It also reflects the degree of risk taken by the user in that people are more willing to trust a system where the exposure to loss is relatively low and legal factors such as the existence of regulators and compensation bodies.

We see examples of this when organizational systems are Internet-enabled for external users. People have few problems trusting information-giving systems such as timetables and catalogues (low risk) but are more wary of systems where there is potential financial loss. Many people are still reluctant to use Internet banking, even although the technological safeguards are, if anything, stronger than in traditional banking systems. It is noticeable that many new entrants to banking enabled by the Internet have not been successful. Rather, users have preferred known banks because of their reputation. Here trust is clearly engendered by a known brand rather than any technical characteristics of the bank's information systems.

In this chapter, we will not be concerned with these broader issues of trust but, rather, will focus on trust from a technical perspective. However, we will argue that, for systems where the use of defined operational processes cannot be guaranteed or where users can choose whether or not to use the system, there is a need to extend the technical view of dependability to cover broader issues of fitness for purpose and adaptability as well as more traditional properties such as system reliability and availability.

The remainder of the chapter therefore includes four principal sections. Firstly, we discuss the currently accepted technical model of system dependability as applied to organizational systems. We then go on to critique this model and propose a broader model of system dependability that incorporates this model but which extends it to be applicable to domestic and discretionary systems - workplace systems where users have a choice whether or not to make use of them. Finally, we propose ways in which this model may be used in the design process for domestic and discretionary systems.

2. DEPENDABILITY – A TECHNICAL PERSPECTIVE

Dependability is defined as that property of a computer system such that reliance can justifiably be placed on the service it delivers. The service delivered by a system is its behaviour as it is perceptible by its user(s); a user is another system (human or physical) which interacts with the former[1].

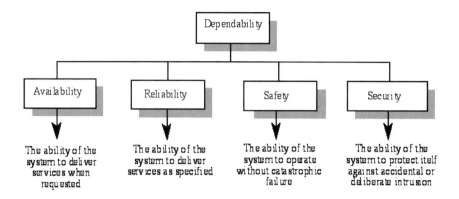

Figure 1: Dependability attributes

The dependability of a computer system is a property of the system that equates to its trustworthiness. Trustworthiness essentially means the degree of user confidence that the system will operate as they expect and that the system will not 'fail' in normal use. A trustworthy system has the potential to be trusted by a user although other factors such as previous experience and the provenance of the system influence whether or not users actually trust the system. As discussed in the introduction, we believe that dependability is by far the dominant factor in influencing whether or not organizational systems are trusted by their users.

Dependability is not a simple, measurable system property but, rather, is a complex property that reflects the fact that simpler properties are inextricably intertwined; it rarely makes sense to consider them in isolation. Figure 1 [2] shows the principal properties that contribute to system dependability:

1. *Availability* The availability of a system is the probability that it will be up and running and able to deliver useful services at any given time.

2. *Reliability* The reliability of a system is the probability, over a given period of time, that the system will correctly deliver services as expected by the user.

3. *Safety* The safety of a system is a judgement of how likely it is that the system will cause damage to people or its environment.

4. *Security* The security of a system is a judgement of how likely it is that the system can resist accidental or deliberate intrusion*s*.

These properties themselves can be decomposed into simpler system properties. For example, security includes integrity (ensuring that the systems program and data are not damaged) and confidentiality (ensuring that information can only be accessed by people who are authorised).

Reliability includes correctness (ensuring the system services are as specified), precision (ensuring information is delivered at an appropriate level of detail) and timeliness (ensuring that information is delivered at the time when it is required).

The principal dependability properties of availability, security, reliability and safety are clearly inter-related. For example, the safe operation of a system usually depends on availability (is the system up and running) and reliability (is the system delivering services as specified). A system may become unavailable because security failings allow external denial of service attacks. If a system that has been demonstrated to be safe is infected with a virus then the system itself has been corrupted; safe operation can no longer be assumed.

As well as these 4 principal dimensions of dependability, other system properties are also sometimes considered under the heading of dependability. These include:

1. *Repairability* System failures are inevitable but the disruption caused by failure can be minimised if the system can be repaired as quickly as possible. If a system is to be repairable, it must be possible to diagnose the problem, access the component that has failed and make changes to fix that component.

2. *Maintainability* As systems are used, new requirements emerge and it is important to maintain the usefulness of a system by changing it to accommodate these new requirements. Maintainable software is software that can be adapted economically to cope with new requirements and where there is a low probability that making changes will introduce new errors into the system.

3. *Survivability* A very important attribute for Internet-based systems is survivability which is closely related to security and availability [3]. Survivability is the ability of a system to continue to deliver service whilst it is under attack and, potentially, while part of the system is disabled.

4. *Error tolerance* This property could be considered as part of usability and reflects the extent to which the system has been designed so that user input error are avoided and tolerated. When user errors occur, the system should, as far as possible, detect these errors and either fix them automatically or request the user to re-input their data

The type of system and its context of use determine which of these dependability properties are most important. For a system controlling a car engine (say), safety and reliability considerations are significant but security is less important because there is no external access to this system. For an e-commerce system, availability and security are usually the most important properties.

Laprie, a leading researcher in system dependability, proposes that, for critical systems used in organizations, the key dependability properties are availability, reliability, safety, confidentiality, integrity and maintainability [1]. He relates these to the system behaviour as seen by an external system user:

"the readiness for usage leads to availability, the continuity of service leads to reliability, the non-occurrence of catastrophic consequences on the environment leads to safety, the non-occurrence of unauthorized disclosure of information leads to confidentiality, the non-occurrence of improper alterations of information leads to integrity, the ability to undergo repairs and evolutions leads to maintainability."

These dependability attributes are one component of Laprie's dependability tree where, as well as dependability attributes, he identifies the means to achieve dependability and the impairments to dependability. This dependability tree is shown in Figure 2.

Randell [4] expands on Laprie's notions of means and impairments in a discussion of faults, errors and failures. Essentially, these terms can be defined as:

Faults. A fault is deemed to be the cause of an error in a system. For example, if a variable in a program has been wrongly set up (say as 1 rather than 0) then this is a fault. Faults, however, need not manifest themselves every time that a program executes – indeed, they may never manifest themselves as, in many programs, sections of code are included to cope with situations that never arise.

1. *Errors*. An error is defined to be an unexpected or unwanted system state. That is, using the above example, when the faulty statement is executed then a part of the system state has a value of 1 rather than the expected value of 0. The fault is the latent condition; the error is its manifestation when the system is in operation.

2. *Failures*. A failure is an external manifestation of an error when some system service behaves in an unexpected way. For example, if the service is to add numbers input by the user but the initial value of the sum is 1 rather than 0 then the final result will be incorrect.

Laprie and Randell have focused on the dependability of critical control and protection systems in their work. Consequently, their views on dependability are influenced the nature of these systems. Their definitions of impairments to dependability embed a number of assumptions:

1. That system failures (defined by Laprie as a deviation from fulfilling the system function) can be recognised when they occur. In a control system, this might be because sensors indicate that a controlled variable is changing in an unexpected way or, sometimes, systems simply terminate execution unexpectedly.

2. That errors (defined by Laprie as 'that part of the system state which is liable to lead to a subsequent failure') can be detected by an external observer who has access to information about the system. For example, system logs may show that a program variable has an unexpected value of −10 rather than +10.

3. That errors arise inevitably from faults (the hypothesised cause of an error). For example, a system fault may be the omission of code to check that an operator input is not negative. Faults in programs are assumed to arise because there has been a failure in the development system. For example, the software testing process may never have checked the system's response to incorrect operator inputs.

Randell proposes that this technical fault-error-failure model of dependability can be applied to the development system for software as well as to the software itself. This leads to a conceptually attractive failure-fault dependency in different systems as shown in Figure 3. Failures in one system inevitably lead to faults in another system that may then manifest themselves as failures.

However, while the failure-fault cascade is certainly valid within computer systems where a failure in a sub-system can lead to a fault in an encompassing system, we are unconvinced that it applies equally to socio-technical systems, such as systems used for software development. The scheme shown in Figure 3 is conceptually attractive but we believe that the reasons why faults are introduced into software systems are more complex than the model implies. We return to this discussion in the following section.

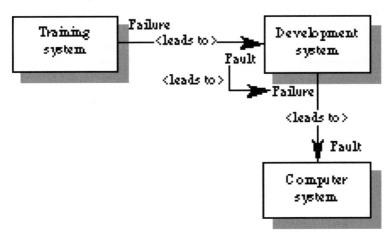

Figure 2. System dependencies

Finally, from Laprie's dependability tree, the means are the ways in which the developers of a computer system can achieve dependability. These are:

- Fault prevention – ensuring that faults are not introduced into a system.
- Fault tolerance – designing the system in such a way that it can continue in operation in spite of the occurrence of faults.
- Fault removal – reducing the number or the seriousness of faults before the system is deployed.
- Fault forecasting – estimating the number, incidence and consequences of faults.

Fault prevention can be achieved through the use of development techniques and tools that identify potential faults at an early stage in the development process or, more simply, by excluding approaches to development that are known to be likely to lead to faults. For example, modern programming languages such as Java do not allow the use of pointers – a programming construct that is notoriously error-prone. Consequently, a large class of faults resulting from mis-oriented pointers simply cannot occur.

Fault tolerance can be achieved in programs by making use of diversity and redundancy. An approach that is used in some critical systems (such as the flight control system in some models of the Airbus aircraft) is based on multi-version programming where several versions of critical systems components are developed by different teams [5-7]. There is an assumption made that the teams are unlikely to make the same mistakes. A checking mechanism is embedded in the system and if a component appears to be producing results that differ from other functionally identical components then it is switched out of the system.

In practice, shared cultural and educational backgrounds as well as problems with clarity of specification means that the practical benefits from this approach are less than theoretically predicted [8]. However, there is no doubt that it does lead to a significant increase in software system reliability.

Fault removal is essentially a development strategy where the goal is to identify faults that have been introduced into the system and then change the system to remove these faults. Different techniques are used to achieve this from very comprehensive system testing through to mathematical proof that a program meets its specification. For most large, complex computer-based systems, fault detection and removal is the most time-consuming and expensive part of the development process.

Fault forecasting does not, in itself, help achieve dependability but helps us make judgments of whether or not the system is sufficiently dependable. Examples of fault forecasting techniques include fault seeding and system reliability modeling[9] [10]. It is essentially impossible to achieve a system that is completely fault-free and pragmatic considerations mean that systems are usually delivered with known (and unknown) faults. Fault forecasting allows the organizations developing and using the system to make judgments about when the risks of failure resulting faults that have not been identified or repaired are acceptable.

3. DEPENDABILITY - A HUMAN PERSPECTIVE

In technical models of dependability, such as the Laprie/Randell model, humans are considered to be system elements that can be treated in the same way as other software or hardware elements. In his paper, Laprie recognises the importance of human operators but discusses them in terms of 'interaction faults' resulting from 'human errors'. Failures on the part of humans in the operational system lead to these interaction faults which result in unexpected computer system state and hence computer system failures. Similarly, as suggested by Figure 3, failures in the development system as a result of human errors lead to the introduction of faults in the operational system.

Human 'errors' and the relationships between these errors and system failures have been extensively discussed by authors such as Reason [11]and Rasmussen [12]. Rasmussen discusses different types of human errors such as skill-based, rule-based and knowledge-based errors and Reason, in his 'Swiss Cheese Model' relates human error to system failure. He suggests that human errors lead to system failures when they bypass the checks and protection built into a system. Researchers in human psychology argue that so-called 'human errors' [13, 14] arise because the systems designers did not consider the practicalities of system operation in their design. Although we do not discuss dependability from the perspective of human error here, this body of work suggests that failures resulting from human errors have complex causes and should not be considered in the same way as failures deriving from faults in hardware or software components.

If we consider broader socio-technical systems and apply the technical dependability model to the people in these systems, it is our contention that the fault-error-failure model breaks down. Recall that failures are unexpected behaviour, errors are undesirable system states and faults are the causes of an error. The basic problem arises because, for people, the notions of fault, error and failure are inapplicable:

Failure recognition People are not automata and they use their intelligence to discover many different ways of doing the same thing. An action that might be interpreted as a failure for one person (such as an air traffic controller placing aircraft on a collision course) might be part of a dependable operational process for another (the ATC may have a reliable method of ensuring that they will move one of the aircraft before any danger ensues[17]). Clearly the failure is   recognised when the near miss occurs but how much earlier could it have been recognised? Was the failure placing the aircraft on a collision course or failing to subsequently separate the aircraft?

Error identification. How can we tell if an unwanted state has resulted in the failure? The notion of explicit state is one that is particular to computer systems and is difficult to apply outside these systems. For example, we cannot monitor our brains to identify the erroneous state that has arisen nor can we keep records of how a set of thought processes led to some action being taken.

Fault recognition. What was the fault that resulted in the human error? Was it a training fault or something more fundamental? People are not deterministic and their emotional and physical state profoundly affects their behaviour. The notion that failures in the development process lead to faults in the 'system' clearly doesn't apply to people. The development process for people from conception (fusing of genetic histories) through nurture to education and training is so extended and complex that identifying the 'fault' that resulted in a consequent failure is impossible.

For some classes of highly automated system, where operational processes and tightly defined and operators are highly trained, then the benefits of adopting a consistent view of dependability that encompasses both people and computers may outweigh the disadvantages of treating the

CRITERIA	HOME CONTEXT	ORGANISATIONAL CONTEXT
USAGE	Ad Hoc Uncontrolled	Systematically Controlled
STANDARDISATION	Legislative and Product Specific	Standardised with Organisational Environment
PROCESSES	Uncontrolled and Ad Hoc	Controlled and Systematic
OPERATORS	Untrained and Unskilled	Training Available
OPERATIONS	Unrestricted and Ad Hoc	Restricted and Systematised
ACTIONS AND ACTIVITIES	Undefined and Uncontrolled	Predefined and Limited
SAFETY	Suggested but Difficult to Enforce	Controlled through Systems

Table 1: Home and Organisational Differences

[17] In studies of air traffic controllers, we actually observed this control strategy.

human operators in a simplistic way. However, within organizations, there are many systems that are discretionary whose use is not constrained by organizational processes and where users do not face sanctions if these are not used. For those systems, the notion of what is mean by a human 'error' or 'failure' is more difficult. If a user does not read a system user guide and hence makes an input error is that a human failure? Or, is this a system failure because the designers have made invalid assumptions about the reality of system use?

Of course, the ultimate discretionary systems are those that we have in our homes. For those systems, there are no organizational constraints – we are free to do what we wish with systems and to discard them if we are unhappy with them. We believe that the simple technical model of dependability as discussed in the previous section does not apply to domestic and discretionary systems. Our work on extending this model to domestic systems and the lessons learned for system dependability and trust is the topic of the remainder of this chapter.

4. DOMESTIC SYSTEMS DEPENDABILITY

For domestic systems, the users of the system are central to the design and central to the consideration of dependability. In the home, people do not follow defined operational processes, system users may vary widely and within the same home there may be both techno-phobes and techno-philes. The dependability of home systems is played out daily through the routines and situated actions of the people in the home. Therefore, we contend that the requirements of dependability in the home setting are derived from different roots from traditional dependability models of software design. To achieve dependability, we must take an approach that integrates the user and environment with the technology rather than considering dependability as a property of the technology alone.

In contrast to organizations where technologies and processes are limited, within the home people can choose whether or not to use technology, how to use it and where they wish to use it. People do not read instruction manuals, are not trained in the use of domestic technologies and the use of these technologies often depends on their previous technology experience. For example, on early video recorders the process of setting up a timed recording was difficult and error-prone. Although this has been much improved on modern machines, a large number of people simply do not use pre-recording because their previous experience was that it was beyond their capabilities.

In organizations, activities tend to be set in regular procedures, such that work begins at prescribed times. The organizational system has regular processes through which activities must follow. Dependable operation may rely on this timing. For example, in a hospital, a surgeon in a hospital can usually assume that appropriate pre-operative procedures have been carried out. A significant difference between the organizational system and the home system is that processes and timing are far more flexible and adaptive in the home. Home routines are often unplanned and lacking rigid structure, although foreseen events, such as children's music lessons, may be planned and approximately situated into a daily/weekly/monthly schedule.

Table 1 outlines some of the differences between technology use in organizations and the home environments. Clearly, this is a generalization and the criteria are not applicable to *all* organizations or *all* homes. However, it essentially summarises what we see as the key differences between these settings, namely the uncontrolled nature of the home.

The overall dependability of an organizational socio-technical system that includes a computer-based system is derived from the dependability of the computer system and how it is used. The controlled nature of the organizational environment means that usage of a computer-based system can be controlled and mandated.

In the home, however, the dependability of the socio-technical system, that is the user plus the technology, depends primarily on how (if at all) the user *chooses* to use that technology. For example, if an elderly person is offered a communication aid that they cannot fit into a pocket of their normal clothing, they may choose not to carry that aid. Therefore, the availability of the communication aid system is limited because the user can't always carry it around. The communication aid itself may be dependable, but the overall *system* of helping with communication is not.

The dependability of systems extends beyond the hardware and software into the social and lived experience of the home dweller. As Lupton and Seymour [15] suggest, technology becomes part of the self-concept for the user and therefore it is essential that dependability does not just mean that a system behaves according to the expectations of its designers. Systems therefore have to be designed so that they are *acceptable* to users and so that they can use them for their intended purpose. We should not underestimate the difficulty of this design problem in domestic settings.

A dependability model for domestic systems

It is our contention that the techno-centric model of dependability that is exemplified by Laprie's dependability tree needs to be developed and extended for it to be applicable to domestic computer-based systems. We have proposed an augmented model that is based on a number of field studies of people in their homes [16]. Our work, in fact, has focused on a specific type of domestic system namely assistive technology systems for the elderly. However, we believe that it has more general applicability to any type of computer-based system that is used in the home to deliver what the people in that home consider to be important services.

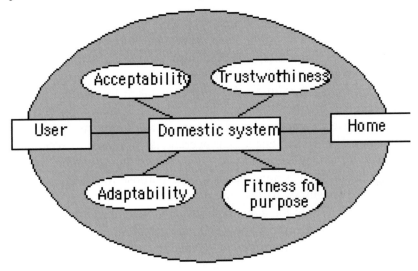

Figure 3. Dependability attributes of a situated AT system

Fundamentally, techno-centric dependability models exclude the user and the user's environment from considerations of what dependability means. These models assume that the system will actually be used as intended by its designers. The technical model of dependability can consider a system that meets its specification to be dependable, even if it is practically useless and never used. We generally reject this view (not just for domestic but for all systems) and believe that we should not just be concerned with dependability *in* use but also dependability *of* use. By this, we mean that it is not enough for a system to be dependable in that it meets its specification and operates according to that specification. The system must also be accepted by its users and used for its designed purpose. Dependability, therefore, is not just a technological consideration but also a holistic notion that applies to the technology and its practical use.

For domestic systems, we need to consider the dependability of the socio-technical system as a whole including the user, the home environment and the installed technology. We propose that the dependability characteristics of domestic systems should be considered under 4 headings as shown in Figure 4:

- *Trustworthiness* The trustworthiness of a system reflects whether or not the system will behave as intended by its designers and as expected by its users. We consider this attribute to be the equivalent of 'dependability' in Laprie's model. That is, it includes the traditional dependability attributes of availability, reliability, etc. However, we suggest below that these may need to be re-interpreted to take into account the specific characteristics of domestic systems.

- *Acceptability* The acceptability of a system reflects whether or not that system fits in with the user's everyday life and environment. We argue that a system that cannot be integrated with normal activities will not be accepted and so will not be used. Therefore, it is essential that system characteristics that affect its acceptability such as the system learnability and aesthetics are considered in the design process.

- *Fitness for purpose* Fitness for purpose is taken for granted in most of the dependability literature but, socio-technical system failures regularly arise because a computer-based system does not meet user requirements so that users have had adapt their operational processes to accommodate the system's inadequacies [17, 18]. When the use of a system is discretionary, then it must be fit for the purpose intended by its users; otherwise they simply will not use it.

- *Adaptability* Within the home both the environment and the user's of the systems change. People's knowledge and capabilities change over time. This is particularly true for elderly people whose vision, hearing and memory tend to decline as they age. Therefore, if system dependability of not to degrade, then it must be able to evolve over time, generally without interventions from the system's designers.

Now let us examine each of these characteristics in more detail to assess what they might mean for domestic, computer-based systems.

Trustworthiness

In the context of domestic systems, we consider the trustworthiness of a system to correspond to the technical notion of dependability as defined by Laprie. That is, the trustworthiness reflects the systems availability, reliability, safety, confidentiality, integrity and maintainability. However, the nature of home systems as assemblies of relatively cheap, off-the-shelf components, the fact that home users are not systematically trained in the use of these systems and the nature of the home itself means that these dependability characteristics have to be re-interpreted for domestic systems:

Availability and reliability

As far as availability and reliability are concerned, we need to consider two classes of domestic system namely critical and non-critical systems. Critical systems are those that supply a critical services such as some assistive technology systems that help elderly or disabled people or control systems for power, external security, etc. Non-critical systems are systems such as entertainment systems where failure is inconvenient but does not pose any real threat to people in the home.

For critical systems, availability and reliability are critical attributes. An elderly or disabled person's quality of life may be dependent on their assistive technologies and failure of these systems has severe implications for them. For non-critical systems, availability and reliability are perhaps more critical for the system vendor rather than the system user. Failures of these systems can mean that buyers will reject that company's products in future.

However, domestic technology system designers are faced with a challenging problem when trying to build systems by with high-levels of availability and reliability. Systems are mostly composed of off-the-shelf devices where the system designer has no control over the engineering of these devices. For example, consider a situation where a system is to be installed to allow a disabled person to see visitors, communicate with them by voice and to automatically unlock the door if they are to be allowed in. A domestic television is to be used as the display device. This system may involve integrating a set-top box on the television with an external video camera, a voice system and an electronically controlled door lock. These are provided by different vendors and the failure of any one of these components can result in overall system failure.

Cost is often the dominant factor in manufacturing domestic systems so lower quality standards may be applied to systems components and external interfaces may not be provided. Typically, hardly any information may be available about device reliability so designers must trust manufacturer specifications, which, in our experience, are often optimistic.

Safety

Clearly safety is a very important factor in domestic systems and home technology must pass rigorous standards for electrical safety. However, few products can dictate how they should or should not be used in a domestic setting. A large number of domestic accidents result from inappropriate use of equipment. For example, accidents have occurred because people try to use a hairdryer while they are taking a bath, because they try to clean equipment while it is switched on, etc. The critical factor in home safety is rarely the equipment itself but how it is actually used.

Given that most domestic systems are low power systems that conform to electrical safety standards, we consider that the risks of injury associated with failures in computer-based home systems are relatively low. This does not mean, of course, that we should install unsafe systems – however, it does suggest that it is not worth incurring very high costs in activities such as detailed product safety analysis. Rather, it may be more productive to think about 'design for misuse' and try to design these systems so that potentially unsafe ways of using them are made as difficult as possible.

Confidentiality and integrity

If a system is to be dependable, a user must be able to trust that system to keep personal information confidential and to ensure that the information is not lost or corrupted. This is equally true for organizational or domestic systems. While the need for integrity goes without saying, the issue of confidentiality is much more difficult in situations where elderly or disabled people depend on monitoring technology that alerts relatives and carers when a problem arises. These users often value their privacy and wish to maintain the confidentiality of their personal information. On the other hand, this may compromise the safety of the overall system as it may limit the speed and type of response in the event of a problem. The level of confidentiality in a system therefore cannot be fixed but has to be programmable and responsive to an analysis of the events being processed by the system.

Maintainability

Maintainability is the ability of a system to undergo evolution with the corollary that the system should be designed so that evolution is not likely to introduce new faults into the system. We distinguish here between maintainability as the process of making unanticipated engineering changes to the system and adaptability, which is the process of changing a system to configure it for its environment of use. It is now the case that the low-cost of much domestic equipment means that that replacement rather than maintenance is the norm so software and hardware changes and upgrades are unlikely. Therefore, we consider maintainability under the adaptability attributes that we discuss later.

Acceptability

Acceptability reflects whether or not a domestic system fits in with the user's abilities, personal preferences, environment and routines of everyday life. The notion of acceptability was initially conveyed through an advocate of Universal Design (UD), an approach to design that advocates that designers should design for all ages and skills. Sandhu [19] presents a diagrammatic representation of system acceptability within a Universal Design context (Figure 5). Systems that are not acceptable to users will simply be discarded even in situations where their functionality is clearly of some value.

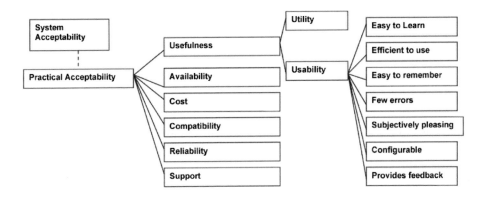

Figure 4. Sandhu's system acceptability model

Sandhu's diagram illustrates that for systems to meet his Universal Design criteria there are a considerable number of attributes and properties that the system and designer must address that are comparable to those derived by software engineers considering dependability. The model that Sandhu proposes situates the user and the product within the same contextual model so reflects our views on the central significance of the user when considering system dependability.

Our view of acceptability takes a simplified view of Sandhu's model as we consider some of his acceptability characteristics such as reliability, availability and configurability under other headings such as trustworthiness. Essentially, we consider that a system will only be acceptable if the user feels that the benefits that accrue from the system justify the costs and effort of buying, installing, learning to use and using the system. We therefore consider the principal acceptability characteristics to be:

- *Usability* It must be possible to use the system on a regular basis without error and without having to re-learn how to benefit from the system. This suggests that user interfaces should be intuitive and should not be based on modes or complex sequences of actions.
- *Learnability* It should be possible to learn to use the system relatively easily with no steep learning curve before any benefits can be gained from it. Again, this highlights the needs for intuitive interfaces that reflect the most common ways in which the system might be used.
- *Cost* The system should also be within the budget of the person allowing for maintenance and repair costs in the future.
- *Compatibility* The system must be compatible both physically and electronically with other systems that are installed in the home. Systems should, essentially, be 'plug and play' and users should not

have to understand the details of interfaces to make different products work together.

- *Efficiency* The effort and time saved by using the system must significantly exceed the effort involved in making use of it.
- *Responsiveness* The system must respond in a timely fashion to user requests and provide feedback on its operation to the user.
- *Aesthetics* If a system is to be actively used in the home, it should be aesthetically pleasing, blending in with the décor of the existing home and the user's taste.

Of course, these factors are not just relevant to domestic systems but apply in many cases, to organizational settings. The difference, however, is that in organizational settings resources may be available to pay for ways to cope with the deficiencies in the technology. Problems of acceptability may be addressed through training and the adaptation of operational processes. However, we strongly believe that, in this area, the design of organizational as well as domestic systems would benefit if system designers paid more attention to the acceptability of these systems in their intended environment.

Fitness for purpose

The fitness for purpose of a domestic system reflects the extent to which that system meets the real needs of its users. This is particularly important for systems, such as assistive technologies for the elderly or disabled. These are not mass-produced consumer commodity systems but are systems that are designed and tailored specifically for an individual set of disabilities. If the systems do not address the specific problems faced by the user, they are essentially useless.

Fitness for purpose is related to but distinct from acceptability. A domestic technology system may be acceptable to a user but if it is not carefully tailored to their specific needs then the compromises that have to be made in using the system may lead to system failures. For example, a voice-activated system may be installed to help elderly users set off an alarm in the event of accident or illness. This system may work reliably so long as the user's voice is strong enough but if it does not take into account the fact that the elderly person's voice may be weakened in the event of an accident then it is not fit for its intended purpose.

Of course, this is not just an issue for domestic system but a more general dependability concern. For organizational systems, dealing with this concern is seen as a specification issue i.e. failure to meet real needs is equated to a specification failure. Given that the level of specification that is used for organizational systems is totally impractical for domestic systems for the elderly or disabled, the issue of fitness for purpose cannot be addressed in this way. Rather, the system has to be designed to evolve during installation and use to take into account the routines of the user's life and the particular characteristics of that user and their home.

Adaptability

Homes and the people living in these homes change with time [20]. Spaces are reconfigured to cope with changing demands and tastes, new people come to live in the home, children grow up and the capabilities of elderly adults may decline as they grow older. Consequently, the requirements of users in the home for domestic systems are constantly changing. If systems cannot be adapted *in situ* to meet new requirements they will become less and less used and, hence, less dependable.

We can identify three types of modification that may be made to domestic systems:

- Addition of new equipment. This can be in addition to existing equipment or can replace obsolete devices. Given the relatively low costs of domestic equipment, this will often be the most cost-effective way to modify a system.
- System configuration or re-configuration by its users. In this case, the user (or someone with technical knowledge) adapts the system using built-in capabilities for adaptation. For example, if a person's eyesight degenerates, then the default font size on a screen that they regularly read may be increased.
- Configuration or re-configuration of a system by its supplier. In this case, the supplier or installer of the system may visit the home to make the system modifications. Alternatively, if the system can be connected to a network, then remote upgrades of the software may be possible. This is already commonplace for mobile phones and digital TV set-top boxes.

Of course, it is well known that dependability problems in computer systems regularly arise because of errors made during system maintenance. These occur in spite of extensive quality control and testing mechanisms that are in place. There are no such mechanisms in the home so clearly the potential for undependability after modification is significant. This fact, along with the need to support system change leads to the following adaptability attributes:

1. *Configurability* This attribute reflects the ability of users or equipment installers to adapt the system to cope with a range of human capabilities such as variable hearing, eyesight, balance, etc.

2. *Openness* This attribute is concerned with the system's ability to be extended with new equipment, perhaps from different manufacturers.

3. *Visibility* This attribute reflects the extent to which the operation of the system can be made visible to users and installers of that system. This is particularly important when problems arise as it increases the chances that these problems can be diagnosed without expert assistance.

4. *User repairability* This attribute reflects the extent to which system users can repair faults in the system without specialist tools or knowledge. This is important for domestic systems as it means that users or helpers can fix problems without the need for an external service call. Thus the system can be brought back into operation quickly and the overall availability of the system is increased.

5. DEPENDABILITY, TRUST AND DISCRETIONARY SYSTEMS DESIGN

We have argued that, for domestic systems, we need to extend the notion of technical dependability as developed for organizational systems to embrace broader notions of acceptability, fitness for purpose and adaptability. The question now is: how can this broader dependability model be used to help system designers create better systems? That is, how do we design systems that, within a socio-technical context, are more likely to be trusted by their users?

Although the focus of our work has been domestic systems, we are convinced that the domestic dependability model is equally applicable to 'discretionary systems' in organizations. Professional users in organizations, such as doctors or engineers, who choose to use systems to support their work, are often unwilling to change their ways of working to accommodate these systems. As in the home, they have rhythms and routines of daily work and they expect their computer systems to fit in with these. They become extremely frustrated if they have to change how they work because of the computer system and, in such circumstances, will simply discard the system. Therefore, we argue that the dependability model for domestic systems may also be applied to discretionary workplace systems.

We believe, that for discretionary systems design, there are a number of ways in which the dependability model may be used:

1. As a way of focusing communications with potential system users.

2. As a way of organising and presenting observational studies.

3. As a checklist for designers of discretionary systems.

4. As a means of assessing existing technology and classifying problems and deficiencies in that technology.

The problem of discovering user requirements for a system is recognised as the most difficult issue in computer systems engineering [21]. The essential difficulty is that system users really don't really know what they want from a system. This problem is particularly acute for discretionary systems where there is no strictly defined process that users must follow to do their work. Even in situations where the users have a fairly clear idea of what they would like, they are poor at articulating the practical constraints on the operation of the system. The advantage of using the model that we propose here to structure communications with potential users is that it integrates functional characteristics (fitness for purpose) with non-functional characteristics (trustworthiness and acceptability). Furthermore, it highlights the importance of evolution and change (adaptability) so allowing the discussion to consider not just the immediate user requirements but how these requirements might change.

A related use of the model is to help organize and present field studies in the home or workplace. Field studies (ethnographies) collect a large volume of data about the rhythms and routines of everyday life and work including data on the use (or the lack of use) of technology. We are not suggesting that the model itself drives the ethnography. Rather, it becomes useful once studies have been completed as it allows the ethnographer to organize his or her data in such a way that it can be communicated to the potential system users or to system designers.

Both of these uses of the model are appropriate in situations where a system is being developed for use in a specific setting with a clearly identified set of users. This may be a discretionary system for professionals (e.g. problem reporting system for anaesthetists) or a specially constructed system to support a disabled person in their home. However, many domestic systems, in particular, are developed and marketed as generic products that are intended for use in a wide variety of different situations.

The danger here is that designers of these generic products focus on the product technology and the functionality that it delivers without paying sufficient attention to how it will actually be used. We see this in all sorts from products from mobile phones to video recorders and in the invention of a range of devices for 'the home of the future' such as smart fridges and heating systems. Such systems often include unnecessary and unwanted functionality that serves to confuse normal operation of the device. The dependability model that we propose, with its focus on the user and use of the technology, provides a checklist to designers that helps them consider how the technology will be used. From the model, we can derive questions such as:

- How will the user learn to use the system?
- Can they get some benefit from the system without reading an instruction manual?
- Is there a need to interface this system with other systems in the home or workplace?
- How will the system provide feedback on its operation to users?
- What user-level configurability will be supported in the system?
- How will users (with different ability and experience) access this configurability?
- How can users find out what the system is doing?

Finally, an immediate use of the model is as a way of assessing existing systems and classifying the problems that arise with these systems. It can be used in this way with one-off systems such as systems intended to help a disabled person, with workplace systems used by a group of professionals or with generic products. In the latter case, the model can be the basis of a user survey to elicit information about what users like and don't like about a system.

To illustrate how the model might be used, consider a situation where a system is to be installed in a housing complex for elderly people that is intended to help them communicate informally and share information. It makes them aware of who is available and interested in talking, provides a messaging facility and access to an electronic noticeboard that maintains information that is potentially of interest to all residents.

It is not possible to provide a complete analysis of this system here but the snapshot below shows how the classification in the model can highlight issues that have to be considered by system designers.

Attribute	Issue	Proposal
Confidentiality and integrity	Some users are concerned that it will be possible to 'eavesdrop' on private communications.	This is true but addressing the problem adds to the complexity of the system. Inform users that the system is not intended for private conversations.
Maintainability	Inevitably, there will be system software failures and the software will have to be restarted. Repairs and updates will be required. However, at least some of the users will not be able to do any installations themselves.	Provide a remote diagnostic and maintenance facility so that updates are possible without user intervention. Provide a (large) restart button on the device.
Learnability	Many users have minor problems with short-term memory. Hence, learning how to use the system can take some time.	Provide all users with a quick reference card. Arrange 'buddies' so that people help each other to learn to use the system.
Compatibility	Each flat in the complex has an alarm system that can be used to call for help if an emergency arises. Ideally, it should be possible to activate this from this system.	Requires further analysis to see if system protocols are compatible.
Aesthetics	Users are short of space and mostly have traditional decoration in their homes.	Use a tablet-PC and thus avoid the need for electronic boxes. All communications should be wireless.
Configurability	Some users suffer from arthritic fingers and have difficulty pointing at small targets.	The user should be able to increase or decrease the size of all buttons and menus in the system.

6. CONCLUSIONS

This paper has discussed traditional notions of system dependability that have arisen from research into computer-based control and protection systems. These have highlighted the importance of system characteristics such as reliability, availability and safety. Building on this work, we have proposed broader notion of dependability for systems, such as domestic systems, where users choose whether or not to use these systems. We argue that dependability is not just a technical system attribute but also includes those factors that influence the user's choice of whether or not to use a system. If a system is not used, it is not meeting its designer's intentions and hence, we argue, it is not dependable.

We believe that the domestic dependability model is an important contribution to broadening the notion of system dependability and has real practical value in the analysis and design of domestic and discretionary systems. We are currently gaining experience in the use of the model in the design of a communications system for elderly people and anticipate that this will allow us to extend the approach. Extensions may include a discussion of impairments – what stops a system being used – and design guidelines that provide more detailed advice for system designers.

ACKNOWLEDGEMENTS

We would like to thank Age Concern, Barrow; MHA Penrith, Dundee Social Work and Aberdeen Social Work departments as well as a number of elderly system users and potential users who helped us understand their needs for domestic systems. The research was sponsored by the EPSRC under the DIRC Inter-disciplinary Research Collaboration on system dependendability.

REFERENCES

1. Laprie, J.-C. Dependable Computing: Concepts, Limits, Challenges. in 25th IEEE Symposium on Fault-Tolerant Computing. 1995. Pasadena: IEEE Press.
2. Sommerville, I., Software Engineering, 6th edition. 2001, Harlow, UK: Addison-Wesley.
3. Ellison, R.J., et al., Survivable Network System Analysis: A Case Study. IEEE Software, 1999. 16(4): p. 70-7.
4. Randell, B., Facing Up To Faults. Computer J., 2000. 45(2): p. 95-106.
5. Avizienis, A., The N-Version Approach to Fault-Tolerant Software. IEEE Trans. on Software Eng., 1985. SE-11(12): p. 1491-501.
6. Avizienis, A.A., A Methodology of N-Version Programming, in Software Fault Tolerance, M.R. Lyu, Editor. 1995, John Wiley & Sons: Chichester. p. 23-46.
7. Randell, B. and J. Xu, The Evolution of the Recovery Block Concept, in Software Fault Tolerance, M.R. Lyu, Editor. 1995, John Wiley & Sons: Chichester. p. 1-22.

8. Brilliant, S.S., J.C. Knight, and N.G. Leveson, Analysis of Faults in an N-Version Software Experiment. IEEE Trans. On Software Engineering, 1990. **16**(2): p. 238-47.

9. Littlewood, B., Software Reliability Growth Models, in Software Reliability Handbook,, P. Rook, Editor. 1990, Elsevier: Amsterdam. p. 401—412.

10. Musa, J.D., Software Reliability Engineering: More Reliable Software, Faster Development and Testing. 1998, New York: McGraw-Hill.

11. Reason, J., Human Error. 1990, Cambridge, UK: Cambridge University Press.

12. Rasmussen, J., The definition of human error and a taxonomy for technical system design, in New Technology and Human Error. Chichester: Wiley. , J. Rasmussen, K. Duncan, and J. Leplat, Editors. 1987, John Wiley and Sons: Chichester.

13. Norman, D.A., The Psychology of Everyday Things. 1988, New York: Basic Books.

14. Norman, D.A., Human Error and the Design of Computer Systems. Comm. ACM, 1990. **33**(1): p. 4-7.

15. Lupton, D. and W. Seymour, Technology, selfhood and physical disability. Social Science & Medicine, 2000. **50**(1851-62).

16. Sommerville, I., et al. A Dependability Model for Domestic Systems. in SAFECOMP 2003. 2003. Edinburgh, Scotland: Springer.

17. Edwards, K. and R. Grinter. At Home with Ubiquitous Computing: Seven Challenges. In Proc. Ubicomp 2001. 2001. Atlanta, Georgia. Springer.

18. Miller, C., K. Haigh, and W. Dewing. First, Cause No Harm: Issues in Building Safe, Reliable and Trustworthy Elder Care Systems. In Proc. AAAI-02 Workshop on Automation as Caregiver. 2002. Edmonton, Canada.

19. Sandhu, J., Multi-Dimensional Evaluation as a tool in Teaching Universal Design, in Universal Design; 17 Ways of Teaching and Thinking, J. Christopherson, Editor. 2002: Husbanken, Norway.

20. Dewsbury, G., et al. Designing Dependable Digital Domestic Environments. In Proc. HOIT 2003: The Networked Home and the Home of the Future. 2003. Irvine, California.

21. Kotonya, G. and I. Sommerville, Requirements Engineering: Processes and Techniques. 1998, Chichester, UK: John Wiley and Sons.

Chapter 9

UNDERSTANDING AND SUPPORTING DEPENDABILITY AS ORDINARY ACTION

Alexander Voß[1], Rob Procter[1], Roger Slack[1], Mark Hartswood[1] and Mark Rouncefield[2]
[1]*School of Informatics, The University of Edinburgh*
[2]*Department of Computing, University of Lancaster*

1. INTRODUCTION

In this chapter we are concerned with the ways in which people within organisations experience dependability, how dependability is routinely achieved through 'ordinary action', and what this could mean for the design, development and implementation of dependable IT systems. Our programme of investigation into these matters has a number of related threads, which we will address in turn.

First, we are interested in the *in-vivo* work of living with systems that are more or less reliable and the practices that this being 'more or less dependable' occasions. The situated practical actions of living with systems (e.g., workarounds and so on) are important to us in that they show how society members[7] experience dependability as a practical, day-to-day matter.
In particular, we seek to explicate what dependability means in an everyday language sense, and to provide an analysis of the ways in which systems come to be seen as dependable and the work members are called upon to perform to make them more or less dependable. This is not intended as a remedy or corrective to 'professional' uses of dependability, but to demonstrate the value for IT professionals of looking at what, following Livingston [14], we call the 'lived work' of working with more or less dependable systems. By this we meaning attending to the 'what is this?', 'what to do?' and 'what to do next?' of practical problem solving; it draws our attention to the nature of candidate solutions and the fact that not just anything will do. Just as Livingston's mathematicians cannot divorce their

K. Clarke, G. Hardstone, M. Rouncefield and I. Sommerville (eds.), Trust in Technology:
A Socio-Technical Perspective, 195–216.

proof accounts from the work undertaken to prove the theorems (diagrams, notes and the like), so the workers in our case study below cannot divorce what they have done from what the problem was. It is through this that solutions become *accountable* in the sense that people can give reasons why this or that worked and these become parts of the used-before-and-seen-to-work repertoire of candidate solutions.

To illustrate how dependability is realised in and as a part of members' ordinary actions – the 'routine' but nevertheless skilful responses to both expected and unexpected problems – we draw on material from an ethnographic study of control room work and IT systems implementation in a manufacturing plant. Instances of undependability in this setting are quite frequent but are not normally catastrophic. Rather, they are 'normal, natural troubles' that occasion situated, practical investigation and repair. This is in contrast to much of the extant literature, which has focused on dependability issues as fatal issues, e.g., studies of such cases as the London Ambulance Service [1] or Therac-25 [13].

The first part of our study points to some of the worldly contingencies of production management that control room workers routinely deal with as a part of their work [19]. More precisely we might say that all plans are contingent on what, following Suchman [17], we call 'situated actions'. In particular, we show how the practical implementation of a production plan is a production worker's formulation, produced in response to issues concerning the 'local logics' of day-to-day production management. By this we mean to emphasise the dynamic yet situated nature of knowledge and plans, the 'minor actions, minor decisions and minor changes', upon which the organisation rides [2]. Such local logics attend to the incompleteness of knowledge on both organisational and spatial-temporal levels – that which is an acceptable solution *just here and just now*, with these circumstances and in this organisational context as a basis for proceeding *right now*. Decisions are made in the fabric of both real space and time. This stands in marked contrast to the rationalist view of planning where plans stand as directives for future actions produced out of a systematic analysis of the possible options and constraints on their application and which can then be passed on for implementation as schedules for production to be followed literally as a 'script for action'. Our findings lead us to support the argument that the implementation of plans is always a practical and situated activity, the character of which emerges in action [17]. This view emphasises the incompleteness of knowledge and the set of circumstances – more or less intended, arbitrary, uncontrolled or unanticipated – which affect action [6].

In the second part of our study, having looked at the use of IT systems and related practices in the control room, we turn to the implementation of these systems and their configuration in what constitutes the socio-material basis for production work. Here, the day-to-day activities of the plant's own IT staff come to the fore. The case study material shows how their work is closely related to production work and how dependability of the overall production process is a concern shared by IT and non-IT professionals in the plant. As in the case of the control room workers, one might say that the activities of the plant's IT staff are situated and that for them, too, dependability is a contexted matter.

We conclude by considering how the understanding gained from witnessing at first hand members' experience of dependability as a practical, day-to-day matter might be taken up and applied more widely to the design, development and implementation of dependable IT systems. In particular, we point to the problem of the 'design fallacy', the assumption that more dependable IT systems can be achieved by more sophisticated processes of *a priori* requirements analysis and design. Instead, we propose *co-realisation* as an approach to building highly dependable, work affording artefacts, which is based upon creating a shared practice between IT professionals and system users that is set within the context of use [7].

2. METHODOLOGY

The research was based on ethnomethodologically informed ethnographic methods which, with their emphasis on workplace studies and the 'real world, real time', day-to-day character of work, have become popular in the study of organisational life and information and communications technology in recent years [10]. The use of ethnographies of work has been notably successful in the field of Computer Supported Cooperative Work as a tool for informing IT systems design (e.g., [9]).

The central characteristic of the ethnographic method is the researcher's detailed observation of how the work actually 'gets done'. Its focus is upon the circumstances, practices and activities that constitute the 'real world', situated character of work and the recognition of the tacit skills and cooperative activities through which work is accomplished as a day-to-day, practical activity and it aims to make these processes and practices 'visible'. This approach to work as a socially organised phenomenon is designed to illuminate the rationale brought by people at work to the various tasks, 'problems' and 'things to do' that they are confronted with in the course of their daily working lives. The defining feature of this kind of study is the immersion of the researcher in the work environment where a non-presumptive record is made of all aspects of the day-to-day work over an extended period of time. In this way a 'thick description' is built up of the situated working practices.

3. THE CASE STUDY

The case study organisation, EngineCo, produces mass-customised diesel engines ranging in size from 11 to 190 kW. Production in the plant was designed to work along a strict production orthodoxy and large parts are automated. Since the plant was built in the early 1990s, significant changes have been made to keep up with changing customer demands and to keep the plant operational in a difficult economic environment. The organisation makes heavy use of a wide range of information technologies and, to a large extent; their operation depends on complex ensembles of these technologies. Ethnographic studies of the working practices of control room workers have been conducted over the course of the last two years as a predicate for IT systems design activities [18]. Interviews with staff were recorded, and notes made of activities observed and artefacts employed. The data also includes copious notes and transcriptions of talk of members (i.e., regular participants in the work setting) as they went about their day-to-day work.

The production environment at EngineCo is shaped according to a just-in-time (JIT) production orthodoxy. Material is delivered to an external logistics provider that operates a high-shelf storage facility near the plant on EngineCo's behalf. Upon EngineCo's order, the logistics provider delivers parts to the plant. Consequently, the plant itself was not designed to store large numbers of parts, containing buffer spaces for only four hours of production. The layout of production is basically linear, with an engine picking up its component parts as it moves from one side of the plant to the other. The production of engines is divided into two main steps: the basic engine is produced on an assembly line while customer-specific configuration is done in stationary assembly workspaces.

Central to production is the assembly control host which controls all processes within the plant, interacting with local systems in the various functional units of the plant (e.g., assembly lines) as well as with the company's ERP system (SAP R3). The assembly control host is custom-built rather than being part of the ERP system. It has been developed and is now operated and maintained by an external IT service provider, which has personnel located in the plant. A basic precondition for production to work along the lines of the JIT regime is that all parts are available in time for production. This notion of *buildability* is the key concept in the production management orthodoxy at EngineCo. Located within the plant, an assembly planning department is responsible for the buildability of engines, assuring that all component parts as well as the various pieces of information needed (such as workers' instructions) are available before production starts. They are also responsible for scheduling production orders in time to meet the agreed delivery dates. Assembly planners create a schedule for production taking into consideration their knowledge about the current status of the plant, upcoming events and the requirements of control room and shop floor workers.

4. DOING DEPENDABILITY: NORMAL NATURAL TROUBLES

Due to problems with the availability of certain parts, especially crankcases and because of ever increasing customer demands, the notion of buildability was renegotiated [18] in order not to let the plant fall idle. Today, there are 'green'; 'orange'; and 'red' engines in the plant that are respectively: strictly buildable; waiting for a part known to be on its way; and waiting for something that is not available and doesn't have a delivery date. Where, previously, buildability was a verifiable property of an engine in relationship to, e.g., the inventory, now buildability is an informed prediction based on workers' knowledge about various kinds of socio-material circumstances. So, for example, control room workers must take into account the interests of workers on the floor, for example avoiding a long string of potentially problematic engines, e.g. ones that need more work than others and would affect their engines per hour performance target. Control room workers effectively share responsibility for ensuring that engines are buildable with the assembly planning department as is illustrated by the following extract from the control room shift book:

From the shift book:
As soon as crankcases for 4-cylinders are available, schedule order number 56678651 (very urgent for Company X).
Engines are red even when only loose material is missing.

This first example shows how control room workers effectively assign material to orders and how their decisions may be influenced by various contingencies. Choosing the order in which to schedule engines is a situated accomplishment rather than a straightforward priority based decision wherein the importance of the engine dictates its order. Control room workers need to attend to the way scheduling an engine might influence the 'flow' of other engines through the plant and take into consideration the workload a particular type of engine places on workers on the shop floor, i.e., they have to attend to the 'working division of labour' [16]. The second example refers to a problem with the plant IT systems, which does not allow them to start production of engines that are missing loose material (e.g., manuals). Clearly, while a missing crankcase effectively prevents production of the engine, loose material is not needed until the engine is actually shipped to the customer (and perhaps not even then in very urgent cases).

By redefining details of the working division of labour, EngineCo has effectively addressed a situation that was impossible to predict during the original planning of the plant. This is not to say that the notion of buildability has ceased to exist. Rather, the general notion as originally inscribed in working practices has, by appropriation, been localised to take into consideration the 'worldly contingencies' – situations which arise in and as a part of the day-to-day practical work of the plant and its members and which are not, for example, involved with setting up a new system or introducing new machinery or practices – of production in EngineCo's plant. Where, previously, buildability was a verifiable property of an engine in relationship to the inventory, now buildability of 'orange' and 'red' engines is an informed prediction based on members' knowledge about various kinds of socio-material circumstances.

In our research we have found a series of expectable, normal, natural troubles whose solution is readily available to members in, and as a part of, their working practices. That is, such problems do not normally occasion recourse to anything other than the 'usual solutions'. Usual solutions invoke what we call *horizons of tractability*. By this we mean that a problem of the usual kind contains within it the candidate (used-before-and-seen-to-work) solution to that problem. These problems and their solutions are normal and natural and putatively soluble in, and as a part of, day-to-day work.

> **From the shift book:**
> SMR [suspended monorail] trouble 14:15 to 16:30, engines not registered into SMR, took 25 engines off the line using emergency organisation.
> Info for Peter: part no. 04767534, box was empty upon delivery, so I booked 64 parts out of the inventory.

The emergency organisation involved picking up the engines by forklift truck and moving them to a location where they can be picked up by the autonomous carrier system. A number of locations have been made available for this purpose where forklift truck drivers can access the assembly control host to update the location information for the engine they just reintroduced into the system. This is one of many examples where non-automated activity leads to a temporary discrepancy between the representation and the represented, which has to be compensated for. The second example illustrates the same point. Updating the inventory in response to various kinds of events is a regular activity in the control room and the fact that control room workers have acquired authority to effect such transactions is witness to the normality of this kind of problem compensation activity. Workers are also able to assess the potential impacts of seen-before problem situations and they take measures to avoid them:

From the shift book:
Carrier control system broken down 10:45–11:05 resulting in delayed transports, peak number of transports in the system = 110
If in the carrier control system you can't switch from the list of transport orders to the visualisation, don't reboot the PC if the number of transport orders is more than about 70.

In the first two lines of the above example, workers report on problems with the system that controls the autonomous carriers that supply material to the workstations in the plant. The recording of a breakdown in the shift book is a way to make this incident accountable to fellow workers, including those working on another shift. The entry contains a number of statements that, on the surface, seem to be rather uninformative. However, they point to a number of normal, natural troubles that can result from this particular incident such as material being stored in places that are far from the workstations where it's going to be needed. This will affect the length of transports for some time after the root problem has gone away. The result of this is that since transports take longer, more of them will queue up in the carrier control system. Such 'ripple effects' are quite common in this production context. In effect, because of the breakdown of the control system, the 'transport situation' might be considered problematic for quite a long time. The next extract can be read in this same kind of context as being part of the process of workers' making sense of, and responding to, the potential undependability of the carrier control system. It has become part of the local practice to avoid certain actions that might result in the breakdown of the carrier system if the 'transport situation' is regarded as problematic by control room workers:

From a video recording of control room work:
Pete: Hey, the carrier control is still not running properly. Let's not run the optimisation, ok Steve?
Steve: We didn't run it this morning either, because we had 40 transports.

Other problems that are not susceptible to these remedies are also interesting to us in that they demand a solution – members cannot remain indifferent to their presence – but that solution is not a normal or usual one (by definition). In order to keep production running, members have to find and evaluate possible solutions quickly, taking into consideration the present situation, the resources presently available, as well as, ideally, any (possibly long-term and remote) consequences their activities might have:

From fieldwork notes:
A material storage tower went offline. Material could be moved out of the tower to the line but no messages to the assembly control host were generated when boxes were emptied. Control room workers solved this problem by marking all material in the tower 'faulty' that resulted in new material being ordered from the logistics provider. This material was then supplied to the line using forklift trucks. [...] A material requirements planner called to ask why so many parts were suddenly 'faulty'.

Such situated problem-solving results in work-arounds that are initially specific to the situation at hand but may become part of the repertoire of used-before-and-seen-to-work candidate solutions. They may be further generalised through processes of social learning [20] as members share them with colleagues or they might get factored into the larger socio-material assemblage that makes up the working environment. This process of problem solution and social learning, however, is critically dependent on members' orientation to the larger context, their making the problem solution accountable to fellow members and their ability to judge the consequences.

The plans that members come up with within this horizon of tractability do not usually work one way only – it is our experience that an unexpected problem can become a normal problem susceptible to the usual solutions in, and through, the skilful and planful conduct of members. That is to say, the boundaries between the types of problem are semi-permeable (at least). The order of the potentially problematic universe is not similarly problematic for all members, different members will view different problems in a variety of ways and, through the phenomenon of organisational memory [12], this may lead to the resolution for the problem in, and through, the ability to improvise or to recognise some kind of similarities inherent in this and a previous problem.

It is important to note that problem detection and solving is 'lived work' and that it is also situated. That is, it is not to be divorced from the plans and procedures through which it is undertaken and the machinery and interactions that both support and realise it. Working practices and the structure of the workplace afford various kinds of activities, which allow members to check the proper progress of production and to detect and respond to troubles. These very 'mundane' (i.e., day-to-day) activities complement the planned-for, made-explicit and formalised measures such as testing. As in other collaborative work (see e.g., [8]), members are aware of, and orient to, the work of their colleagues. This is supported by the affordances of their socio-material working environment as the following example illustrates:

From a video recording of control room work:
Oil pipes are missing at the assembly line and Jim calls workers outside the control room to ask if they "have them lying around". This is overheard by Mark who claims that: "Chris has them". He subsequently calls Chris to confirm this: "Chris, did you take all the oil pipes that were at the line?" Having confirmed that Chris has the oil pipes he explains why he thought that Chris had them: "I have seen the boxes standing there".

Here, the visibility of situations and events within the plant leads to Mark being aware of where the parts in question are. The problem that the location of the parts was not accurately recorded in the information system was immediately compensated by his knowledge of the plant situation. Likewise, Jim's knowledge of working practices leads him to call specific people who are likely to have the parts. Mark's observation makes further telephone calls unnecessary[8].

Video recording continued:
Now that the whereabouts of the oil pipes has been established, the question remains why Chris has them. Mark explains that this was related to conversion work Chris is involved in at the moment. This leads Jim to ask if there are enough parts in stock to deal with the conversion work as well as other production orders. Mark explains how the inventory matches the need.

Having solved the problem of locating the parts, there is the question of how the problem emerged and what further problems may lie ahead. It is not immediately obvious that Chris should have the parts but Mark knows that Chris is involved in some conversion work resulting from a previous problem. Again, awareness of what is happening within the plant is crucial since information about the conversion work is unlikely to be captured in information systems, as the work Chris is carrying out is not part of the normal operation of the plant. Rather, it is improvised work done to deal with a previous problem.

Jim raises the question of whether enough oil pipes are available to deal with the conversion work as well as normal production. Again, it is Mark who can fill in the required information and demonstrate to Jim how the parts in the inventory match the needs. As Jim comments in a similar situation: *"What one of us doesn't know, the other does."* Problem detection and solving is very much a collaborative activity depending on the situated and highly condensed exchange of information between members. By saying that Chris has taken the parts from the line, Mark also points to a set of possible reasons as members are well aware who Chris is, where he works and what his usual activities are.

> **Video recording continued:**
> Since it was first established that parts were missing, production has moved on and there is the question what to do with the engines that are missing oil pipes. Jim and Mark discuss if the material structure of the engine allows them to be assembled in 'stationary assembly'.

Workers in the plant are aware of the material properties of the engines produced and are thus able to relate the material artefact presented to them to the process of its construction. In the example above, Mark and Jim discuss this relationship in order to find out if the problem of missing oil pipes can be dealt with in stationary assembly, i.e., after the engines have left the assembly line. They have to attend to such issues as the proper order in which parts can be assembled. The knowledge of the material properties of engines also allows members to detect troubles, i.e., the product itself affords checking of its proper progress through production (cf. [8]).

> **From a video recording of control room work:**
> Jack has 'found' an engine that; according to the IT system has been delivered to the customer quite a while ago. It is, however, physically present in the engine buffer and Jack calls a colleague in quality control to find out the reason for this. "It's a 4-cylinder F200, 'conversion [customer]' it says here, a very old engine. The engine is missing parts, screws are loose ... if it's not ready yet – I wanted to know what's with this engine – it's been sitting in the buffer for quite a while."

Here, the physical appearance is an indication of the engine's unusual 'biography'. This, together with the fact that the engine has "been sitting in the buffer for quite a while" makes the case interesting for Jack.

These worldly contingencies are interesting for us since they invite consideration of the 'seen but unnoticed' aspects of work – that is, those aspects which pass the members by in, and as a part of, their day-to-day work but which, when there are problems or questions, are subject to inquiry (e.g., have you tried this or that? Did you do this or that? What were you doing when it happened?). The answer to such questions, especially to the latter, illustrates the seen-but-unnoticed character of work in that, when called upon to so do, members can provide such accounts, although they do not do so in the course of ordinary work.

5. DEPENDABILITY AND IT SYSTEMS IMPLEMENTATION

Having looked at dependability as a concern in the work of control room workers, we now turn to the work done by IT professionals in the same setting. IT systems in the manufacturing plant are built, configured and operated by a small IT department located in the plant, an external IT subcontractor with on-site staff, as well as various other external suppliers, some of which also have staff located on-site permanently. Work with and on IT systems is a daily concern of various IT and non-IT workers in the plant and an effective integration of various technological offerings and working practices can be seen as a key concern which critically affects the success of the overall production process.

As with the use of IT systems in this setting, the development and operation are also situated accomplishments. The sheer complexity of the overall socio-technical system that forms the basis for production makes it impossible to apply formal modelling and reasoning techniques on a global scale. These may be employed locally, depending on the local needs. For example, the design and operation of material storage towers moving material weighing up to a ton is clearly safety-critical. As one of our interviewees comments:

From an interview with the head of the local IT department:
"In the area of goods handling you have to react at particular times because of reasons of security at work. It just must not happen that the rack feeder moves on and on because the computer is busy doing something else ..."

Consequently, the building of such systems is an area where traditional approaches to dependability such as formal specification and reasoning techniques may be employed. Also, such systems need to be inspected and certified by the German safety authority Technischer Überwachungsverein (TÜV).

In other areas, real-time requirements may not be as strict as work safety is not an issue. However, availability and the quality of the products are issues and there are clear tradeoffs between the operating characteristics of, e.g., a testing field control system measuring the operational parameters of an engine and the costs of buying and operating this equipment. Also, it is not only economics that makes other, potentially less dependable systems attractive:

From an interview with the head of the local IT department:
"Finding a programmer for the operating system OS/9 is a catastrophe.

You are stuck with [the supplier] and can't do anything about it. In the meantime, PCs have become so fast that they can now do what they cannot normally do because of the operating system, namely service all those measurement channels fast enough [...] With OS/9 machines another problem is the network cards."

Clearly, there are benefits of using widely available components rather than more specialised ones in terms of the availability of the products but also in terms of the availability of the knowledge (here in the form of trained programmers) needed to operate them. Another example is the use of Ethernet as a field bus system on the shop floor. In theory, the characteristics of Ethernet make it an unsuitable choice for real-time control of manufacturing:

From an interview with the head of the local IT department:
"Ten years ago [people from the central IT department] said, I'd see that I will fail with this, it just could not work with Ethernet."

In practice, its wide availability and low price has not only made Ethernet an attractive alternative to more expensive solutions like Token Ring systems but it has also made it possible to configure the network in ways that offset the undesirable characteristics of the network technology: through appropriate segmentation, the number of collisions can be minimised and more recently the introduction of network switches has practically eliminated this problem. An additional dimension in the decision concerning which network technology to employ on the shop floor is that of technology ownership. While traditional field bus systems such as Profibus are often maintained by shop floor maintenance personnel, Ethernet with its relative complexity is often the preserve of IT departments:

From an interview with the head of the local IT department:
"That means, the central IT department has expanded more and more downwards, so to say, with their knowledge and [shop floor maintenance workers] couldn't counter that because they didn't have any experience [...] they don't have a network analyser [... the] knowledge is too complex [...] different standards, different responsibilities."

It is important to note that IT staff and production workers share a concern for the overall dependability of the production process. It is thus not possible to draw any non-arbitrary line between what the control room workers do and what people in the IT department do. (In fact, control room and local IT department belong to the same organisational unit.) The practical coordination between the various players (IT staff, production worker; company employee, external contractor) is crucial for continued and dependable operation, and for further development of IT systems and working practices. The following fieldwork material illustrates how problem solutions can get factored into ongoing systems development as well as how they can adversely affect the success of the system:

From an interview with one of the system developers responsible for the ongoing development of the assembly control host:
[Such a complex system] will always have flaws somewhere but if the user has to work with the system and there's a problem he will find a work-around himself and the whole system works. [...] The whole works, of course, only if the user really wants to work with it. If he says: "Look, I have to move this box from here to there and it doesn't work. Crap system! I'll let a forklift do this, I will not use your bloody system" then all is lost. Then our location information is wrong cause the driver doesn't always give the correct information; then it will never fly. [...] If they come to us and say that something's not working, we will say "oh! we'll quickly have to create a bug fix" and, for the moment, I'll do this manually without the system, then it works, the system moves on, everything stays correct, the whole plant works and if the next day we can introduce a bug fix, the whole thing moves on smoothly.

IT systems development and production work go hand in hand and the successful operation of the various systems controlling production depends on maintaining enough shared understanding of 'how things should be done'. This shared understanding, e.g., that the information stored in the assembly control host should match the situation on the shop floor, that problems and workarounds should be communicated to the developers, is what members orient to in their work and it is this to which they appeal when asked to make their work accountable. In situations where problems arise, the effort of coordination can be highly condensed as the following transcript shows:

From fieldwork notes:
An IT systems operator comes into the control room and asks if there are problems with the computer system at the logistics provider. Jim looks at his process visualisation system and notes that there are a number of unacknowledged requests recorded for commission boxes, which indicates a problem. He discusses a number of possible causes for the problem with the operator who then returns to his office while Jim phones workers at the logistics provider and asks them if their IT systems are working: "Do you have problems with your system? I have unacknowledged requests for commission boxes and for assembly line parts." Having learned that the logistics provider does not seem to have problems, he then walks over to the operators of the local systems to discuss the issue with them. When he comes back into the control room, he comments, "They will phone [the central mainframe and network

operators in another town]." I ask Jack about the counters in the process visualisation system and he explains: "This counter here normally goes back to zero immediately. It takes a bit longer for the assembly line parts." Some time later, Jim asks the local operators about the status of the problem. He comes back and says, "Things should be fine again." Indeed, now the counter that first indicated the presence of the problem is back to zero again. Later, Jim gets a phone call from one of the workers at the logistics provider asking about the previous inquiry regarding the problem. Jim informs him that the problem has been found and that it was due to a faulty router device.

Having established that there is a problem with the communication between EngineCo and the logistics provider, workers can draw upon their repertoire of candidate explanations, one of them being that the logistics provider's IT system is offline. Phoning their colleagues serves not only to determine if this is the case but also to alert them to the problem situation. Likewise, in the context of 'how things are done here', the news that "they will phone [other operators]" means that control room workers need not take further action for the moment. Of course, after some time, they would have been called to initiate an existing emergency organisation had the problem not been solved in a relatively short time. It may seem surprising that an IT systems operator should turn to the users of the system to inquire if there was a problem. However, the operation of complex IT systems is somewhat opaque even to IT professionals and control room workers are well placed to contribute to the discussion. They also know whom to call at the logistic provider to determine if the problem was due to a fault in their system.

6. DEPENDABILITY AS A MEMBERS' PHENOMENON

A central problem for us is the manner in which the term 'dependability' has been used in the professional literature. We argue that there is a need to complement this with a consideration of the ways in which dependability is realised as a practical matter by members and over time. This is not to say that we reject notions of dependability offered by this literature or that our comments here are incommensurable: the point is that we want to look at dependability and similar terms by doing an ethnography of what it means for a system to be reliable or dependable as a practical matter for society members engaged in using that system with just the resources and the knowledge they have. That is, we are interested in what it means to be dependable or reliable in context. In other words, while we are interested in the notions of dependability invoked in the 'professional' literature and these inform our discussions, we argue that we should consider how society members experience dependability in context. Indeed, it is our contention that such lay[9] uses are important for understanding what we could mean by 'dependability'. Our aim here, then, is to bring forward the lay uses, the practical procedures and knowledges that are invoked in working with more or less dependable systems and to consider this alongside 'professional' uses of terms and the metrics that realise them. This is not to suggest that 'professional' metrics and definitions of dependability have no value but that their use in everyday language is limited.

Our aim is to focus on what it means to live with more or less dependable systems, and to do so in the natural attitude through everyday language and situated actions such as repair. As for humans, for machines the notion of being dependable is an accountable matter.[10] It is also a matter that might well occasion workarounds or other situated actions, which we should consider when examining what we call the 'logical grammar' of dependability. By this we mean the ways that the concept might be used. Consider "this machine is totally undependable, let's buy it" – such a use cannot be said to be acceptable except as an ironic utterance. Uses such as "you cannot always depend on the machine but we usually find ways of making it work" point us to the ways people treat notions such as dependability not simply as common understandings but as common understandings intimately related to practical actions. Our study of control room work shows that in a strict sense the system is not 100% reliable but in showing how members make it work, we aim to provide a complement to such metrics and to show the work of making systems dependable. This is also our reason for recommending doing an ethnography, since it is only by so doing that we might see the workarounds in action and come to know just how the system is unreliable or cannot be depended on.

As practical matters, dependability is important for members; yet the senses in which members treat such terms seems to be missing in the dependability literature. We argue that if one examines everyday language uses of these terms (and others), the benefit will be in a fuller appreciation of what it means to work with (or around) such systems. Consideration of technology in its (social) context illuminates the practical actions that make technologies workable-with and which realise horizons of dependability as society members' objects. Such an exercise might appear as if it is trivial – playing with words – but we find value in it in that it shifts attention to how people cope with technology, and away from metrics and measures that find their use in the technical realm, but which have little value on the shop floor. They also show us something of the 'missing what' of making technologies reliable or dependable, the practical actions that occur, the workarounds, the procedures adopted and so on. In other words, we want to present a consideration of the ways in which dependability is ad hoced into being. It is only by doing the ethnography that such features might be found. We might be seen as providing an outsider's comment on something that has been professionalized and fine-tuned, yet we would argue that such issues are of merit to professionals and that they should be examined in considering what we mean by 'dependability'. Perhaps the consideration of such terms in everyday language will be 'therapeutic' in the sense that it opens up some elbow room in which to do the kinds of ethnographic work that illustrates how knowledge is deployed within the working division of labour and how members in settings such as EngineCo treat knowledge as a practical resource for making more or less dependable systems work. This directs our attention to knowledge in and as a part of practical action and we would argue forms a complement to the work currently being undertaken in the area of dependability.

7. DEPENDABILITY AS ORDINARY ACTION

We found within the day-to-day operation of the EngineCo plant a series of sources of undependability as expectable troubles whose solution is readily available as ordinary action. That is, these problems and their solutions are 'normal and natural', invoking a search through a repertoire of seen-to-work-before candidate solutions. Problems not susceptible to these remedies also demand a solution. In order to keep production running, workers have to find and evaluate possible solutions quickly, taking into consideration the present situation, the resources presently available, as well as, ideally, any (possibly long-term and remote) consequences their activities might have. Such situated problem-solving results in workarounds that are initially specific to the situation at hand, but may become part of the repertoire of used-before-and-seen-to-work candidate solutions. They may be further generalised through processes of social learning as workers share the various 'local logics' with colleagues. This process of problem solution and local logics, however, is critically dependent on members' orientation to the larger context, their making the solution accountable to fellow workers and their ability to judge the consequences.

We observe how production plans, and formal production logics, such as buildability, are treated as resources for the situated accomplishment of production, being oriented to, and used with skill and judgment, in order to get the work done. This is done in the knowledge that workers may be required to account for a decision, or make a case in ways that can be seen and understood as complying with production objectives and rules. In this sense, production plans are less a device for directing production than a template for publicly accounting for it. This is not to repeat a common misconception to the effect that 'plans are useless'. As Schmidt [15] reminds us, the role of formal constructs such as plans in cooperative work remains deeply misunderstood. We take seriously Schmidt's injunction to pay close attention to the differential role of plans in organisational life:

"Instead of merely observing in case study after case study that procedures are impoverished abstractions when confronted with the multifarious and contingent nature of practical action; it is necessary to investigate precisely how they stipulate the articulation of cooperative work, how they are interpreted and used, designed and adapted by competent actors 'who have to live with them from day to day'."

Control room workers take advantage of the separation of planning systems and assembly control systems to make interventions in the unfolding production plan. This separation facilitates, to paraphrase Bowers et al. [3], 'production from within' – emphasising methods used in the control room and on the shop floor that constitute the local accomplishment of the work. Underlying much current work on production planning and management systems is the notion that to achieve the prescription of a task, everything must somehow be rendered uniform and predictable. This pursuit of uniformity manifests itself in numerous ways. Yet our observations of production management work make clear that any attempt to see this as simply following the script is wholly unwarranted. Furthermore, a prime conception at play in rationalist view of planning is that there is a sequence of tasks that together make up a definitive version of best practice. However, the actual achievement of any production plan makes it clear that all that this is, at best, a contingent version of best practice.

If the aim of production planning technology is to embed knowledge properties in systems, then production knowledge needs to be captured and managed in a way that will make it accurate, available, accessible and effective. Such a task is hardly trivial and our concerns are precisely with the conceptual and empirical issues that need to be understood before such projects become feasible. In pointing out the divergence of plans and actual production we are not being critical of the principle of planning. Rather, we are suggesting that its orthodoxies should perhaps be accompanied by complementary analysis of a more qualitative kind.

8. CO-REALISING DEPENDABILITY IN IT SYSTEMS

Our detailed understanding of what dependability means, and of how it is achieved in practice, would not be possible without the use of ethnographic studies of the workplace. We argue that it is therefore important to consider how the insights offered by ethnographic inquiry might be taken up and used by IT professionals. However, the translation of ethnographic analyses of work practices into IT system design work has remained problematic (e.g., [4,5,11]). So far, many of the attempts to do this have fallen foul of the design fallacy, i.e., that better, more usable and dependable IT systems can be produced by putting more effort into *a priori* requirements capture and design processes. In contrast, our approach has been to put forward a way of re-shaping IT systems design and development practice around the principles of ethnomethodology and the ethnographic method. Co-realisation is an orientation to building IT systems that emphasises the importance of creating a shared practice between IT professionals and users that is grounded within the context of use [7]. We argue that co-realisation enables, for example, members' day-to-day concern for dependability to be integrated with ongoing design and development activity. It is therefore interesting that there is much that is consonant with the concepts of IT systems design and development as co-realisation in the way that EngineCo's IT staff go about their work on a daily basis.

The work of the plant's IT staff illustrates how dependability is a practical issue in the development and implementation of large, complex IT systems. Building working ensembles of technological components, social relations and working practices is the challenge that IT practitioners face. They have to act on limited knowledge and with limited control as they try to configure together offerings from diverse sources. They need to consider not only the here and now, but also the trajectory of technological development, both within the organisation and outside it. In all this, they have to act with the limited resources available to them in the 'here and now' and need to consider the moves that other players make as their pursue their (often conflicting) aims. Day-to-day IT systems development and implementation thus has the character of situated action and any plans that members devise are provisional, subject to reconsideration as the need arises.

IT staff at EngineCo depend on their understanding of 'how things are done here' and 'what our problems are currently' to determine what is to be done. For example, change reports produced by local IT staff are indexical in that they do not contain everything that is needed to make sense of them, but point to a number of contingent circumstances that competent members can refer to. Likewise, control room workers' statements about problems refer back to what we might call the 'biography' of the plant and its IT systems. EngineCo's IT staff need to be competent members in the workplace in order to make sense of these statements without having to resort to lengthy negotiations about what they mean. Such pay offs of 'being a member' are what we seek to promote and amplify when we advocate pursuing IT systems design and development as co-realisation.

Co-realisation asserts that the character of day-to-day work and the workarounds involved needs to be understood in context in order that one can design dependable, work affording systems. It therefore calls for creating a shared practice between members and IT professionals that is grounded in the lived experience of members, and a commitment to 'stick around and see what happens' once a new IT system or artefact is deployed. Co-realisation attends to the design of work and work affording artefacts as a pair – the way that the system is designed is reflexively related to the configuration of work and it is possible for members to suggest changes in both system and practice. The 'logical grammar' of co-realisation demands that IT professionals take an interest in the way that a system is used, that they look beyond the design phase and the 'fix the bugs' phase to the ways that new systems are used and integrated into the wider socio-technical infrastructure. Elsewhere, we describe our experiences of following co-realisation in the design, development and implementation of IT systems in EngineCo and other settings [7].

9. CONCLUSIONS

Our approach to dependability is to regard it as a worldly achievement that requires one to look at the practices that exist in and as a part of its achievement. This is why we recommend 'doing the ethnography' to show what it means to live with systems that are more or less dependable. Through examination of the 'lived work' of working with undependable systems (including the workarounds etc. that this involves) we aim to complement existing work in this area.

We have argued that the study of dependability can be enhanced and strengthened by attending to everyday uses of the term and by focussing on the work that goes on to make systems more or less dependable. We do not argue that ethnographic studies should replace the work currently undertaken under the rubric of dependability, but that there is what we would call a 'missing how' that needs to be addressed and that this can be done satisfactorily in and through ethnographic research on the procedures and situated actions involved in making systems dependable. There is also a sense in which the study of dependability can be developed through the securing of a deeper understanding of the practices by which it is constituted. Ethnographies of the making of dependability measures/metrics might be useful in that they afford those involved the opportunity to reflect on their practice.

We have provided examples of how practical actions such as workarounds contribute to the notion of dependability. If we ask "What does 'this system is dependable' mean?", members' answers will reflect their experiences with the system in context. Dependability is not some inherent system property as the same artefact can be seen as being undependable from other points of view and the 'being dependable' can not be carried into some other context, i.e., if the system were to be taken into another plant, it might turn out to have features that are very much undesirable in this setting. That is to say, dependability is not simply an inherent property of the system itself but of the work in which it is enmeshed. We can, therefore, speak of the 'lived work' of dependability in that, having done the ethnography, we can see that there is a reflexive relationship between work practice and dependable systems. The aim has been to demonstrate not that 'professional' discourses of dependability have no place in our considerations, but that there is an important practical counterpart to these in lay notions of dependability and the work practice that goes on in and as a part of working with (un-)dependable systems. It is our recommendation that researchers consider this often neglected component when employing these concepts.

The case study has illustrated how dependability is a situated concept and that when we consider the constitution of dependable systems, we must keep in mind the settings in which such systems are used and the accompanying work practices. When we look at the work of the EngineCo plant, for example, we find that the workers engage in a series of situated practical actions in order to have the system be reliable. These findings speak to the essentially fragile nature of plans as scripts for action and how the agility of the work practice, predicated on the autonomy accorded to plant workers, is necessary to keep the system running. The more or less dependable system that comprises the plant requires workers to be accorded autonomy in order to have things work. We have focused attention on the ways that this goes on and how reliability and dependability are practical outcomes of the deployment of knowledge by control room and shop floor workers in an organisation whose production orthodoxy requires agility to repair its rather fragile nature and to make it work.

Finally, our findings have illustrated how the creation of dependable socio-technical systems critically depends on the day-to-day interaction between users and IT professionals as they collaboratively track down troubles and work to come up with solutions, as temporary fixes, changed working practices (e.g., stable work-arounds) or changes to the IT system. We have seen, for example, how EngineCo's own IT staff apply their understanding of the work of the control room and shop floor in the ongoing implementation of IT systems within this particular context. The importance of the situated character of this understanding is taken up and amplified in our proposal for re-shaping IT systems design and development work as co-realisation, a shared practice involving users and IT professionals that is grounded in the context of use. We have argued that by following co-realisation we are more likely to be able to ensure that members' perspectives on dependability find their way into IT systems and artefacts. Since, as we observed, the boundaries between the normal and the unexpected, the dependable and undependable are permeable, IT systems design and development should not be conceptualised as a one-off process. Whilst it is true that current IT systems design and development methodologies conceptualise design and development as an evolutionary process, what is still not widely appreciated is the connection of design and development with actual work practice. This is what co-realisation sets out to achieve.

ACKNOWLEDGEMENTS

The research reported here is funded by the UK Engineering and Physical Sciences Research Council (award numbers 00304580 and GR/N 13999). We would like to thank staff at the case study organisation for their help and participation.

REFERENCES

1. P. Beynon-Davies. Information systems failure and risk assessment: the case of the London Ambulance Service Computer Aided Despatch System. In *Proceedings of the European Conference on Information Systems*, 1995.
2. D. Boden. The business of talk: organizations in action. Cambridge: Polity Press, 1994.
3. J. Bowers, G. Button and W. Sharrock. Workflow from within and without: Technology and cooperative work on the print industry shop floor. In H. Marmolin, Y. Sunblad and K. Schmidt (Eds.), Proceedings of the Fourth European Conference on Computer-Supported Cooperative Work. Kluwer Academic Publishers, September, p. 51–66, 1995.
4. J. Blomberg, J. Giacomi, A. Mosher and P. Swenton-Wall. Ethnographic Field Methods and Their Relation to Design. In D. Schuler and A. Namioka (Eds.), Participatory Design: Principles and Practices. LEA, 1993.

5. G. Button. The ethnographic tradition and design. Design Studies, vol. 21(4), July, 2000.
6. T. Dant and D. Francis. Planning in organisations: Rational control or contingent activity? Sociological Research Online, 3(2), 1998.
7. M. Hartswood, R. Procter, R. Slack, A. Voß, M. Büscher, M. Rouncefield, P. Rouchy. Co-realisation: Towards a Principled Synthesis of Ethnomethodology and Participatory Design. *Scandinavian Journal of Information Systems*, 14(2), 2002.
8. M. Hartswood and R. Procter. Design guidelines for dealing with breakdowns and repairs in collaborative work settings. *International Journal of Human-Computer Studies*, 53:91–120, 2000.
9. C. Heath, M. Jirotka, P. Luff and J. Hindmarsh. Unpacking collaboration: the interactional organisation of trading in a city dealing room. *Journal of Computer Supported Cooperative Work* 3:147–165, 1994.
10. J. Hughes, D. Randall and D. Shapiro. Faltering from Ethnography to Design. In *Proceedings of the ACM Conference on Computer Supported Cooperative Work (CSCW'92)*, ACM Press, 1992.
11. J. Hughes, V. King, T. Rodden and H. Andersen. The role of ethnography in interactive systems design. *Interactions*, p. 56–65, April 1995.
12. J. A. Hughes, J. O'Brien and M. Rouncefield. Organisational memory and CSCW: supporting the 'Mavis' phenomenon. In *Proceedings of OzCHI*, 1996.
13. N. Leveson and C.S. Turner. An investigation of the Therac-25 accidents. *IEEE Computer*, 26(7):18-41, 1993.
14. E. Livingston. The Ethnomethodological Foundations of Mathematics. Routledge, Kegan, Paul, London, 1986.
15. K. Schmidt. Of maps and scripts: the status of formal constructs in cooperative work. In *Proceedings of the ACM Conference on Group Work*. ACM Press, 1997.
16. W. Sharrock and J. Hughes. Ethnography in the Workplace: Remarks on its theoretical basis. In *TeamEthno-Online*, Issue 1, November 2001. Available at http://www.teamethno-online.org/Issue1/Wes.html (accessed 14th Feb. 2002).
17. L. Suchman. *Plans and Situated Actions: The Problem of Human-Machine Communication*. Cambridge University Press, 1987.
18. Voß, R. Procter and R. Williams. Innovation in Use: Interleaving day-to-day operation and systems development. In *Proceedings of the Participatory Design Conference (PDC'2000)*, T. Cherkasky, J. Greenbaum, P. Mambrey, J. K. Pors (Eds.), p. 192–201, New York, 2000.
19. Voß, R. Procter, R. Slack, M. Hartswood and R. Williams. Production Management and Ordinary Action: an investigation of situated, resourceful action in production planning and control. In *Proceedings of the 20th UK Planning and Scheduling SIG Workshop*, Edinburgh, December, 2001.
20. R. Williams, R. Slack and J. Stewart. *Social Learning in Multimedia*. Final Report of the EC Targeted Socio-Economic Research Project: 4141 PL 951003. Research Centre for Social Sciences, The University of Edinburgh, 2000.

---

[18] This and the related notion of membership point to the skills people have, what they know and do competently in a particular setting. In this usage we also stress mundane, banal competence as opposed to professionalised conduct.

[19] Another example of the mutual monitoring that goes on in control rooms and similar facilities is to be found in [3].

[20] By 'lay' we do not suggest some impoverished version of a term, but a necessary complement to the 'professional' uses to be found in the literature.

Chapter 10

THE DIRC PROJECT AS THE CONTEXT OF THIS BOOK

Cliff B Jones
University of Newcastle upon Tyne

1. THE DIRC PROJECT AS THE CONTEXT OF THIS BOOK

As explained by Graham Button in the Introduction, this book is one outcome of a large project aimed finding ways to increase the Dependability of *Computer-Based* systems. The purpose of this concluding chapter is to put what has been presented above into the context of that wider endeavour. In particular, the initial organization of DIRC's research into *Project Activities* and *Research Themes* is explained together with the logical split of the six year span of the project into analytic and synthetic phases. In conclusion, some observations are offered on interdisciplinary research – how it has been tackled and how it has evolved during the DIRC project.

This "postscript" on the current book also serves to indicate other books that we expect to produce from the DIRC project.

There is certainly no need to reiterate the insightful points made by Graham Button about the content of the preceding chapters. Furthermore, it is to be hoped that the reader has by now read at least the majority of the contributions and understood how they provide evidence for:

K.Clarke, G. Hardstone, M. Rouncefield and I. Sommerville (eds.), Trust in Technology:
A Socio-Technical Perspective, 217–224.
© 2006 *Springer. Printed in the Netherlands.*

- *Trust* as a practical matter;
- Its necessary influence on designers who wish to achieve Dependability in an overall complex system;
- The reader will certainly have seen ample evidence of the role of ethnographic studies.

In the initial planning of what became the DIRC project, we identified a number of specific activities that we wished to pursue. Some of the researchers were motivated by technical goals like understanding notations for specifying and reasoning about the real time aspects of systems or for reasoning about the probability of failure for a system built from diverse components. Others wanted to conduct experiments in psychology that would produce results about human performance whose statistical significance could be measured. Many of the researchers who have authored the chapters of this book wanted to conduct ethnographic studies. Common to all of the researchers involved was an excitement about – and commitment to – interdisciplinary research.

We initially planned a number of *Project Activities* (PA) which, relative the six year time frame of the overall DIRC project were to be shorter term. One of these PAs was an exploratory study of what was called "Open Source" development. This PA ran only one year; the thrust of the conclusions can be seen in Gacek (2001) (indeed, the very title of this paper indicates our overall reservations about OSS as a panacea). The other PAs each ran for about three years. The studies reported in this book were conducted within two of these PAs.[21] The PAs were the focus of DIRC's interaction with organizations external to the five universities involved in the consortium.

In addition to the relatively short term activities, the initial project planning identified a number of hard problems to which we certainly wanted to make a contribution but whose final resolution we accepted was unlikely even in six years. These *Research Themes* (RTs) were five in number: Responsibility, Structure, Risk, Diversity and Timeliness. Each was characterized by the interdisciplinary view that there it was possible to look at the issues raised either from the technical questions relevant to the computer system or from the user side and consider the human implications. We recognized the five themes as both pervasive and hard but felt that we had an interdisciplinary team of researchers who could rise to the challenge of making a real contribution to the topics. At least in the spirit of tackling

---

[21] A full account of the Activities and lists of relevant publications can be found on the DIRC WWW site www.dirc.org.uk under "Mid-term Report".

challenging objectives, it seemed worth trying. We set several goals for that portion of our research conducted under the themes:

- it was necessary that some small group functioned as a "conscience" for the theme and made sure that work on it was conducted whenever appropriate;
- the people involved were to collect the "wisdom" that came from the other activities within DIRC;
- ultimately, there should be one or more books which recorded the knowledge about each research theme.

One of the five chosen RTs was *Responsibility*. Without doubt, this is a challenging topic. It is clear that designing a system, which is to be successfully used by professionals like those in health care, requires a thorough understanding of the responsibilities of different players. John Dobson tackles some of these issues in Chapter 3 of this book but we are not yet in possession of a way or recording and manipulating facts about responsibilities. Notions of *Trust* are connected with the way individuals discharge their responsibilities. It is however clear that more research is required on the overall RT of *Responsibility*.

To discharge the promise to fit this book into the wider context of the DIRC project, it is perhaps important to spend more time on the other research themes which are less the focus in the current book.

The RT on *Structure* offers the required two-way view because one can look at the "architecture" of technical systems and one can discuss the organizational and human organizations into which a technical system must fit. On the technical side, studies of "architecture description languages" are of interest but so are, say, the trade-offs between using a customizable (generic) system versus a custom built application. This choice could have a major impact on flexibility to evolve the system (generic systems offer a range of variability but can be rather inflexible beyond that envelope). The topic of *Evolution* is extremely important for any Computer-Based system: the very act of deploying such a system will result in changes of usage; furthermore the impact of numerous external forces like legislation, standardization and integration with other systems will create needs for a system to evolve.

It is equally important to understand how the organization into which the technical system is to be embedded is structured. A hospital is organized differently from an army and there are obvious reasons for some of the differences. (Some of these differences relate to *Responsibility*. Of course, the RTs are not separable concepts.) Aspects of an organization that are crucial to understand before one can hope to design a system which will be usable include how the organization checks for – and limits the flow of – errors. A crucial point made in this book is the adaptation of humans to systems which never achieve complete technical accuracy: up to a point, humans are extremely good at tolerating imperfection – providing their trust is not destroyed.

One can again easily see the technical versus human views in the RT *Risk*. It is possible to do purely technical, statistical, calculations about the risk of a system failing under certain circumstances. But it is also essential to look at how humans view risks. After railway accidents like that discussed in Chapter 6, proposals are often discussed whose cost (per injury) would far outweigh the preparedness of society to invest in reducing the appalling accident rates on the roads. Our perception of risk is not purely arithmetic. If one is designing a system that is to be dependable, it is important to realise that the human participants might make decisions which surprise the designer.

A key tool to improve the Dependability of any system is redundancy. In hardware, "triple modular redundancy" is used so that a two-out-of-three voting system will deliver the correct answer if one component is malfunctioning. This approach is valuable because electronic or physical components tend to decay and fail at different rates. The Achilles heal of TMR is "common mode failure" and, for example, running the same software three times is not going to offer useful redundancy. The RT on *Diversity* is studying many aspects of the topic. For example, the vexed question of how much useful diversity results from having separate groups of programmers write programs to the same specification has been studied. One might suspect that computers and humans are so different that diversity could easily be obtained by having a technical component checked with a human approval. In some cases, this is probably true but there is a danger in some situations that an operator will become bored and just accept the computer recommendation. More worryingly DIRC researchers have uncovered undesirable effects in "advisory systems" which are supposed to support the interpretation of medical images. Diversity is both a technical and extremely delicate issue. This is a convenient place to mention that researchers in DIRC are not only interested in the process of developing dependable systems; there is also a strong focus on the *assessment* of Dependability and the independence of safety case arguments is also being studied.

The final one of DIRC's RTs in this listing is *Timeliness*. Again, one can look at precise timing specifications of a (real-time) computer system; on the other hand, one can study how people handle timing constraints on their behaviour and tolerate (or otherwise) delays in getting results from technical systems. This RT has been a productive collaboration between computer scientists and psychologists.

As indicated above, the topics studied in the RTs interact heavily but it is our expectation that one or more books will record our conclusions on each RT separately.

It would be reasonable to view the first half of the six-year DIRC project as being analytic in the sense that a significant proportion of the effort was spent in understanding the dependability characteristics of complex computer-based systems. This is certainly a characterization of the majority of this book. Since the mid-term review, there has been more emphasis on synthetic aspects of our research into Dependability. The move to put more emphasis on RTs was presented and approved at DIRC's mid-term review. Although others beyond the original PAs had been proposed and in part had begun, there was also approval of a move away from the rather large PAs which were used in the first half of project's lifespan: *Targeted Activities* (TAs) of less than a year are now being used to help study gaps in our understanding which are identified in the RTs.

Perhaps more profoundly, the synthetic phase of DIRC is committed to offer "development methods" for the creation of dependable systems. This is an extremely ambitious goal. The introductory chapter has identified the broad scope of systems being considered in DIRC and Chapter 8 of this book looks at computers in a home environment (where one cannot fire an inept operator!). So these methods cannot be purely technical. Graham Button writes persuasively about "Ethnography as a Design Methodology" and it is clear that DIRC researchers are equally committed to this attitude about system understanding. John Dobson's Chapter 3 in this book moves towards method and Martin&Sommerville's Chapter 7 uses Patterns that could inform system design. The collection of methods that we hope to document will then make proposals about the comprehension and design of complex socio-technical systems.

REFERENCES

1. Gacek, C., Lawrie, T., and Arief, L.B. (2001) The Many Meanings of Opeb Source. CS-TR 737 Department of Computing, University of Newcastle on Tyne.